T0305494

Social Cohesion and Welfare States

Aiming to go beyond reiterating the stereotypical narrative of the rise of welfare states, this interdisciplinary book examines the long-run historical processes of the development of the welfare state. It focuses on the complex political, social, economic, and institutional transformations which give rise to these peaceful and cohesive societies.

Welfare is crucial to the story of peaceful social integration and this book explores and explains this vital connection, taking a non-linear view of the history of moving from fragmentation to peace with comprehensive welfare institutions. Chapters collectively focus on three central areas: (a) types of socio-political fragmentation; (b) the interconnection of social, political and economic forces that led to the institutionalisation of integrationist processes and policies (including redistributional welfare systems); and (c) how this new institutional development helped achieve, or failed to achieve, social peace and welfare. The international panel of expert contributors provide case studies from a rich variety of country contexts, including Germany, South Africa, the Netherlands, Austria and the Nordic countries.

This thought-provoking collection of essays is well suited for advanced students and researchers in social history, economic history, political economy and social policy.

Christopher Lloyd is Emeritus Professor of Economic History at the University of New England, Australia, was Guest Professor at the Finnish Centre of Excellence in Historical Research at the University of Tampere, Finland, and is now an Adjunct Professor of social science history at the University of Helsinki. His current interests include the history of democratic socialist regimes.

Matti Hannikainen is Senior Researcher at the Finnish Labour Archives and Adjunct Professor of economic and social history at the University of Helsinki. His current interests include the history of the Social Democratic Party in Finland. Hannikainen has also studied economic crises and the welfare state, especially the history of the Finnish pension scheme.

Perspectives in Economic and Social History
Series Editors: Andrew August and Jari Eloranta

Credit and Debt in Eighteenth-Century England
An Economic History of Debtors' Prisons
Alexander Wakelam

Luxury, Fashion and the Early Modern Idea of Credit
Edited by Klas Nyberg and Håkan Jakobsson

The Nordic Economic, Social and Political Model
Challenges in the 21st Century
Edited by Anu Koivunen, Jari Ojala and Janne Holmén

North Eurasian Trade in World History, 1660–1860
The Economic and Political Importance of the Baltic Sea
Werner Scheltjens

A History of Cold War Industrialisation
Finnish Shipbuilding between East and West
Saara Matala

Social Cohesion and Welfare States
From Fragmentation to Social Peace
Edited by Christopher Lloyd and Matti Hannikainen

For more information about this series, please visit www.routledge.com/series/PESH

Social Cohesion and Welfare States

From Fragmentation to Social Peace

Edited by Christopher Lloyd and Matti Hannikainen

LONDON AND NEW YORK

First published 2022
by Routledge
4 Park Square, Milton Park, Abingdon, Oxon OX14 4RN

and by Routledge
605 Third Avenue, New York, NY 10158

Routledge is an imprint of the Taylor & Francis Group, an informa business

British Library Cataloguing-in-Publication Data
A catalogue record for this book is available from the British Library

Library of Congress Cataloging-in-Publication Data
Names: Lloyd, Christopher, 1950– editor. | Hannikainen, Matti, editor.
Title: Social cohesion and welfare states : from fragmentation to social peace / edited by Christopher Lloyd and Matti Hannikainen.
Description: Abingdon, Oxon ; New York, NY : Routledge, 2022. | Series: Perspectives in economic and social history | Includes bibliographical references and index.
Identifiers: LCCN 2021058209 | ISBN 9781138587540 (hardback) | ISBN 9781032235004 (paperback) | ISBN 9780429503870 (ebook)
Subjects: LCSH: Welfare state—History. | Civil society. | Social integration. | Consensus (Social sciences)
Classification: LCC JC479 .S62156 2022 | DDC 361.6/5—dc23/eng/20220318
LC record available at https://lccn.loc.gov/2021058209

ISBN: 978-1-138-58754-0 (hbk)
ISBN: 978-1-032-23500-4 (pbk)
ISBN: 978-0-429-50387-0 (ebk)

DOI: 10.4324/9780429503870

The OA version of chapter 2 was funded by University of Jyväskylä.

Contents

Contributors

Marcel Boldorf

Professor of German history at the University Lyon 2 Lumière, France. He received his PhD from the University of Mannheim with a doctoral thesis on welfare policy in the German Democratic Republic. In 2003, he passed his habilitation in Mannheim with a comparative analysis of the transformation of the Silesian and Northern Irish linen industries (1750–1850). His research focuses on German and European economic history from the 18th to the 20th century. Recent studies are dedicated to the economies of World War I and II in a European and worldwide perspective. He is affiliated to the research projects on the Nazi past of German Reich ministries. Further research interests are the institutional analysis of industrialization and social and welfare policies.

Jari Eloranta

Professor of Economic History, Helsinki University, Finland; Secretary-General of the International Economic History Association; Meetings Coordinator, Economic History Association; Editor of Perspectives in Economic and Social History (Routledge): www.routledge.com/series/PESH. His research interests include cost and impact of conflicts; evolution of states; small states and trade in the 18th, 19th, and 20th centuries; Nordic economic history; and business history as a discipline.

Susanna Fellman

Professor of Business History (Torsten and Ragnar Söderberg Chair in Business History) at the School of Business, Economics and Law at the University of Gothenburg, Sweden. Her research interests are the professionalization and modernization of management and competition policy and cartels in a historical perspective. Her most recent book (co-edited with Martin Shanahan) is *Regulating Competition – Cartel registers in the twentieth-century world* (Routledge 2016). Fellman has also carried out research on family business and labour-market issues.

Matti Hannikainen

Senior Researcher, The Finnish Labour Archives and Adjunct Professor in Economic and Social History, University of Helsinki. He has studied wages and unemployment in Finland during the Great Depression of the 1930s, the history of the Finnish pension scheme, and social spending in Finland in the long-term perspective. Hannikainen is currently studying the history of the Social Democratic Party in Finland from the 1950s onwards.

Sakari Heikkinen

Emeritus Professor of Economic History at the University of Helsinki, Finland. His publications include *The Labour and the Market* (1997). His current research interests are long-term economic growth in Finland compared with Sweden, as well as labour markets in Finland and Sweden during the Great Depression.

Reino Hjerppe

Professor of Economics and Director General (retired) for the Government Institute for Economic Research (VATT) in Finland. He worked as a principal academic officer of the World Institute for Development Economics Research of the United Nations University 1994–1995. In addition, he has held several civil service and academic posts. His major research interests are macroeconomics and the economics of the public sector.

Riitta Hjerppe

Emerita Professor of Economic History at the University of Helsinki, Finland. She was the president of the International Economic History Association from 2006 to 2009 and is now the honorary president of the International Economic History Association. Her main research interests are Finland's historical national accounts, economic growth, economic, and social history of large and small enterprises and foreign direct investment in Finland.

Christopher Lloyd

Emeritus Professor of Economic History, University of New England, Australia; Adjunct Professor in Social Science History, Helsinki University, Finland. His research interests include the long-run history and future of social democratic welfare capitalism, the historical political economy of Australia, comparative settler capitalism within global history, and the theory and methodology of social science history.

Jari Ojala

Professor of Comparative Business History and Dean at the Faculty of Humanities and Social Sciences at the University of Jyväskylä, Finland. His areas of expertise include economic, business, and maritime history and he has published research in major journals of these fields. He is the co-editor, together with Anu Koivunen and Janne Holmén, of the anthology *The Nordic Economic, Social and Political Model – Challenges in the 21st Century* (Routledge, 2021).

Jarmo Peltola

Senior Research Fellow, Faculty of Social Sciences, Tampere University, Finland and Adjunct Professor in Economic and Social History, University of

Helsinki. His most important research includes a three-volume study: *The Depression of the 1930s in the Industrial City* (2008). In his new project (2015–2020), he is writing the history of Finlayson Cotton Mill (1820–2000), which was the biggest mill in Finland during the inter-war period.

Johanna Rainio-Niemi
Associate Professor in Contemporary History, Helsinki University, Finland. She specializes in comparative European histories and has studied the traditions of democracy and the state and the procedures and ideas of consensus-building in smaller European countries, including especially Austria, Finland, and the Nordic countries. Her publications include *The Ideological Cold War. The Politics of Neutrality in Austria and Finland* (Routledge, 2014).

Oriol Sabaté
Beatriu de Pinós Fellow, Department of Economic History, Institutions, Politics and World Economy, University of Barcelona. His research interests include state capacity, public policy, taxation, military conflicts, and Latin American and European economic history in the 19th and early 20th centuries.

Jeroen Touwen
Associate Professor in Economic and Social History and Vice Dean of the Faculty of Humanities at Leiden University, The Netherlands. His previous research was on 19th- and early 20th-century Indonesian economic history, and his current research focuses on the Dutch economy in the 20th century, with an emphasis on political economy. He is interested in the comparative characteristics of Dutch capitalism, as observed in labour relations, employer interest organization, welfare state development, and economic government policy. This research resulted in various articles in refereed journals and a monograph titled *Coordination in Transition. The Netherlands and the world economy, 1950–2010* (Brill, 2014).

Grietjie Verhoef
Professor in Accounting, Economic and Business History in the Department of Accountancy at the University of Johannesburg, South Africa. She has published 25 book chapters, 76 peer-reviewed articles, and two monographs. Her research specialization is on the development of corporate business in South Africa and Africa, the development of financial institutions in Africa and South Africa, and voluntary savings organisations, colonial economic growth, and the development of the insurance industry. Her monographs are *The History of Business in Africa. Complex discontinuities to emerging markets* (Springer, November 2017) and *The power of your life. The Sanlam century of insurance empowerment, 1918–2018* (Oxford University Press, 2018).

Introduction

Christopher Lloyd and Matti Hannikainen

Social fragmentation and social conflict are widespread phenomena and seem to always accompany the onset of economic transformation. Countries that are now advanced and relatively peaceful were once also conflicted and fragmented, and much of the world has always remained fragmented and conflicted. How did the transforming countries and regions of the world, beginning in the early to mid-19th century in parts of Western Europe, North America, and Australasia, move, in various ways, from social fragmentation and social conflict to stabilization and democratic social peace? While the rise of state (or public) welfare sectors since the late 19th century is a major theme in this economic, political, and social transformation of the advanced capitalist countries, there is more to the story. Our aim in this project is not simply to yet again write the history of the rise of welfare states. That has been done many times already. We aim, rather, to examine the *historical processes* whereby certain fragmented and undeveloped societies became peacefully integrated through endogenous processes of *political, social, economic, and institutional transformation*. This has been a rather rare phenomenon in human history and cannot simply be explained by reference to the rise, as if by magic, of advanced welfare systems. Welfare is crucial to the story of peaceful social integration, of course, but the connection has to be explored and explained in particular cases.

A good case can be made that most welfare states were to a large extent the product of social peace and social pressure, not the other way around. The emergence of comprehensive welfare states depends on socio-political consensus and compromise. Notwithstanding the significant Bismarckian case (explainable by the exceptional circumstances of the attempted *authoritarian* incorporation of part of the new working classes into the militaristic state), the emergence of welfare regimes depended on a general social consensus on and economic-fiscal capacity for the growth of a taxing and spending state. The consequences of the Great War were a related impetus in some places for the expansion of the state capacity, through mass human and material mobilization and the welfare system (extensively examined in Obinger et al. 2018). But welfare states had begun to emerge endogenously, often at the local level and with regional differences, before the Great War, and the demonstration effect of those innovations was already occurring.

DOI: 10.4324/9780429503870-1

Thus, one central issue concerns the origins of peaceful social integration, in some places before the Great War, in others in the inter-war period (some of which were destroyed in the 1930s and 1940s), others in the 1940s and 1950s, and another of the interconnected causes of social welfare systems. The earliest cases of welfare regimes (e.g. Australia, the UK, Denmark, Weimar Germany, 1920s' Vienna, Sweden) exhibit a close connection between the emergence of a democratic social consensus, an ideology of egalitarianism, and the building of a welfare system.

We are not aiming to produce a work of peace research as is commonly understood. That is a large field, with many institutes and journals, which concentrates mainly on the present world and on interstate, as well as intrastate, conflict. How to achieve peace through deliberate international intervention is the main concern of that field. Of course, the discourse of peace research should take a long-term historical approach for through that view it can be found that the conditions for the emergence of and consolidation of social peace are rather complex and endogenous: essentially a product of collective agency within certain specific contexts. As such, it cannot really be manufactured from outside, as the sorry history of interventions has shown.

Overcoming fragmentation and becoming socially peaceful and cohesive was a process of, among other forces, social compromises in differing contexts. Without compromises, resulting from various forces (including sometimes authoritarianism) initially and ultimately resting on social and political legitimacy and shared sovereignty, and a necessary degree of economic prosperity to enable a sizeable tax state to develop, there could not be peace. And the tolerant compromises had to be sustained if the peace was to survive. Furthermore, the nature of the social compromises is important. Some are more inclusive, egalitarian, and tolerant than others, and some are more fragile than others.

Thus, what we can see from the early 20th century onwards is the emergence of certain socio-political and institutional movements to resolve fragmentary differences in the interests of social cohesion. Some attempts failed for a time and were later successful (e.g. Germany and Austria). Everywhere we look in the history of what became the advanced and peaceful societies we see the social divisions – class, religion, ethnicity, gender, wealth, access to power, and so on – eventually being submerged in processes of socio-political compromises, democratization, tolerance, and the building and consolidation of strong capacious state institutions of education, health, welfare, and public provision generally. Consensus was easier to build and consolidate with increased social spending. Inclusion and amelioration for the losers of structural change helped maintain the peace. And, as mentioned, these peacebuilding processes were sometimes subverted and fell apart into worse conflict. Examples are the cases of Austria and Germany in the inter-war period and Yugoslavia in the 1990s.

In the early 21st century, there is a new crisis of the integrationist public sector and of social peace. The ideological and institutional attack by certain ideologues, policymakers, and politicians on the socio-economic roles of the state and public sector in the advanced West, in a manner and degree not seen since the pre-1940 era of *laissez-faire*, has come as the culmination of a growing trend towards marketization, anti-state ideology, economic neo-liberalization, and growing inequality of the past few decades and has been accelerated by the public fiscal crisis consequent to the bailouts of the Great Recession after 2008. At the same time, integrally linked with the unresolved problems of the Great Recession, there has been a rise of political extremism in advanced countries and a trend towards social fragmentation, in part caused by the large-scale unregulated movements of people, driven by war and poverty in the still-fragmented societies towards the advanced, attractive countries. The high degree of internal social peace that the West achieved in the post-war decades, during the golden age, is now declining. Relative social fragmentation has become a significant issue again. Social peace is always fragile, and its consensual foundation has to be preserved consciously and collectively.

While the 2008 global economic and financial crisis was a major shock to the world system, it did not have a lasting effect on the ideological anti-state hegemony of the era from the 1980s onwards (cf. Crouch 2011). And the global environmental crisis had not yet fully impacted public and political consciousness. By 2017, however, notwithstanding the ideology of neo-liberalism, the recent fiscal, ideological, and demographic developments had not succeeded to any great degree in reducing the scale of public sectors and the interventionist roles of states to anything near the kind of political economy that ruled before the 1940s. The seriousness of the global environmental crisis, however, was rising to the top of the political agenda with the Paris Agreement. The vast wildfires of Australia, the US, Siberia, and the Amazon in 1918–20, beyond all previous experience, raised a new urgency in recent years but not yet an existential one as far as dominant political power and ideology are concerned. The global pandemic, however, has produced a major fiscal response beyond anything seen after 2008 and enough to produce the end of the neo-liberal fiscal conservatism of the era from the 1980s. In 2021, the welfare state seems to be under re-activation in the West for the first time since the 1970s, and the public sector seems to be in a process of reconstruction again.

A longer-term perspective, such as developed by Edward Nell (1988), Vito Tanzi (2011) Vito Tanzi and Ludger Schuknecht (2000), and Peter Lindert (2004), to mention a few, sees the rise of the public sector as a highly significant global phenomenon of the past century, which is still continuing in many newly industrializing countries. Taxation and public spending since the 1940s, as well as regulatory intervention (for and against free markets), have empowered many national governments to become chief actors and structural determinants in the lives of their people. Public education, healthcare, unemployment protection, and pensions are the cornerstones of modern welfare states. Economic transformation, public expenditure, and high standards of living seem to have formed a symbiotic socio-economic system of capitalism in advanced Western and some other Organisation for Economic Co-operation and Development countries. The details of the particular routes of state formation and state–democracy relationships are crucial for understanding how this occurred, and cases are discussed in this volume.

The picture of welfare systems in other regions is mixed. Some developing democracies have more austere welfare systems than others, and some states strive to modernize without developing into democracies. Of course, there are a few significant rich-country exceptions to the public sector/development nexus, and furthermore, the place of democracy within that historical process is a highly contentious matter. While no country has achieved high income through economic and social development and socio-economic diversification (i.e., what is usually called modernization) without also becoming more or less constitutionally democratic, certain resource-rich countries (such as some Middle Eastern and North African states) also do have high average (if very unequal) incomes but are not economically and socially developed in the normal sense, being authoritarian as well as lacking large public sectors. And authoritarian developing (low- and middle-income) states, such as Thailand, China, and Vietnam, oppose democratization as supposedly dangerous to national unity and certainly dangerous to the power of the ruling class and party elite. Pressure from below for social reform is fiercely resisted. On the other hand, some other developing countries have long been or recently have become consolidated and more or less inclusive parliamentary democracies, such as India, South Africa, and Indonesia.

All the contributors herein are providing chapters that take an interdisciplinary and long-run historical approach. It is essential to explain the nature of the erstwhile fragmentation (social, ethnic, political, economic, etc.) and how historical processes evolved to overcome (or not) these divisions and their resulting conflict and oppression. We see it as essential to take a non-linear view of the history of the move from fragmentation to peace with comprehensive welfare institutions. Indeed, it's the history (complexity, contingency, agency, non-linear structuration) that has always mattered.

Therefore, the chapters herein are constructed as contributions to the topic by focusing on three things:

a) an account of the kinds of socio-political fragmentation as the context in each case;
b) the interconnection of social, political, and economic forces that led to the institutionalization of integrationist processes and policies, including redistributional welfare systems; and
c) how this new institutional development helped achieve, or failed to achieve, social peace and welfare.

The causal/historical interconnections are a (perhaps the) most significant issue for the broad social science history approach taken in this book. Uneven economic development, societal fragmentation and inequality, thwarted democratization, and authoritarian (often ethnic and cultural) oppression, are, and long have been, the destabilizing causes of large-scale violence. The Great Recession since 2008, the collapse of the global commodities boom in 2014–15, and the pandemic crisis have exacerbated the problem of social fragmentation in many places, but this is far from being a new problem. In current public and scholarly debates, globalization, fading economic growth, an ageing society, and increasing migration are big challenges that Western societies are expected to face during the coming decades. And the problems facing developing countries in this context are significantly greater. Furthermore, the global environmental crisis is looming in the background.

Thus, the comprehension of the inter-causal connections of the aforementioned factors has to be wide enough to address the issue of how the ways in which these did actually interconnect did lead to a remarkable transition from fragmentation to lasting social peace, however fragile today, in the most advanced countries and whether this can be replicated in the newly transforming societies. How did that happen? What can history teach us about this? Are there certain commonalities to the paths that all transforming, industrializing societies take, especially regarding their public sectors? Or are there quite distinct paths to economic development and modernization, including some that do not lead to extensive public social welfare and liberalization. Maybe that is an intermediate stage? Recent history in certain Asian states would seem to indicate that movement towards democratic social peace is the long-run tendency, closely associated with economic advancement, as evidenced by Taiwan most clearly.

This book is designed to examine these issues both generally and particularly through a series of historical cases that together focus on this complex set of interconnected forces. The focus is, indeed, on taking a historical approach that, first, attempts to build from cases to try to reveal the complexity of the many transition paths that have resulted in the early 21st century in the large public/state sectors that we see today in advanced countries. Second, the aim is thereby to provide a possible outline of a general approach to the intersecting dynamics of economic and social transformation, social fragmentation, state activism in socio-economic issues, and the rise of public-sector welfare regimes in response to both social need and social conflict.

References

Crouch, C. (2011). *The Strange Non-Death of Neo-Liberalism*. Cambridge: Polity Press.

Lindert, P. (2004). *Growing Public: Social Spending and Economic Growth Since the Eighteenth Century*. Cambridge: Cambridge University Press.

Nell, E. (1988). *Prosperity and Public Spending: Transformational Growth and the Role of the State*. London: Unwin and Hyman.

Obinger, H., Petersen, K., & Starke, P. (eds.) (2018). *Warfare and Welfare: Military Conflict and Welfare State Development in Western Countries*. Oxford: Oxford University Press.

Tanzi, V. (2011). *Government Versus Markets: The Changing Economic Role of the State*. Cambridge: Cambridge University Press.

Tanzi, V., & Schuknecht, L. (2000). *Public Spending in the 20th Century: A Global Perspective*. Cambridge: Cambridge University Press.

1 From social fragmentation to peaceful social cohesion

Historical and future themes

Christopher Lloyd

Social peace and emancipation

Beginning in the early 20th century a few economically advanced Western states began to develop democratic welfare regimes with the aim of stabilizing and building peaceful, egalitarian societies. Social peace is an essential condition for and a concomitant of social cooperation and emancipation, just as the reverse is also true. But the precise meaning and content of emancipation are contested in theory and practice. The long-lived and evolving republican tradition has supported peace and equality as enlightened freedom from domination but has always struggled to define the content of this freedom because of a lack of understanding of the power of *economic class domination*, as well as political and social domination. As argued in the following, radical socialist republicanism always placed *economic emancipation* at the centre of the project for emancipation.

A state of common violence and domination has characterized almost all societies for thousands of years and still does in large parts of the world, as stated in a calm but chilling way by Acemoglu and Robinson (2019, Ch I), echoing Hobbes. The greatest Western thinkers from Socrates, Plato, and Aristotle to today have striven to understand the possibility of and processes for constructing social integration and peace out of a generalized state of social fragmentation and violence. How the complex dialectics of human nature, social relations and social classes, culture, economy, and government intersect over time has always been the fundamental issue for social and political philosophers, social and political theorists, historians, and students of society generally. The "solution" proposed for overcoming social fragmentation and dissipation (or of what we might now call social entropy), which was usually thought of as an ever-present potential within society supposedly owing to human base instincts, traditionally involved the contradictory imposition of a sovereign's monopoly coercive power over violence, individual liberty, and collective social agency.[1] Such power always had to be exercised in collaboration with the dominant social faction or class.

Socially cohesive, inclusive, egalitarian, and democratic social peace is a highly desirable state for almost all individuals, as well as for collective humanity, but

DOI: 10.4324/9780429503870-2

has rarely been achieved or sustained. Imperfect approximations have existed and still do, but in 2021, the future does not look very hopeful regarding the sustenance of the existing regimes, establishing new ones, and bringing about peace in the world generally.[2] A vital component of social peace is a sufficiently egalitarian material foundation for social life such that all members of society can feel there is not just the possibility of an adequate material standard of living for all persons but also a just distribution of the material basis of individual and social life. Ideas and feelings about a just distribution are closely interconnected with ideas of sufficiency and equality.

All the themes that have been and are still central to the construction of ideal socially cohesive and peaceful societies – solidarity, democracy, sufficiency, equality, justice, humaneness, tolerance – came to the fore over time as a particular but fragile constellation in Western political thinking and action in the 19th century and have continued ever since to animate political discourse and political behaviour in all countries and regions of the world. Together they can be combined in the general concept of "social justice". But this is a very contentious concept, just as much of political discourse and debate is contentious. Indeed, many governments, acting as the instruments of narrow and greedy sectional interests, are openly hostile to equality, inclusion, and social justice. As argued in the following and elsewhere, the emergence of *very large-scale societies built on commitments to social justice* should be understood as a revolutionary development in societal history,[3] of equal significance with Agricultural and Industrial Revolutions. Large-scale cooperation has always been desired and perhaps possible but thwarted by unequal class power.[4]

In the 20th century, the achievement of "social justice" as an emancipatory project became a prime animator of the political action of social liberals, socialists, and communists in different ways.[5] Their ideologies and class projects shared a concern to achieve social welfare through the construction of state-based redistributive welfare regimes that would achieve a sufficient degree of material equality and security for all citizens in terms of income, health, housing, and education, as well as a high degree of individual freedom in the liberal democratic variant of political movements. "Freedom from want" became a prime aim of the proponents of welfare regimes, and through political transformations (even revolutions), such regimes became synonymous with welfare states that strove (not always very successfully) to establish equality of material living standards and a system that guaranteed material and social security throughout the whole life of all citizens. But "freedom from want" did not necessarily include emancipation in the sense of social and human rights or liberation as they came to be understood in Western liberal democratic thinking by the late 20th century.

Cohesive democratic social peace is much more than the traditional republican ideal of an absence of violence and social domination or the existence of universal voting. Democratic social peace requires a conscious public desire for and acceptance of integration, equality, and solidarity of political and social rights of all people. The enlightened ideal was of human equality. Social peace of a sort can be imposed (at least temporarily) through repression, but this is far from the social ideal. Conflict, disintegration, and inequality of power have been normal features of societies ever since medium- to large-scale societies emerged millennia ago. Through a contingent but rapid transformation, however, as a response to generalized social crises, a small number of previously fragmented and conflicted societies did become more or less democratically and peacefully integrated in the early 20th century out of backgrounds of class, religious, and ethnic divisiveness and violent contention. Instead of a new repressive hegemony or the ruin of the contending classes (*à la* Marx and Engels), the conflicts that arose out of the severe crises that each of these countries experienced led to democratic, peaceful more or less transformative *social compromises* with a sufficient degree of social solidarity to seem stabilized. These were *historic settlements* of class and nationality (although imperfect according to an abstract extraneous standard) and were institutionalized in radically new ways in order to ensure a continuing peace. Forces of collective agency of popular power were contingently able to construct these new institutionalized forms of popular sovereignty. In some cases (such as Australasia and Scandinavia) the transformative settlements endured despite further crises in the 1930s and 1940s. In other cases (notably Vienna and Germany), the peaceful settlements, while less secure, were improving until the crises of the 1930s destroyed them. In some other cases (including the Netherlands, Denmark, and Norway), peaceful democratic societies were constructed but were then destroyed through foreign invasion and the imposition of militaristic fascism and had to be reconstructed after 1945. In the post-1945 era, of course, the integrated, inclusive, and democratic peaceful structure spread to other Western countries in a rather more pervasive development. The British case of the late 1940s, for example, was rightly seen by some of its intellectual and activist progenitors[6] as, indeed, a *revolutionary* outcome for social integrative progress, just as the earlier developments in Australia, Vienna, Germany, and Sweden should also be seen as social democratic revolutions in comparison with what preceded them.[7]

Industrialization, democratization, and social justice

From the early to mid-19th century onwards, the coerciveness of the authoritarian state or sovereign, which had been re-established in Europe by the Restoration after the French Revolution and Napoleonic conquests, began to be undermined in some places through the emergence of the great solvent of industrialization. Indeed, the *material foundation* for the emergence of democratic social cohesion and peace as an ideal and a political program was industrialization. Viewed in the perspective of very long-run economic and social history, industrialization was and is a truly transformative revolutionary process that completely alters not just the material productive process of society but all the social and political relations and institutions of a society as well. Primordial forms of economic and social life are turned upside down and abolished. New social classes are created, and old ones are not just threatened but often swept away. As the industrial transformation has spread around the world, it has, to a greater or lesser extent, speeded up in its transformative (but very uneven) effects, especially the raising of material prosperity and rapid urbanization of erstwhile poor agricultural societies in some regions. But industrialization (or, more generally, "economic development") is not something that can easily be engendered by deliberate private or government action although the role of governments has become increasingly central to the process as it has become clear that state policies can play a vital role in greatly improving the quality of material life of the populace, albeit at the price of growing inequality. Thus while largely unrestricted and rapidly growing private investment, and incorporation of new labour forces in developing zones, with ever greater production for sale in global markets, has been the socio-economic structure of industrialization, states came to play an ever-greater role in organizing and directing the process for competitive purposes of national capitalist businesses.

Notwithstanding a communist interregnum in some places, the industrialization process has always been driven by the development of *capitalist* relations of production that have displaced older forms of socio-economic relatedness and institutionalization. Industrialization has, in fact, been the culmination of a much older emergence and evolution of capitalist relations from late medieval times. The private pursuit of profit through investment and then the further investment of those profits to accumulate further capital is one of the hallmarks of capitalism. Another is the use of capital for the employment and exploitation of wage labourers who have no other means of livelihood than their own labour capacity, having been displaced from older forms of self-employed production. A third dimension has been the extraction of and transformation of ever-greater supplies of raw materials and energy sources. All these features together over time produced a world-straddling force of trade and investment, centred initially on north-western Europe, that eventually set the context for a worldwide technological and organizational transformation in the already-existing systems of handicraft textile, iron production, and ceramics. Thus was modern industry engendered along with an industrial working class required to work the new industrial and extraction sites. The working classes became over the course of the 19th century the most important force in the socio-political history of industrializing and extraction zones. The social justice ideology and political program of socialists (and their communist variant) grew out of working-class demands for an end to exploitation, for social security, and for democracy. The primordial social and institutional structures of erstwhile agrarian societies became the sites of great class contestation as industrialization developed and subaltern demands were resisted by the dominant landed and capitalist classes.

The *foundational political condition* for achieving the aforementioned desirable state is liberal democracy, for democracy enables popular sovereignty and the possibility of capturing of state power with the aim of using it to achieve greater social justice. But democracy is always imperfect in an unequal world.

"True democracy" in the sense of popular, egalitarian, decision-making, and control is very difficult if not impossible to achieve. The ceding of decision-making to an elected parliament with its associated state administration and state-centred factions of social classes, places limits on popular sovereignty and the achievement of true egalitarianism, especially if the state is not reconstructed as an egalitarian force. Representative democracy is, of course, only partial democracy, albeit a step forward from authoritarianism. Many democratic socialists and social liberals of the late 19th and early 20th centuries knew this to be so, but the question for them was of the best strategy to achieve subaltern class domination if and when they constituted the large majority of the advanced capitalist societies. Seizing state power through elections was, for the leading advocates of democratic socialism, only the first step in the advanced Western states in the early 20th century, most notably the Australasian countries, Britain, Canada, the US, Germany, Austria, France, the Low Countries, and the Nordic countries. Of course, there was considerable disagreement among democratic socialists and social liberals at that time, but such activists and organizations were distinguishable by about 1912 from those parties that openly advocated insurrection to achieve the socialist future. Violent revolution was considered unnecessary if and when power would fall into the arms of the reformers through economic and political evolution, aided by popular working-class agitation and growing workplace power. This outcome was more or less achieved in Australia by 1910 and in Germany and Vienna by 1920, which were the most advanced democratic countries or zones by that time. But reformatory rather than insurrectionist politics, in order to be successful in the face of the pre-existing bourgeois/landlord state had to have a sufficient social base in the populace – a base of agreement about equality of and access to a just material life. This could only come about with a strong social class organization and compromise from the bottom up within a sufficiently developed capitalist economy. (Agrarian societies are unable to produce these kinds of class outcomes as the long history of the violent crushing of peasant revolts shows.) Furthermore, nations and societies as such do not achieve political development and democracy for nations and societies have no agency as such but are semi-organized complex collectives of small-scale social structures, large-scale social classes, socio-political factions, powerful networks of economic and clan loyalties, institutional entities, and so on that require new institutionalizations of solidarity in order to cohere together in new peaceful ways. The agency of groups and classes is always the force making for social advancement, but these have to develop collective consciousness and coherence of action in order to achieve popular power in a world of unequal power and oppression.[8]

As became abundantly clear from the late 19th century, there is no necessary relationship between industrialization and a particular form of socio-political regime, as Barrington Moore argued as long ago as 1966. Indeed, uneven and diverse regimes have coexisted with industrialization. Nazi Germany, Imperial Japan, the Soviet Union, and Communist China have demonstrated that rapid industrialization can be achieved by authoritarian states, especially if combined with large-scale private capital, as shown most markedly by China in the past 30 years. Liberalism and democracy are not necessary to achieve rapid economic development. But are they necessary to the building of peaceful social cohesion and comprehensive welfare states? None of the aforementioned states established welfare regimes that aimed at achieving social justice, equality, and socially cohesive peace for all citizens. Rather, they have been repressive regimes that have aimed to prevent popular political movements from challenging the power of small, self-perpetuating, greedy, and brutal ruling elites not really interested in social justice and welfare but only in internal and external hegemony, intermixed with racist nationalism. Nevertheless, these regimes have understood very well that the continuation of their authority depends on a continuation of their legitimacy as organizers of ongoing prosperity for the mass of the population. Repression is not a policy that will maintain ruling elite power forever, as has been shown in several Asian states (e.g., Taiwan, South Korea, Indonesia) in recent decades. This was not sufficiently understood by the ruling elites of the old agrarian regimes of Europe in the late 18th until the early 20th centuries. Popular expressions of discontent became salient everywhere, increasing in times of economic crisis caused by depressions and wars, although it took decades and major catastrophes before liberal democracy could be firmly established against the old regimes, and even then, those regimes have retained some residual power everywhere, even into the 21st century.[9]

Liberalism and socialism

Liberalism and socialism developed in parallel as the dominant new political ideologies from the early 19th century under the global influences of the American and French Revolutions. Oppositional political movements espousing synthetic and syncretic combinations of these ideas, with their foundations in the new social classes deriving from capitalism and industrialization, challenged the old imperial/agrarian and emergent industrial elites as the century progressed. Then the great crisis of 1914–18 undermined and delegitimated the old regimes, opening the door for the new ideologies and radical political movements. Their relative success in the early 20th century in some advanced Western states, notably Australia, Weimar Germany, Vienna, and Sweden, revealed what was possible for social justice and peace when the combination of democratic politics, constitutionalism, socialist ideas, and growth of the taxing-and-spending state could be achieved against the entrenched opposition of hegemonic regimes of agrarian/industrial power. Then, in the wake of the concatenated disasters of the 1929–45 era, the late 1940s witnessed the regime of social democratic state welfare becoming entrenched throughout most of the advanced Western-world state structures of production, welfare, and redistribution became the centres of the advanced Western model, around which a political consensus converged. Keynesian economic management, increasing taxation, public ownership, and "cradle-to-grave" welfare were central features in most advanced states.[10] Full employment and economic growth characterized the "*trente glorieuses*".

Meanwhile, the international socialist movement, founded as a radical opposition to capitalism and landlordism, divided over the necessity or otherwise of insurrection and the imposition of a one-party state to achieve the future socialist society of egalitarianism in the face of reaction from agrarian and capitalist elites. The split between the Russian and German social democratic parties and their greatly differing roles in the revolutions of 1917–18 (Russia) and 1918–19 (Germany) sundered the international socialist movement in an irreparable way with lasting consequences for the Weimar Republic especially. Lenin's and Kautsky's ideological separation (one-party dictatorship of the proletariat versus democratic socialist republic) led to very different left parties and outcomes in Eastern and Western Europe. But while the Leninist model degenerated into the Stalinist totalitarian state, the Kautskian social-democratic republican state never reached its promise of democratizing the whole of society, although the Swedish "peoples' home" came closest. Liberal rather than radical socialist democracy, in which the state retained a powerful self-interest around which the new elites of management and politics coalesced, became the dominant structure.

Importance of the symbiosis of democratic state/universal humanism and against neo-liberal "rights"

Is general material sufficiency and political equality enough for social cohesion? What about class, ethnic, religious, cultural, linguistic, and gender equality and cohesion? These human dimensions became increasingly significant as the material/civil dimension of the welfare state was supposedly "achieved". The humanist dimension to social life that encompasses different forms of identity and integration cannot simply be submerged into the welfare state, for material provision does not necessarily incorporate human provision and, in any case, material provision has never been distributed equally by any, even the most democratic, states. Issues of human inequality of class, racial, religious, gender, and ethnic dimensions have always bedevilled and undermined the strength of welfare regimes. Welfare states, with their foundations in concomitant national movements, have struggled to balance the demands for welfare with the demands for inclusion and equality of rights for all the population. Social democratic and labour parties have found it difficult to maintain their political salience as both the industrial working class has declined numerically and the new humanist/intellectual middle class and its precarious wing have grown. In the late 20th and early 21st centuries, large-scale immigration to and emigration from the advanced states have placed new pressures on the processes and institutions of welfare and integration in the advanced states. In addition, the looming crisis of climate change is necessitating a great shift away from many traditional modes of employment and lifestyle.

The problem of diminished left politics and consequent attacks on the welfare state in the 21st century is traceable to conflicts over the emergence of new and reconstructed nation-states in the late 19th and early 20th centuries. Nation-states were abstractly conceived by new elites as ideally ethnically united polities, but this was rarely the case in reality. From the beginning of the early 20th century, the agenda of social liberals and democratic socialists in the most advanced states was the construction of a state governance regime that combined direct facilitation of economic development and full employment, combined with democracy and welfare. These themes formed a holistic democratic socialist idealization if not always with full practical effect. The earliest cases of such a developmental state in Australasia (before 1915), Germany (1920s), and especially "Red" Vienna (1920s, but not extending to the rest of Austria) and later Sweden (after 1932) were explicitly democratic socialist in ideology. The structure was further cemented through the victorious cooperative experience of the anti-fascist war and the adoption of Keynesian economic and public policy that reinforced the active role of the developmental state in the post-war decades. Furthermore, the ideal of welfare solidarity incorporated the idea of equality of contribution in the newly enlarged taxing-and-spending state, and so the possibility of welfare dependence was intolerable in the idealized society of equality. The problem became more acute when the golden age of full employment and Fordist production declined and economic stagnation returned from the 1970s. A market solution of economic liberalism was adopted in which the ideal of equality and solidarity was replaced with a neo-liberal individualist imperative of competition and the resultant possibility of inequality and social outcasts. The new discourse of "liberal rights" was conjoined with moralistic "liberal obligations" (Whyte).

Central to the question of welfare construction from the beginning of welfare states was the question of humanist tolerance and inclusion. All the earliest formations were lacking in tolerance of ethnic and religious minorities. The tolerance and inclusion of minorities of various kinds were, from the beginning, a problem for all interventionist welfare states, which strove to unite their nation in a harmonious and unitarian manner. Nationalism was always present and has usually influenced political movements inimical to humanistic inclusion. The social and political equality of women did, however, over time become more advanced in these states with liberalization, although still leaving a large gap with the degree of inclusion of men. The question of tolerance and universality of human rights came to the fore more as the 20th century progressed. The most developed welfare states in the post-war era – in the Nordic region – were also the most ethnically homogeneous and as that homogeneity declined due to non-European immigration from the early 21st century so were the stability and social cohesion challenged. The idea of the inclusive multi-ethnic (or multicultural) society and state developed much further (albeit imperfectly and with contestation) in the erstwhile Anglo settler liberal societies (Australia, Canada, New Zealand), which had always been sites of mass immigration.

Moreover, the rise of neoliberal ideology to practical power from the 1980s, claiming to be a movement of individual human rights against "interfering" states, has been a powerful force for exacerbating inequality via marketization[11] and allowing the tyranny of markets to undermine democracy, social welfare, and cohesion. A direct consequence has been stagnant economies, growing inequality, and right-wing populist particularistic-authoritarian ideology that works to reduce the universality of welfare regimes[12].

Political modernization and the end of history: the false stages theory

The once-pervasive concept of "stages" to help explain the history of societies and economies is dangerously misleading, for it contains a teleology, which is always unscientific and ahistorical. The concept of "modernization" can also be used in an ahistorical and even teleological manner, for it can imply that there is a direction to history, especially since the 17th century when fundamentally transformative geopolitical and economic forces, originating in western Europe, began to impact the whole world. European imperialism and later European industrialization tied the whole world together, driven by capitalism's relentless search for materials, markets, and labour. But this process was not modernization in the sense of "becoming modern" and being modern, which was a socio-political and cultural process of individuation and rejection of the past and all primordial relations. Social process was one of constant change in which "all fixed fast relations were dissolved" (Marx). The mode of existence for such metropolitan cohorts was a form of precarious and illusory freedom of a liberal kind. But there was nothing inevitable about this state of society or culture, even though capitalism was the driver. In much of the uneven and variable world system, the other social relations cemented by the penetration of metropolitan capital were ones of degradation and "backwardness", the escape from which could only be achieved by a powerful developmental state acting as the instrument of local class control, either of bourgeois or subaltern origin, such as seen recently in various forms in China, South Korea, Taiwan, Singapore, and Vietnam. In these cases, the global economy was useful for exports but not imports. These states are not ones of "modernity" in the sense of Western liberal modernity, but they have their own forms of "modernity" which is appropriate in the eyes of their regimes for successfully allowing their people to rise from poverty. Without such strong states that would not be possible, as we see elsewhere in those "backward" parts of the world that have not yet been able to break free from the clutches of metropolitan domination and allure. Thus, there is no stages process leading to economic development and welfare and certainly not an "end to history". And even within those societies that achieved economic advancement and modernity, there are severe limits to the liberation and social enrichment of peoples.

Combined and uneven development: the international division of labour and the barriers on the road to the spread of the "Western model"

Development within the world system of the past century or so certainly has had its dark and degrading side in the periphery. As all the world has become capitalist, "marketized", and individualized since the 19th century, the globally systemic integration through the capitalist transformation has affected all parts and people of the world in multiple ways so that a great unevenness of the development became a chief characteristic of the process. The economic development of the core, the rise of the new global imperialism, and the eventual emergence of advanced, more or less peaceful states (out of earlier violent imperialistic states) came at the great cost, perhaps even as a systemic necessity, of inequality within the system as a whole. Backwardness and peripheralization were certainly central characteristics of the system. In the late 19th and early 20th centuries, backwardness within Europe and later East Asia was sometimes advantageous because it enabled the possibility of "leaping over" earlier stages of industrial development to institute innovatory and larger scale structures, particularly through close integration between capitalist (and later communist) states and economic systems, as Trotsky and Gerschenkron argued.[13]

But other parts of the world were zones of extreme plunder and exploitation, including large-scale trade in slaves or semi-slaves until the 21st century. Thus, the question of whether and how the backward (undeveloped) regions and zones of the world would be able to participate in development and modernization by catching up became a fundamental problem for state-focused economic and intellectual actors from the early stages of the process once it began in the UK. Britain's leadership in industrialization was the only case of 'first mover'. All other states, classes, and regions have been required to catch up if they wish to share in the benefits (as well as power) of economic development and its flow-on effects in geopolitical and social structures. All the advanced states have indeed caught up (which makes them "advanced"), and there has been a high degree of convergence in their incomes per capita and in their neo-liberal political development in the late 20th century.[14] Some erstwhile undeveloped states, particularly in East Asia, have overcome their backwardness with spectacular growth trajectories and even the beginnings of welfare states, such as in Taiwan and South Korea. The key to their success has been a strong centralized state with a nationally focused developmental policy. But many of the rest of the people of the world in Africa, other parts of Asia, and Central America have been excluded from the road to affluence and welfare because of a combination of exploitation through uneven value chains of investment and trade, centred on the rich countries, and ruling elites who have been happy to connive in and consolidate the exploitation of their own people. In the most extreme cases, some rulers have actually greatly enriched themselves while locking their people into abject poverty. A further category of states has also been unable to develop into the advanced stage because of their rentier socio-political structure arising from dependence on an abundance of oil and gas. These states depend on a pool of semi-servile imported labour without rights or prospects of socio-economic advancement. In the 21st century, the revolutions in transport (shipping and airfreight) and telecommunications have shrunk costs and time to an absolute minimum so that production can be located anywhere that labour is at its cheapest. As John Lanchester (2021) has pointed out,

> [t]he single biggest enabling force behind the global economy might as well be invisible, even as it drives down workers' pay and living conditions, as it contributes to climate change, as it reshapes the planet's economic geography. And, of course, it helps to keep stuff cheap. Shipping is a modern miracle of efficiency, interconnection and technology. It might also be the definitive example of modern capitalism, at the moment of its peak supremacy over labour.[15]

Given the foregoing discussion, there is good reason to doubt that most of the rest of the world's countries and regions can catch up in the present context and by which processes they could possibly converge with the advanced countries, not only in economic development but also in democratization, with all it implies for relative social consensus and peace. In the foreseeable future of the structural processes that presently exist, given the great shift in local and global geopolitical institutionalization that has occurred as a consequence of the ways in which the advanced states developed,[16] catch-up is increasingly difficult. That is, the world system of the first great transformation that produced the advanced states by the early post-war decades has been replaced by a different global system that is much more structurally hostile to further socio-economic transformation in peripheral zones but more conducive to the advancement (i.e. wealth accumulation) of the new corporate main actors within the core regions and their dependent (usually rentier) elites of the backward zones. While the original processes of advancement produced, at first, a world system of imperial and trade power that did eventually transform by the 1950s into an international system in which interventionist states became the main actors, those states, however, were very differentiated in their agency within the system. The hope, then, that all peripheral states would develop and become advanced through globalization has been thwarted, however. This is notwithstanding the South Korean, Taiwanese, Chinese, and Vietnamese partial successes so far, which are perhaps exceptions proving the rule of growing unevenness within the world system and within each state.[17] Many peripheral states were and are weak institutionally and dominated by external forces, as well as by internal comprador, rentier, and exploitative elites that have made it very difficult for them to develop the social agency to institute development strategies, assuming the elites wish to do so.[18]

Despite the great transformation of North-East Asia in recent times (the second great transformation after the North Atlantic and Western Europe), much of the world remains impoverished, conflicted, and authoritarian. About 1 billion people live below the barest measure of poverty of $2 per day, and about 3 billion are now wage workers, dependent on selling their labour time rather than producing their own livelihoods through self-employment. The efflorescence of capitalist accumulation after 1989–92 is proletarianizing the rest of the people of the world but not improving their quality of socio-economic or political life in many places.[19] Most of these new wage workers are located in the poorest regions. The much-vaunted rhetoric of "lifting billions from poverty" through development is a hollow promise. During this process, inequality has grown rapidly almost everywhere. Indeed, especially since 2008, stagnation has afflicted most of the world economy and now exacerbated by the COVID-19 crisis. There has been no democratic success in this era – authoritarianism has actually increased against democratizing attempts in the Middle Eastern and North African states, for instance, and growing anti-liberal movements in Central and Eastern Europe.

In addition to these structural problems of political economy, are two equally or even more significant interconnected problems of the global system: climate change and demographic change. Mark Blyth (2016) recently summarized the situation:

> The world cannot burn 60 to 80 percent of remaining known carbon fuel stocks without causing catastrophic warming. But under capitalism, this is exactly what the world will do. Carbon taxes will do little to change this reality.
>
> Add to this . . . an aging developed world with huge pension liabilities and a climate-shocked developing world of young people who have nowhere to go, and its little wonder that the Organisation for Economic Co-operation and Development has forecast stagnant growth for the global economy for the next 50 years and an almost 40 percent rise in inequality in the world's rich countries.[20]

Given these conditions of the global system, the problem of how the less developed parts of the world can escape from poverty, social fragmentation, and endemic conflict, and achieve development, democratization, and social peace, requires not only a combination of new and old historical knowledge, theorizing, and critical thinking but, moreover, new forms of collective social action in all parts of the global system. The agency of subordinate classes and non-state actors in their resistance to local and global domination within peripheral states is central to this question, as are existing and new global institutions of justice, human development, and climate mitigation that can perhaps provide a space for state-based advancement. Some degree of conflict on the road to socio-economic advancement may be unavoidable, as the historical experience of all the advanced states has revealed, but avoiding or ameliorating that conflict and establishing the rule of law and strong state institutions focused on development, more or less free from rentier compromise with advanced capital, are essential to the future. The current situation throughout much of the less developed world is not promising and, indeed, is worsening.

The return of fragmentation and the road to the future: globalization and the decline and revival of the interventionist democratic and universalizing state

The radical welfarist critique of and opposition to capitalist inequality and exploitation reached its apogee in the West in the late 1940s to late 1960s but steadily declined in most of the world from the late 1970s. Neoliberal quasi-authoritarianism in the Western world and quasi-fascism in the communist and post-communist East became dominant from the 1980s. The social democratic state and social form withered in much of the Western world. The neo-liberal "revolution" and its associated decline of the power of the interventionist democratic state empowered metropolitan capital to globalize: to find global sources of cheap labour, raw materials, and consumer goods and open new markets for high-tech industrial and consumer goods. But the Western globalization strategy began to unravel from 2008 and especially as the Far Eastern industrialization boom flooded the world with all kinds of consumer products.

Indeed, the era of the Western hegemony of the social democratic state began to lose its salience from the stagflation crisis of the 1970s which was widely blamed on the scale and supposed inefficiency of the state sector and its tax needs. An ideology and corresponding political opposition to the welfare state and its Keynesian macroeconomic policy prescriptions arose from the late 1970s – neo-liberalism advocated a reduced state sector, privatization for efficiency of public services and infrastructure, erosion and even elimination of labour unions, and removal of regulatory restrictions in some areas of economic and social life. Neo-liberalism succeeded in becoming ideologically and politically hegemonic throughout not just the advanced world but also the developing world and eventually even in the former Eastern bloc after the fall of communism in the 1989–92 era. The erstwhile reformist social democratic left was captured by this new rightward shift towards freeing markets and, in some cases (e.g. Australia, New Zealand, the UK, Canada, Sweden, the Netherlands), were chief implementers of the new public policy regime. Even the Chinese Communist Party shifted away from presiding over a state-owned and managed economy to a partially privatized quasi-state capitalist system with massive private capitalist accumulation and a rapidly transforming industrialization process, driven by export demand and internal wage suppression of the mass migrant labour supply that had been pulled out the backward agrarian sector.

At certain moments, then, over the long term, the Western transformations changed in such a way as eventually to make the intersection of elite and popular agency in the advanced states more integrated within the process. Historic institutionalised compromises in the interests of the sharing and promotion of greater prosperity have been characteristic of these states. General prosperity was essential as a precondition. The leaders and ideologies of social democratic/labourist parties have been crucial to this process of channelling class anger and seeking compromises with capital. That is, a popular shared consciousness was constructed into more or less consensual forms that attempted to transcend the old sources of conflict in more humanistic, egalitarian, and redistributive ways.[21] This was a social development made possible only by the process of economic prosperity that generated sufficient social surplus and a sufficiently increased standard of living for workers through their organizational pressure and universal education while at the same time not threatening the returns to capital. Mass working-class organizations and comparative solidarity were essential drivers, even in the US in the 1930s' period of New Deal compromises. Of course, these working-class pressures failed in the short term in many places in the 1920s and 1930s, which were highly conflicted decades in many Western countries, due, in large part, to the failures of economic prosperity and constitutionalism. The defeat of fascism and militarism in the 1940s was essential for the further advancement of socially solidarisitic and peaceful outcomes. Just as important were economic prosperity from socio-economic development. Prosperity has always been and is still essential to the compromise. Having relied so strongly on the emergence of strong democratic states, the spread of prosperity, however, has become far less possible with the evolution of the global system since the 1980s. The original primordial capitalist character of the transformation and the continuing role of the old elites in the process was such as to ensure the maintenance of some degree of class power and inequality, which have become exacerbated in recent decades with rising inequality within advanced states and between the advanced and the poorest peripheral regions of the world. The close interconnection between advanced country and peripheral capitalist elites has acted to make much more difficult the institutionalization of developmental states in the periphery.

The decade of the 2020s, however, has already witnessed a concatenation of global crises As Nouriel Roubini (2021) has reminded us,

> [t]he COVID-19 crisis likely will lead to an increase in inequality within and across countries. The more that vulnerable cohorts are left behind, the greater the risk of social, political, and geopolitical instability in the future.

The fires and floods of climate change, the COVID-19 pandemic resulting from the despoliation of nature, and the economic depressions that both are causing, cannot be overcome by individuals, groups, corporations, or even nation-states acting separately. A significant reactivation of state power in both the advanced West and in Latin America, not to mention most of Africa, is required. There have already been the significant beginnings of a new fiscally interventionist state in the West. Moreover, a new form of planetary cooperation is necessary, something that was hoped for from the disasters of 1929–45 and did emerge in a limited form in 1944–45 from Bretton Woods, San Francisco, and New York but could last only 30 years. and the revival of the "Pink Tide" in Latin America is providing some hope for a more equitable future. As Guy Rundle (2021) has opined,

> [t]he turn back to these movements probably represents an aspect of one of the most important things happening in the world today. That's the defeat and discrediting of the classical liberal-social conservative ideology sparked by Thatcherism and Reaganism and carried to new heights first by post-1989 globalisation, and then by post-9/11 consolidation of Western national security states.
>
> Neoliberalism has continued as a process, of course, but the suggestion that it offers some sort of human liberation has gone. . . .
>
> The right has driven the global downward drift of wages, the financialisation of the world economy and a series of decades-long, multi-trillion-dollar wars. They have resorted to a cod-populism, which, in the home of cod-populism, appears to have been exposed more rapidly than elsewhere in the non-Latin West.[22]

Thus, the end of neo-liberalism has not yet arrived, notwithstanding the signs of rejection in some places, in the US most remarkably, with the Biden administration's willingness to fund a sort of social new deal, the judgement of which is still to be made. Chile, once touted as the poster child of neo-liberalism, has suffered a devastating experience from the corona pandemic, thanks in part to the failure of the right-wing regime to introduce sufficient social assistance because of the commitment to austerity,[23] but a popular backlash against the regime has led to a new possibility of deeper democratization and constitutionalism.

The climate crisis (long in the making), the pandemic crisis, and the conjoined economic crisis are together already producing new ideological streams of political activism and public policy. On one hand, social fracturing is being greatly exacerbated, manifested most notably in the rise of right-wing fanatical anti-social movements of quasi-fascistic racism in many countries and the great enrichment of billionaires, profitting from the crisis. The Trump phenomenon was the most visible manifestation of a right-wing populist reaction. It's clear that such radicals are pursuing a strategy of entryism to try to subvert the central institutions of the liberal bourgeois state, as Nina Kruscheva (2021) has pointed out. On the other hand, new progressive/leftists thinking about the role of the welfare and interventionist state is being reconfigured intellectually and practically in support of a regime that combats class inequality.[24] The policy of austerity is being seen as no longer appropriate (it never was) to deal with the economic and social needs arising from the COVID and climate crises. But these streams of thought and activism are not simply a return to the social democracy and then Keynesianism that were products of industrial working-class organization from the late 19th century. The industrial working class and its unionization have declined numerically and institutionally such that it is no longer able to pose a serious opposition to capital within the advanced West.

The new forms of Western left organization often have a populist and spontaneous (albeit peaceful) rather than a solidified institutional form, and their capacity to engage with and influence bourgeois state power is very limited.[25] New democratic social movements that are aimed at capturing state power (such as grew in the early to mid-20th century), with the express purpose of overcoming and transforming the foundations of the global climate and economic crises, are still in an inchoate state. Nothing has yet emerged that can replicate the erstwhile power of organized labour and its political strength. The strength of global capital and its neo-liberal ideology has long co-opted the old social democratic/labour parties so that in their current forms, they cannot institute the progressive or even radical democratic program that the current situation demands. The consequence is the steady erosion through privatization and profit gouging of public services in health, welfare, and infrastructure, almost everywhere. The neo-liberal revolutionaries did succeed in capturing the state in the 1980s, just as some social democrats and communists had in the early 20th century. Can the new socialist green progressivist humanism bring about a similar revolution? Can social democracy/democratic socialism be rebuilt institutionally and ideologically sufficient to challenge the global order? The new dominance of post-materialist values means that the old ideology of redistribution and economic justice through the tax state/welfare system cannot be politically salient. Can a new emancipatory project of justice be constructed beyond the past of social democracy? As Roberto Frega (2021) has argued, there has to be a new synthesis of ideology, a practical (mundane) program, and an appeal to a new (dialectically constructed) broad social constituency.

An essential element in any new left political organization aiming to reorganize society in an inclusive, peaceful, welfarist, and egalitarian manner has, *in the first place*, to have a full appreciation and articulation of the persuasive power of three related sets of ideas:

- radical socialist republicanism that has a new central theme of the necessity of an environmental ideology within socialism;
- universal humanism that goes beyond the limitations of multiculturalism and national citizenship, which are used as a means of both inclusion and exclusion of individuals; and
- a new global political economy that builds on theoretical and empirical understandings of the system (such as combined and uneven development) and seeks to grasp the ways in which exploitation and inequality can be overcome through international political action.

Building this new intellectual synthesis for future politics will necessitate, first, a new view of Marx's valuable insights, for he articulated a still-vital understanding of the connection between a radical (not bourgeois) republican tradition, stemming from Machiavelli and including Rousseau and Hegel, and socialist democracy. This theme of Marx's has not been fully grasped until recently, being particularly articulated earlier (but largely forgotten) by Karl Kautsky (e.g. 1918, 1924) and then re-emphasized and updated by Michael J Thompson (see recent contributions: 2019a, 2019b, 2019c), one of the most significant contemporary scholars of Marxist themes. Kautsky (1918) argued, in the context of the Bolshevik seizure of power, for a thesis that can be interpreted as radical republicanism:

> The distinction is sometimes drawn between democracy and Socialism, that is, the socialisation of the means of production and of production, by saying that the latter is our goal, the object of our movement, while democracy is merely the means to this end, which occasionally might become unsuitable, or even a hindrance.
>
> To be exact, however, Socialism as such is not our goal, which is the abolition of every kind of exploitation and oppression, be it directed against a class, a party, a sex, or a race.
>
> We seek to achieve this object by supporting the proletarian class struggle, because the proletariat, being the undermost class, cannot free itself without abolishing all causes of exploitation and oppression, and because the industrial proletariat, of all the oppressed and exploited classes, is the one which constantly grows in strength, fighting capacity and inclination to carry on the struggle, its ultimate victory being inevitable. Therefore, to-day every genuine opponent of exploitation and oppression must take part in the class struggle, from whatever class he may come.[26]

Building on this, Thompson's new reading of Marx and Kautsky is persuasive. He has argued[27] that Kautsky's contribution to the defence of socialist republicanism in the wake of the Russian and German revolutions was a defence of a "cooperative commonwealth" in which there would be democratic control of productive forces which would be used for social rather than individual ends. Democratized state power rather than works councils (Soviets) would be necessary to ensure the survival of the democratic commonwealth. The republican principle is essential here for its emphasis on elimination of domination:

> Democratisation and socialisation are now the basic ends towards which any socialist society must seek to maximise for social transformation. This was no domestication of Marxian ideas. Indeed, Kautsky was following what Marx's mature political thought had also maintained. As Marx wrote in 1866:

> The working man is no free agent. In too many cases, he is even too ignorant to understand the true interest of his child, or the normal condition of human development. However, the more enlightened part of the working class fully understands that the future of its class, and, therefore, of mankind, altogether depends upon the formation of the rising working generation. . . . This can only be affected by converting social reason into social force, and, under given circumstances, there exists no other method of doing so, then through general laws, enforced by the power of the state. In enforcing such laws, the working class do not fortify the government power. On the contrary, they transform that power, now used against them, into their own agency. They effect by a general act what they would vainly attempt by a multitude of isolated individual efforts.[28]

The argument for a synthesis of radical socialism, planetary environmentalism, and universal humanist republicanism, then, is not one just for somehow inspiring the cooperative and even revolutionary general zeal of the people, for if that occurs in isolation, it's doomed to failure, as history attests of many cases. Rather, practical collective political action has to be focused on capturing state power through agitation and elections, to begin with, for it is only the state that can be used to achieve the social aims of the transformation into positive liberty and social justice and so one important aim is not to do away with the state but to democratize it and for society as a whole to use it for social benefit.[29] The state *per se* is not the enemy (contra Mouffe, 1992), but the strength of the bourgeois state is very great as the social democratic movement found to its eventual co-option. The creation of a social democratic welfare state could only be achieved through persuading capital that it was in its interests to help do so. The working class became a middle class during the full employment and labour agitation of the *Trente Glorieuse* and, as such, was a greater consumer. The contradiction then within capitalism of the necessity to reduce labour and tax costs in order to compete versus the necessity to fund the tax state and find a market for the products of industry is unsustainable in the long run. Globalization, the crises of 2008 and 2020, and MMT-inspired fiscal expansion in 2021, have postponed the reckoning but as Streeck (2017) and others have pointed out even Polanyi's fictitious commodities have now become fully commodified and there is nowhere else for capital to go to find new sources of uncommodified labour, materials, and even ideas that can be plundered and exploited.

A concerted, intellectually inspired, more or less unified political movement, drawing inspiration from the aims and partial achievements of democratic socialism in the early 20th century, is required. During and after the new peaceful change, the democratized state must be employed to institutionalize the Republic of Democratic Socialist Environmentalist and Universal Humanism. This would mean putting an end to capitalist private greed and exploitation, of course, and the beginnings of a regime with a planetary perspective of socio-political integration around the commonness of humanity,[30] social equality, and the saving of the planet's environment for the survival of humanity and all the species with which we must live in harmony. How realistic is this program? Only time will tell, but social pressure is growing.

Notes

1 An example of the sovereign imposition of peace was Tokugawa Japan from the early 17th century until the mid-19th century, so much so that the nation and particularly the samurai warrior caste lost the organizational and technological capacity to wage war, which had been so characteristic of the preceding era.

2 WPR April 18 (2021).

3 Revolutionary rather than evolutionary because of the comparatively rapid shift as a sort of phase change that occurred in the early 20th century out of very conflicted backgrounds.

4 Boyd and Richerson (2021) have recently argued that it seems likely that Pleistocene foragers regularly cooperated in large groups, perhaps for several hundred thousand years. This suggests that the mismatch hypothesis (i.e. modern human cooperation results from a mismatch between current social environments and those in which our psychology evolved) is incorrect and that the psychology that supports contemporary cooperation evolved to support cooperation in large groups in the past. Given that cooperation in large unrelated groups is rare among vertebrates, this evidence further suggests that the evolutionary mechanisms that gave rise to human cooperation likely depend on the peculiarities of human biology, such as exceptional cognitive ability, combinatorial language, and cumulative cultural evolution.

Thus, the implication is that if there is an evolved predisposition of large-scale cooperation that, nevertheless, does not become operational in most cases of large-scale societies, the explanation must lie in the class domination that arose during the emergence of extensive agriculture in the mid-Holocene. Servile peasant life, normal in ancient and medieval societies, was not extensively cooperative. Thus, intense and large-scale social co-operation only emerges during warfare in ancient and medieval societies and, exceptionally, where village communes can emerge on the basis of free associations of direct producers, such as in the Classical polis. But even there, servile labour provided the foundation for citizen cooperation.

5 Rothstein (1998).

6 Cf. Laski (1943); Morrison (1949).

7 Cf. Lloyd (forthcoming).

8 Acemoglu and Robinson (2019) have argued that there is a narrow corridor to be negotiated between state and society if societal peaceful liberty is to be achieved. But social agency of groups and classes is missing from their argument. They defend a form of libertarian republicanism. But, as argued later in this chapter, liberty has to be more than formal negative liberty of the individual subject freed from domination. Substantive liberty can only be enjoyed within a structure of equal, cooperative social relations. Society as a structure of equality for all is necessary for liberty, but liberty also is premised on obligation and justice. Positive liberty requires a democratic socialist state. Democratic socialist republicanism is defended later in the chapter.

9 Mayer (1981).

10 The US was an exception for although Roosevelt's New Deal had done a great deal to overcome the Depression of the 1930s, it could not be described a social democratic welfare regime, and the country's great political and social inequality derived from the legacy of slavery and the unfettered power of big capital was and is still festering. The US has remained a conflicted and incohesive society as events of 2020 and 2021 have shown.

11 Whyte (2019).
12 Busmeyer et al. (2021).
13 Cf. Rosenberg (2020).
14 Commodity-rich exporting countries with high average incomes but low socio-political and human development cannot be considered as advanced modern states. The issue of whether partially democratic or undemocratic but economically developed states in Asia with weak welfare regimes can be considered modernized is a relevant point that we don't need to debate at this stage.
15 Lanchester (2021).
16 Samuel Huntington (1968) famously argued, which was a representative view of certain Western conservatives, that many developing (mostly postcolonial) states risked chaos by educating their citizens in advance of economic development, which would produce great political instability. Of course, this fails to take account of class pressure from below for education and social advancement within those states and of the globalization of information, and hence, the demonstration effect of the advanced societies on the whole world as the 20th century progressed. On Huntingdon, see Bull (2016).
17 The Chinese case shows clearly the effects of the Communist Revolution in sweeping away the old order of landlordism and feudalism and instituting a powerful, centralized, developmental state with a concerted catch-up agenda (see the following discussion). Which other countries are able to do that in the 21st century?
18 The exploitative elites of many backward states are not truly interested in development for to do so would require policies of equality and social investment that would encourage lower class consciousness and erosion of their own power. This seems clearly the case throughout the Middle Eastern and North African states, most of South Asia, and sub-Saharan Africa.
19 The question of the character of the political economy of the former communist countries is a topic that is still hotly debated. One conceptualization is that these countries were actually state capitalist and that when the regimes collapsed the erstwhile party elites were able to transform themselves easily into private rather than state capitalists. This is most clearly seen in Russia and China, which are now the leading examples of this more developed form of state capitalism.
20 Blyth (2016), 11.
21 Of central significance to these settlements was the fact of ethnic homogeneity in most of the advanced states (except the US, where the settlement did not fully develop and did not outlive the 1940s), not yet subject to mass immigration from outside the core regions. Once large-scale immigration from non-core areas occurred, the settlements began to be threatened and in the 2010s this ethnic "issue" is a major cause of crisis in the advanced states.
22 Rundle (2021), 19 April.
23 Reperger (2021).
24 Cf. Krugman (2020); Tooze (2021).
25 As argued extensively by Hardt and Negri (particularly in 2000 and 2004), this multitudinous spontaneity is supposed to carry social agency but such uprisings in the Arab Spring and Eastern European 'colour revolutions' have not so far resulted in significant new regimes in most places. Indeed, greater repression has occurred in the outcomes of most uprisings. This should have been expected. Peaceful demonstrations, crowds, and riots are almost never successful without large-scale organization, and even the Bastille riot of 1789 could have only symbolic power. The decomposition of the monarchical regime in the face of the intransigence of the Bourgeois Third Estate as an alternative government was much more important. The Paris Commune of 1871 and the 1927 spontaneous riot in Vienna, were crushed for they could not secure a new power regime. The exceptions, such as Paris 1783, St Petersburg March 1917, and Berlin 1918–19, prove the rule that conditions have to be ripe and oppositions very organized if a dual-power decomposition and transfer are to be achieved. The instruments of the state have to change allegiance to the opposition.

26 Kautsky (1918), Ch II.
27 Thompson (2019a).
28 Marx (1866), 80–81; Thompson (2019a), 163–164.
29 A similar argument has been made by Acemoglu and Robinson (2019), but the biggest weakness in their institutionalist approach is in their specification of nation and society, which are not conceptualised in structural but holistic terms. Social classes, class consciousness, and the uneven distribution of social agency are not carefully examined. And *nations* cannot struggle for liberty, only people can, in groups, classes, organisations, and institutions. Thus, the issue of society and social power, so crucial to their account of the "narrow corridor" between state and society, is left at an overgeneralized institutional level. Similarly, the broader republican tradition of overcoming domination also leaves insufficiently examined the social forces that can make for ending domination.
30 Cf. Antweiler (2012).

References

Acemoglu, D., & Robinson, J. (2019). *The Narrow Corridor: How Nations Struggle for Liberty*. New York, NY: Penguin Press.

Antweiler, C. (2012). *Inclusive Humanism: Anthropological Basics for a Realistic Cosmopolitanism*. Taipei: V & R Unipress, National Taiwan University Press.

Blyth, M. (2016). Post-Capitalism: A Guide to Our Future. *Foreign Affairs*, *96*(4), 172–179.

Boyd, R., & Richerson, P. J. (2021). *Large-Scale Cooperation in Small-Scale Foraging Societies*. Pre-print, DOI: 10.32942/osf.io/fxwbr Eco-EvoRxiv Preprints.

Bull, M. (2016). Softening up the State. *New Left Review*, *100*(July–August).

Busmeyer, M. R., Rathgeb, P., & Sahm, A. H. J. (2021). Authoritarian Values and the Welfare State: The Social Policy Preferences of Radical Right Voters. *West European Politics*, *45*(1), 1–25.

Frega, R. (2021). The Fourth Stage of Social Democracy. *Theory and Society*, *50*(3), 489–513.

Hardt, M., & Negri, A. (2000). *Empire*. Cambridge, MA: Harvard University Press.

Hardt, M., & Negri, A. (2004). *Multitude: War and Democracy in the Age of Empire*. New York: Penguin Press.

Huntington, S. (1968). *Political Order in Changing Societies*. New Haven: Yale University Press.

Kautsky, K. (1918) [English Ed 1919]. *The Dictatorship of the Proletariat*. Vienna. www.marxists.org/archive/kautsky/1918/dictprole/index.htm.

Kautsky, K. (1924). Revolution and Counter Revolution in Germany. *Socialist Review* [*The Journal of the Independent Labour Party*], *23*(127). www.marxists.org/archive/kautsky/1924/04/counter.htm.

Krugman, P. (2020). *Arguing with Zombies: Economics, Politics and the Fight for a Better Future*. New York: Norton.

Kruscheva, N. L. (2021). *G I Joe Trotsky*. www.project-syndicate.org/commentary/us-capitol-riot-miltary-infiltration-by-nina-l-khrushcheva-2021-04?utm_source=Project+Syndicate+Newsletter&utm_campaign=2efeed0a71-sunday_newsletter_04_25_2021&utm_medium=email&utm_term=0_73bad5b7d8-2efeed0a71-93472413&mc_cid=2efeed0a71&mc_eid=12d85f95bc.

Lanchester, J. (2021). Gargantuanisation. *London Review of Books*, *43*(8), 3–6.

Laski, H. J. (1943). *Reflections on the Revolution of Our Time*. London: George Allen and Unwin.

Lloyd, C. (forthcoming). *The Revolution of Democratic Social Peace: The Variable History and Necessary Planetary Future of Integrated, Peaceful, Democratic Societies*. Forthcoming from Cambridge University Press.

Marx, K. (1866). *Instructions for the Delegates of the Provisional General Council of the International Working Men's Association*, www.marxists.org/archive/marx/works/1866/08/instructions.htm.

Mayer, A. J. (1981). *The Persistence of the Old Regime: Europe to the Great War*. New York: Pantheon Books.

Moore, B. (1966). *Social Origins of Dictatorship and Democracy: Lord and Peasant in the Making of the Modern World*. Harmondsworth: Allen Lane (Penguin).

Morrison, H. (1949). *The Peaceful Revolution*. London: George Allen and Unwin.

Mouffe, C. (ed.) (1992). *Dimensions of Radical Democracy: Pluralism, Citizenship, Community*. London: Verso.

Reperger, S. (2021). The Pandemic Cannot Be Defeated by Vaccination Alone: The Success of Chile's Vaccination Campaign Has Proved to Be Its Undoing. *International politics and Society*, April 28. www.ips-journal.eu/interviews/the-pandemic-cannot-be-defeated-by-vaccination-alone-5142/?utm_campaign=en_888_20210427&utm_medium=email&utm_source=newsletter.

Rosenberg, J. (2020). Uneven and Combined Development: A Defense of the General Abstraction. *Cambridge Review of International Affairs*, https://doi.org/10.1080/09557571.2020.1835824.

Rothstein, B. (1998). *Just Institutions Matter: The Moral and Political Logic of the Universal Welfare State*. Cambridge: Cambridge University Press.

Roubini, N. (2021). Leaders and Laggards in the Post-Pandemic Recovery. *Project Syndicate*, May 24. www.project-syndicate.org/commentary/covid-recovery-uneven-geography-increased-inequality-by-nouriel-roubini-2021-05?utm_source=Project+Syndicate+Newsletter&utm_campaign=7d09d2fb14-covid_newsletter_05_27_2021&utm_medium=email&utm_term=0_73bad5b7d8-7d09d2fb14-93472413&mc_cid=7d09d2fb14&mc_eid=12d85f95bc.

Rundle, G. (2021). *Viva the Pink Wave! Political Left Stages an Unexpected Comeback in South America*. www.crikey.com.au/2021/04/19/south-america-pink-wave-politics/?utm_campaign=Daily&utm_medium=email&utm_source=newsletter.

Streeck, W. (2017). *Buying Time: The Delayed Crisis of Democratic Capitalism, Second Edition*. London: Verso.

Thompson, M. J. (2019a). The Radical Republican Structure of Marx's Critique of Capitalist Society. *Critique*, *47*(3), 391–409.

Thompson, M. J. (2019b). Karl Kautsky and the Theory of Socialist Republicanism. In G. Kets, & J. Muldoon (eds.), *The German Revolution and Political Theory*. London: Palgrave Macmillan.

Thompson, M. J. (2019c). The Demise of the Radical Critique of Economic Inequality in Western Political Thought. In C. O. Christiansen, & S. L. B. Jensen (eds.), *Histories of Global Inequality*. London: Palgrave Macmillan.

Tooze, A. (2021). The Gatekeeper [Discussion of Krugman]. *London Review of Books*, *43*(8), 23 April 2021.

Whyte, J. (2019). *The Morals of the Market: Human Rights and the Rise of Neoliberalism*. London: Verso.

World Politics Review (2021). Who Will Intervene in the World's Hot Spots? 18 April 2021, https://mailchi.mp/worldpoliticsreview/wpr-insights-hotspots-042821-subs?e=e7eae77a89.

2 Smooth sailing toward more peaceful societies? Long-run Nordic development paths

Jari Eloranta, Jari Ojala and Oriol Sabaté

Introduction

In this chapter, we aim to compare the Nordic societies in a broad manner in the last 200 years in their process of "sailing" (with the implication of rough waters along the way) from social fragmentation to welfare societies. Our main goal is to examine the co-evolution of economic, political, and fiscal factors among the Nordic societies in the long run by making use of recent longitudinal data sets. Even if an in-depth analysis of the interplay of these factors would require further theoretical discussion, extensive quantitative modeling, and qualitative contextualizing analysis, we can map out some key patterns that characterized the shift toward more peaceful and well-functioning societies. First, we focus on the process toward economic and political convergence that took place, with some exceptions, in the latter part of the 20th century. Second, we also examine how these processes of convergence translated into the realm of fiscal and social policies and to what extent they were related to decreasing levels of social fragmentation. The chapter shows that the paths toward welfare states differed among Nordic countries and that some of the pivotal forces and periods were connected to crises, namely, these were not processes that were smooth or inevitable. We conclude with some general findings and a discussion of current-day problems from a comparative historical perspective.

The relationship between the factors leading to economic or social convergence remains a disputed matter in the literature. The foundations of welfare societies today – which Nordic societies typically are classified as – are typically linked to democratic institutions: it is hardly possible to build a welfare society based on a comprehensive welfare state without a democratic society and government.[1] However, the linkages between democratic institutions and economic development are far more difficult to pinpoint.[2] There are several examples in the world today of fast-growing countries without democratic governance structures, and history offers us plenty of evidence of such cases. Similarly, the relationship between the welfare state and economic growth is hard to ascertain. While some authors have warned us about the negative effects of social assistance on growth (for instance, due to lowering work incentives and poverty traps), others have found no such negative effects of

DOI: 10.4324/9780429503870-3

welfare policies.[3] According to Peter Lindert (2004), Nordic welfare states have seemingly emerged as "free lunches", that is, not having harmful economic impacts due to their broad investments in education and societal harmony and their tendency to fund these endeavors via indirect taxes, especially the so-called sin taxes, such as taxes on alcohol and tobacco consumption or from the use of cars.

The Nordic region is indeed an interesting case of study. It has been characterized by relatively fast economic growth, especially during the 20th century (converging to Western Europe despite late industrialization); an early extension of the voting franchise; and far-reaching welfare policies while exhibiting at the same time social and political unrest well into the early decades of the century. Nowadays, the region represents one of the most illustrative examples of welfare state: Finland, Denmark, Sweden and Norway appear (in this order) among the top 10 social spenders across the Organisation for Economic Co-operation and Development (OECD) in 2018.[4] According to the most recent World Happiness Report (2020), people in the Nordic countries seem to have the highest happiness levels on the planet, indicating broad satisfaction in their respective societies.[5] The extent to which Nordic countries can be considered part of a coherent unitary bloc, however, remains dubious.[6]

By using a variety of indicators from recent data collection efforts, we can distinguish certain general long-term patterns. First, most of the convergence toward social peace – here broadly defined as societies with fewer violent crimes and less political unrest as well as extensive civil freedoms – in the Nordic region occurred during the era of fast economic growth and catch-up with the leading Western economies, as well as during the development of welfare states and the emergence and consolidation of functional democratic institutions. Second, some of the key social transformations were connected to industrialization and global conflicts and their aftermath, and those processes eventually helped bring about similar political cultures and welfare institutions among the Nordic countries. Third, the path and timing of the transition into these welfare states, however, differed significantly across the region. We argue that the *Nordic societies evolved through phases from socially fragmented societies toward welfare states through social integration*. Denmark and Sweden appear to be the regional pioneers in developing democratic and welfare institutions, whereas Norway's and Finland's catch-up took place during the post–World War II period. Consequently, the two former attained better levels earlier in most of our indicators of social fragmentation. There is today, however, increasing evidence of rising social fragmentation through polarization in which certain groups in society feel left out of the benefits of the high standards of living and globalization, which, in turn, is a challenge for democracy and might lead to social unrest in the future.

In the following sections, we first explore some of the theoretical dimensions of the linkages among democracy, economic growth, and welfare policies. Then we switch gears to analyze the evolution of these factors in the Nordic region since the early 19th century. This is followed by an examination of the various institutional patterns and indicators of social fragmentation. We specifically look at the extent to which the path toward more peaceful and egalitarian societies took place during periods of democratization, economic growth, and fiscal expansion. We conclude with some overall findings and a discussion of future challenges.

Democracy, economic growth, and welfare states

The amount of research discussing democracy, economic growth, and welfare is vast for each of these topics, and studies that concentrate on their potential causal relationships are on the rise.[7] In particular, institutional economics is by now a well-established field of study, and it has added new dimensions to the debates about the role of informal and formal institutions in economic development, transaction costs, and other considerations about the various structures in the society.[8] In this brief review of the literature, we touch on some of the most important debates on these topics, namely, the relationship among democracy, economic growth, and state intervention, as well as the relationship between these factors and social fragmentation. We concentrate on studies done by scholars among social sciences interested in long-run historical dynamics, showing that the analysis of the institutional continuities and discontinuities over a long period, based on a variety of meaningful indicators, is imperative in analyzing these linkages.

The key question within the interrelationship among democratic institutions, economic growth, and fiscal developments is of a chicken-and-egg type: Does democracy need economic growth or growth democracy? Or are they intrinsically interrelated? And how does the development of state capacity and eventual welfare states fit into this discussion? Adam Przeworski, for example, has shown quite convincingly that democracy does need a stable economic structure, including growth, in order to emerge and succeed – and vice versa: the economies of democratic states tend to grow faster than the undemocratic ones.[9] There are, however, plenty of contemporary studies indicating that economic development alone has not led to democracy in various countries, including China.[10] Democracies, on the other hand, are more likely to emerge in countries that are economically developed, but there are notable exemptions too (for instance, in the case of oil-abundant economies or other types of resource curses).[11] In fact, political and economic factors are fundamentally interlinked, thereby forming endogenous processes that are complicated to pin down and often temporally disjointed. Most of the previous studies, moreover, have not looked at the long-run development patterns and rather focused on the post–World War II period. This period was in many ways exceptional in the history of human societies due to its high economic growth rates and the declining trend in economic inequality within countries (at least until the 1980s).[12]

The role that political and economic factors play in determining the level of government spending and the size of the state more in general has been also a contested issue. For instance, Carles Boix (2001) has argued that the growth of the public sector is a joint result of the process of economic development and the political institutions in place. In his view, economic modernization leads to the growth of the public sector, especially when the state intervenes to provide certain collective goods, while industrialization and aging population increase the demand for social transfers. He also maintains that democracy (with full electoral participation) increases public spending levels, since the potential beneficiaries of the welfare state gain the possibility of shaping the political agenda in their favor.[13] Some authors, however, disagree. Cutler and Johnson (2004), for instance, suggest that autocratic regimes might also implement welfare policies in order to gain political legitimacy. Others do not find any significant relationship between political regimes and public social expenditure.[14]

Another strand of the literature has addressed the opposite causal relationship, that is, to what extent government spending (and state intervention more generally) affects economic performance. For example, Bergh and Karlsson (2010) find a negative correlation between government size and growth in a post-1970 OECD sample, while Romero-Ávila and Strauch (2008) argue that government consumption (but not investment) has negatively affected economic growth in the EU-15 from 1960 to 2001. By contrast, Lindert (2004) has argued that social spending leads to economic growth through more productive use of resources. Acemoglu and his coauthors, as well as Lindert, also take into account the various types of welfare states in these processes, since elites will try to promote social peace and prevailing power structure via redistribution strategies, with the expansion of political voice changing the equilibria in the society.[15]

More recently, the study of the impact of state capacity on economic modernization in the long run has gained traction, with important insights about what the state has meant for the development of modern societies, mostly in the West. As shown by scholars such as Mark Dincecco, David Stasavage, and Philip Hoffman, European states developed superior state capacity in the form of revenue collection, financial systems, and military capacity over centuries, which gave them the opportunity to dominate the globe.[16] State capacity contributed, in turn, to economic growth and modernization. For example, Dincecco (2015) and Dincecco and Katz (2016) suggest that effective states have promoted growth by building up administrative infrastructure (necessary for the protection of property rights and market regulation) and by providing public services. In a similar vein, O'Brien (2011) argues that the capacity to provide external and internal security to investors and innovators contributed to long-run economic growth. The lack of state capacity, by contrast, has been associated with economic decline.[17] Dincecco (2015) also finds in state capacity the roots of the 20th-century welfare states, although the transition toward inclusive welfare policies out of this "capacity" is still an underexplored question.

The debate around democracy and economic growth has been deeply interlinked with that of social fragmentation and conflict. A productive strand of the literature has analyzed the effects of democracy and growth on international and internal conflicts. While there is no clear consensus on the extent to which democracies are more conflict-averse than autocracies, a growing body of evidence suggest that democratic states are less likely to fight against each other.[18] There is more debate on the extent to which the opportunity costs of international trade and economic growth hinders international conflict.[19] Internal conflict and social fragmentation, on the other hand, have been analyzed in an interdisciplinary fashion for a long time. The study of civil wars by such scholars as Theda Skocpol and Barrington Moore, in which the broad foundations of unrest and societal order come into play, has long roots in 20th-century scholarship. They argued that centralized semi-bureaucratic systems of authority combined with state-dependent gentry, a weak national bourgeoisie, a century-old legacy of rural collectivism, and a militant labor movement, provided suitable foundations for 20th-century societal unrest and revolutions.[20] More recently, this argument has been refocused by a war-centered theory that maintains that it was the destructive experience of the wars against advanced industrial nations that destroyed the economies of less developed nations, which eventually experienced revolutions and coups, often leading them on an authoritarian path.[21]

Most of the recent literature on social fragmentation and revolutions has indeed focused on modern ethnic strife, civil wars in the developing world, the role played by nonstate actors, as well as the lingering impacts of colonialism as a broad explanatory force in the persistence of poverty.[22] Most of the literature, quite naturally, has also been focused on societal breakdowns and origins of violence. Along these lines, the past of societal unrest in the Nordic countries (and civil war in 1918 in Finland) has been of interest to international scholars.[23] However, the convergence toward more peaceful societies has received less attention and focused study, outside the creation of the welfare states. Moreover, these studies have not been as interested in long-run transitions toward functioning societies and have rather focused on disruptions in various types of societies. The potentially endogenous processes leading toward social peace have not, thus, been studied enough.

Nordic economies and democracies

Following Eloranta et al. (2014), we begin by examining the economic and democratic patterns of four Nordic nations, namely, Denmark, Finland, Norway, and Sweden.[24] These countries have been often viewed as models for democracy and welfare state. Arguments of "good institutions" in Nordic countries,[25] "to become Denmark" as a model for the rest of the world,[26] or using Swedish development also as an example for business development[27] are a few examples of this phenomenon. Still, however, Nordic scholars have argued that there is no single Nordic model, but rather, each country has developed its own peculiar model to build a welfare state (and democracy).[28] For this reason, in this section, we focus our attention on the periods of convergence and

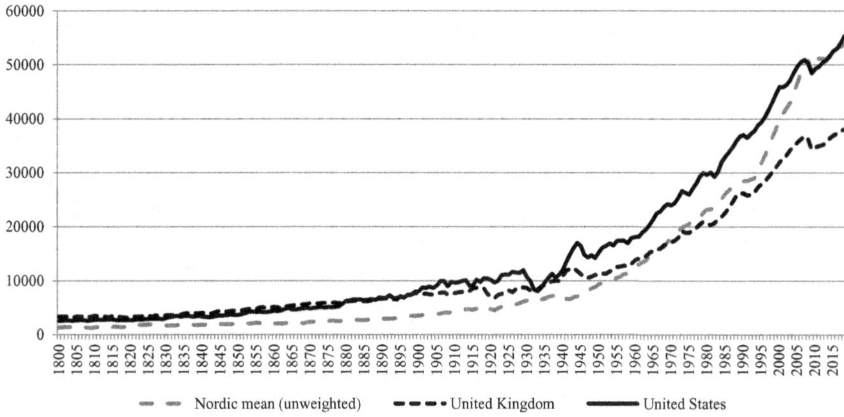

Figure 2.1 Nordic economic growth versus the economic leaders, 1800–2018 (real gross domestic product per capita in 2011US$)

Source: Data compiled by the Maddison Project Database, version 2020 (Bolt and van Zanden, 2020). The country sources are for Finland, Eloranta et al. (2016); for Norway, Grytten (2015); for Sweden, Schön and Krantz (2015); for the UK, Broadberry et al. (2015); and for the US, Sutch (2006).

divergence among the Nordic states, while in the next one, we examine the extent to which these periods were associated with the emergence and consolidation of welfare state policies.

As mentioned earlier, economic and political factors have been found to be important drivers of welfare state policies, and therefore constitute the starting point to our study. We specifically begin in the era when democratic institutions became embedded in these countries – namely, the 19th and early 20th centuries – which is also when they began to experience faster economic growth. Restricted forms of democracy were established in Nordic countries already during the early modern period, but they were heavily discriminatory on the basis of wealth, social class, and gender, and therefore fall outside the limits of any contemporary definition of *democracy*. Most of these early institutions were power-sharing arrangements that provided the first inclinations in their slow transition toward democracies.[29]

As seen in Figure 2.1, the Nordic economies (in average) lagged the UK and the US in the early 19th century, and this gap increased as the latter industrialized quicker. The Nordic catch-up did not begin until the post–World War II period, eventually surpassing the UK in the late 1960s and attaining similar levels to the US in the early 2000s.[30] The Nordic countries, however, did not evolve in unison during this period. Even if they were close to each other in the early 19th century, Denmark soon became the leader of the group during the Second Industrial Revolution (see Figure 2.2). Norway eventually surpassed it in the 1980s as a result of its abundance of natural resources, leading to

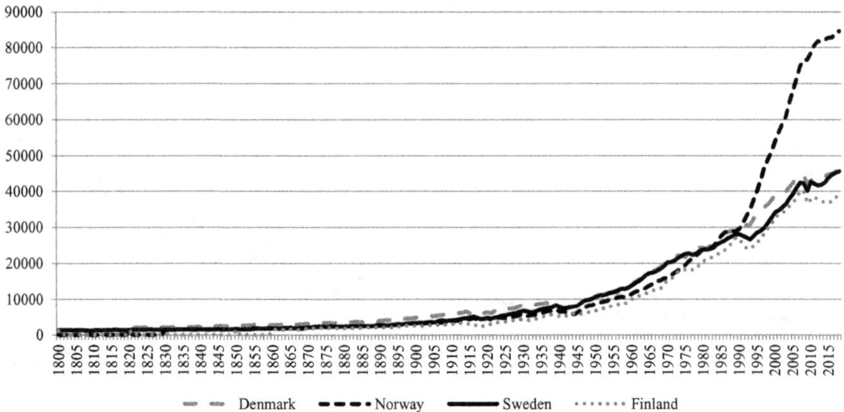

Figure 2.2 Nordic economic growth, 1800–2018 (real gross domestic product per capita in 2011US$)

Source: See Figure 2.1.

a path of exceptional economic growth that set the country apart from the rest of the region.[31] Finland followed a similar pattern compared to its neighbors throughout the period, although at systematically lower levels.

Despite this relatively delayed economic catch-up (at least when compared with the two leaders), the Nordic countries attained high levels of democracy comparatively early. Figure 2.3 displays a composite index (Polyarchy) compiled by the V-Dem Institute and based on Dahl (1998)'s maximalist conception of democracy, in which electoral and non-electoral factors are taken into account.[32] As can be clearly seen, the Nordic countries remained above the European average throughout most of the period, particularly after World War I. Denmark and Norway led the group for most of the time, catching up with some of the forerunners (such as the UK) already in the early 20th century. Sweden and Finland attained similar levels by the end of World War I, although Finland's harsher policies toward the Communist Party and the brief rise of right-wing authoritarianism in the 1930s – although it never reached political leadership – as well as its participation in World War II left the country behind until the 1950s. In general terms, however, we can say that Nordic countries preceded the so-called democratization wave that followed World War I, reaching higher levels than most of their European counterparts by the early 20th century. They were pioneers in extending the franchise to new segments of the population; after 1900, near-full suffrage was achieved in all the Nordic countries in short order, Finland being the forerunner in this development.[33] The highest degree of convergence was achieved in the late 20th century when Sweden and Norway (and, to a lesser extent, Finland) met the Danish standards.

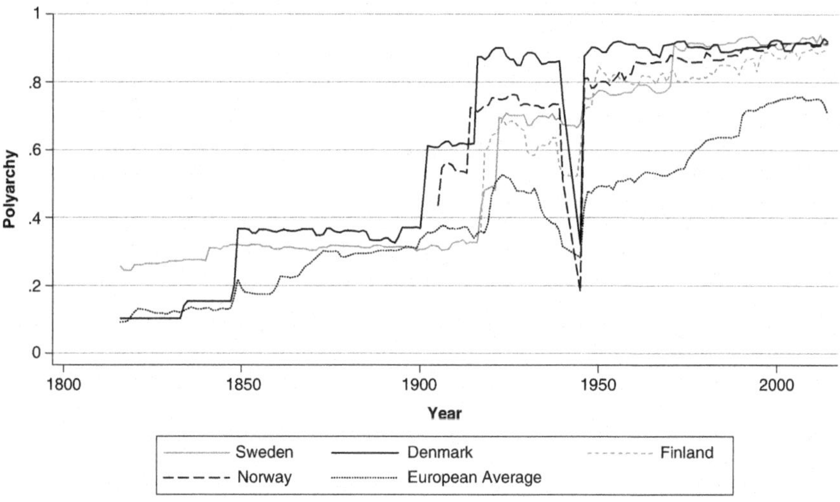

Figure 2.3 Nordic polyarchy, 1800–2016

Source: Coppedge et al. (2018).

The Polyarchy index in Figure 2.3 reflects the extent to which the electoral political process was fair and open to anyone. However, it does not say much about the degree of political participation by society. Table 2.1 presents the evolution of an index of civil society participation, which looks at the involvement of people in civil society organizations and in the nomination of legislative candidates. Vibrant civil societies and social connectedness have been long considered an essential component of stable and functional democracies and even to lower the risk of democratic defection and breakdown.[34] According to this indicator, the Nordic region stands out not only in terms of formal electoral democracy but also in the level of civil society participation. The four countries remained well above the European average since the 1880s, with similar levels among them.[35]

The early extension of franchise and political participation were coupled with the rise of social democratic parties (and other left-wing parties) as relevant political actors, which contributed decisively to advance a welfare state agenda (particularly in Sweden and Norway, where social democrats obtained ample majorities or formed effective coalitions). The importance of labor movements in the political and economic arena can be also observed in Table 2.1, which shows the level of union density across the region. Denmark and Sweden experienced a steady increase until the 2000s and attained higher levels than the European average for most of the period. In Finland, the union density first declined after the Civil War (1918) but caught up to the other countries after

Table 2.1 Civil society participation and union density in the Nordic countries, 1850–2014

	Civil society participation index					*Union density*				
Years	*DK*	*SE*	*NO*	*FI*	*Europe*	*DK*	*SE*	*NO*	*FI*	*Europe*
1880–99	81.4	73.3	..	..	50.5	..	1.9	..	..	4.1
1900–19	86.4	82.0	82.6	81.4	55.4	18.7	11.1	10.8	12.8	11.1
1920–39	92.1	87.3	85.7	81.6	55.8	33.5	35.5	19.8	7.3	24.8
1940–59	92.6	94.8	92.5	88.0	52.7	51.7	64.0	45.3	30.2	42.4
1960–79	97.2	95.7	97.4	95.7	57.5	63.2	71.0	56.6	50.4	49.6
1980–99	97.7	94.8	97.5	97.3	70.9	77.0	82.7	57.3	74.0	45.2
2000–14	97.8	92.4	97.8	97.8	78.6	71.8	76.9	54.7	73.0	32.8

Source: Civil society participation index from Coppedge et al. (2018); union density from Rasmussen and Pontusson (2017).

Notes: DK = Denmark; SE = Sweden; NO = Norway; FI = Finland. Civil society participation is a composite index of four variables, namely, CSO consultation, CSO participatory environment, CSO women participation, and candidate selection. It takes values from 0 to 1 (low to high), although here we present the index multiplied by 100 for the sake of clarity. Union density measures the share of wage and salary earners that were unionized.

the World War II. Norway's unions, on its part, stagnated in lower levels (but still above the European average) since the 1960s and 1970s. Trade unions (and the labor movement in general) have been long considered important agents in the rise of welfare states in Western countries, since they channeled the interests of wage and salary earners through the political process. This, in turn, put pressure on the governments and legislatures to improve social protection and assistance. Norway stands as a notable exception to this Nordic pattern due to its very high levels of economic growth and its lower levels of union density.

Fiscal systems and welfare institutions

Did these processes of economic and political convergence translate into the realm of fiscal and welfare policies as well? First, if we look at the central government revenue patterns, which is a standard measure for state capacity, the short answer is no. Tax revenues as a share of gross domestic product (GDP) increased consistently in Denmark, Norway, and Sweden from the 1930s up to the 1980s, but the former taxed its citizens at significantly higher levels than the latter two since the mid-1960s (see Figure 2.4). Finnish tax revenues, on the other hand, stagnated after reaching their historical peak during World War II. Despite the relatively low levels of economic growth and democracy, the level of taxation was well above the rest until the 1960s. The 2000s witnessed a significant divergence across the region too, with tax revenues soaring in Norway and Denmark while decreasing in Sweden and Finland. Whereas the Danish leading position seems consistent with historically higher levels of democracy, the process of democratic convergence that culminated in the 1990s did not bring about an analogous harmonization of fiscal policies.

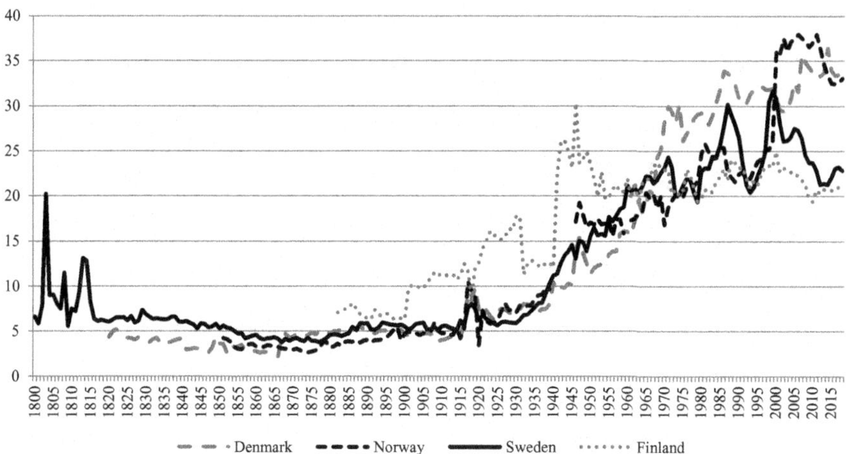

Figure 2.4 Nordic central government tax revenue (as a percentage of gross domestic product), 1800–2018

Source: Andersson and Brambor (2019) for the period 1800–2011. The data set has been extended to 2018 with data from the Organisation for Economic Co-operation and Development (https://stats.oecd.org/Index.aspx?DataSetCode=REV, retrieved on 13/12/2019).

Fiscal divergence, however, was mostly felt at the central government level. If we look at the data available for general government (i.e., including local and regional taxes), the four Nordic countries experienced a very similar evolution since 1965 (see Figure 2.5). A sustained growth during the 1960s and 1970s came to a halt by the 1980s, with Sweden and Norway decreasing their tax burden during the following three decades. Finland was still under-taxing compared to its neighbors throughout most of the period, but it converged upward after the Great Recession (2008). Norway, on the other hand, remained below the rest since the early 1990s, but this trend coincided with its exceptional GDP growth (and thus the amount of revenue collected did nothing but grow consistently throughout most of the period).

How were these tax revenues employed? The two main choices were, of course, guns and butter, so to speak, or warfare and welfare. In general, the choice over public goods (and both of these were imperfect public goods) was to a large extent dependent on the political system in place. Figure 2.6 shows the percentage of social spending at the general level as a share of GDP. Before the 20th century, most of the central government budgets in Western states were allocated for military purposes, and only in the 20th century we do see significant welfare state creation, especially after World War II.[36] The Nordic states expanded the British model of welfare to include new political and social initiatives, which led to the most inclusive welfare states in the world by the end of the 20th century. Although they took some tentative steps in this

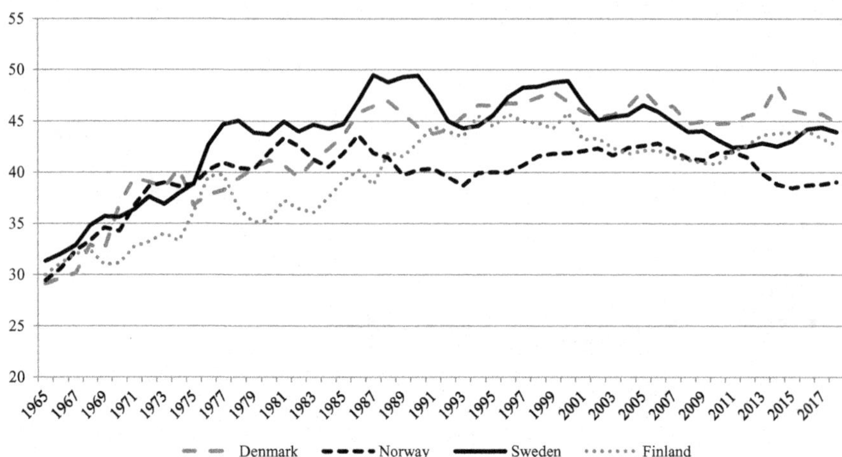

Figure 2.5 Nordic general government tax revenue (as a share of gross domestic product), 1965–2018

Source: Organisation for Economic Co-operation and Development (https://stats.oecd.org/Index.aspx?DataSetCode=REV, retrieved on 13/12/2019).

direction in the 19th century, it was not until the interwar years that the institutional foundations of the welfare states were built in these countries. The 1940s and the 1950s in the Nordic countries were a time of extending the measures already created in the 1930s, especially in Sweden, which developed the most extensive early institutions such as maternity benefits, social insurance, and unemployment benefits. Social spending as a percentage of GDP was still very low in the 1920s in Finland, which was a latecomer with a relative share at about 1 percent, while the leading Nordic country, Denmark, spent three times as much in relative terms. Thus, Finland followed the other Nordic countries at a lag in terms of its welfare state building. After the golden era of the growth of the welfare state in the 1960s, Finland became one of the high-spending states in terms of social transfers. Only Sweden had a higher share before the recession hit the Nordic countries hard in the early 1990s.[37]

Overall, Nordic countries opted for increases in social spending and limited military expenditure, that is, investing in domestic stability and equality. Finland's development since the 1920s is a good case of illustrating the rapid investment in social peace, especially given that it experienced a divisive civil war in 1918.[38] The country that democratized first, Denmark, also led the group in terms of social spending during the early 20th century. Sweden took firmly the lead during the period when its democracy became more entrenched in the 1960s and 1970s. Despite the retrenchment (or the slower growth, in the case of Denmark) in the last three decades, the Nordic countries remain well above

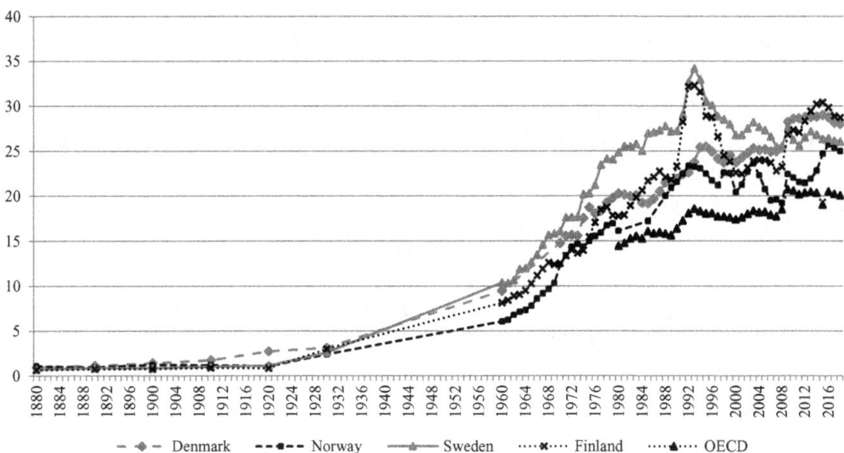

Figure 2.6 Nordic social spending (as a share of gross domestic product), 1880–2016

Source: From 1880 to 1979, *Our World in Data* (https://ourworldindata.org/grapher/social-spending-oecd-longrun?time=1880..2016, retrieved on 13/12/2019), based on Lindert (2004) and Organisation for Economic Co-operation and Development (OECD) statistics. From 1980 to 2018, from OECD (https://stats.oecd.org/Index.aspx?datasetcode=SOCX_AGG#, retrieved on 13/12/2019).

Table 2.2 Nordic social spending, 1980–2018 (position based on social spending/gross domestic product within the Organisation for Economic Co-operation and Development)

Country	*1980*	*1990*	*2000*	*2010*	*2018*
Sweden	1	1	2	7	7
Denmark	6	7	5	2	4
Finland	9	5	8	5	3
Norway	12	8	10	17	9

Source: Organisation for Economic Co-operation and Development (https://stats.oecd.org/Index.aspx?datasetcode=SOCX_AGG, retrieved on 13/12/2019).

the OECD average (which, in 2018, was lower by about 5 to 8 GDP percentage points). Table 2.2 additionally shows the position of each country within the OECD group based on their levels of social spending as a share of GDP. Sweden, Denmark, and Finland stood firmly in the top 10 since 1980, but their relative position changed significantly throughout the period: Sweden moved from being the first social spender to the seventh in two decades, whereas Denmark and Finland climb up to the second and third positions in the 2010s. As mentioned earlier, Norway remained well below the rest due to its higher GDP. While we can hardly talk about a single Nordic pattern, the region stood ahead of most other rich countries for more than four decades.

Were there also similarities in the composition of social spending? As can be seen in Table 2.3, most of it went to pensions and to health services in all four countries. The former gained weight during the 1980–2010 period in Sweden and Finland, while it lost some of its prominence in Denmark. Health services, on the other hand, only gained traction in Norway during this period (together with family-related social assistance). These two budgetary items, however, were also of distinct importance in other OECD countries. What set the Nordic countries apart during this period is the relatively large expenditure in family- and incapacity-related services and transfers, which were consistently above the OECD average.

Table 2.4 summarizes the aforementioned patterns of convergence and divergence in the Nordic region by looking at the coefficients of variation of GDP per capita, democracy, public revenue, and social spending, in different time

Table 2.3 Composition of Nordic social spending (most important categories from 1980–2015 in percentages)

Decade	*Old age*	*Family*	*Health*	*Incapacity*
Denmark				
1980	38.6	13.7	23.8	17.1
1990	36.5	14.7	18.8	16.1
2000	33.0	14.2	22.8	17.4
2010	34.2	12.6	22.8	16.4
Finland				
1980	30.5	11.7	24.1	18.1
1990	29.0	13.1	18.2	16.8
2000	34.1	12.0	19.7	15.5
2010	38.4	11.0	19.2	13.2
Norway				
1980	34.9	11.5	19.9	20.6
1990	31.2	14.7	18.4	21.1
2000	30.3	13.9	24.2	21.4
2010	33.6	14.0	25.5	17.5
Sweden				
1980	29.6	13.8	26.0	17.5
1990	30.8	12.4	19.6	15.8
2000	32.8	11.7	22.7	18.7
2010	34.7	13.4	23.8	15.8
OECD				
1980	32,4	9,2	26,1	14,1
1990	33,4	9,5	26,1	12,5
2000	32,8	10,8	28,4	11,8
2010	34,7	10,8	27,9	10,6

Source: Organisation for Economic Co-operation and Development (https://stats.oecd.org/Index.aspx?datasetcode=SOCX_AGG, retrieved on 13/12/2019).

Table 2.4 Coefficient of variation (average for the period): Nordic gross domestic product (GDP) per capita, government spending, and debt

Variable	*1860–1914*	*1920–1939*	*1946–1970*	*1971–1999*	*2000–2016*
GDP per Capita	0.33	0.30	0.18	0.12	0.33
Democracy	0.21	0.15	0.07	0.04	0.02
Public Revenues (central)	0.28	0.40	0.17	0.17	0.24
Public Revenues (general)	..	..	0.04	0.07	0.05
Social Spending	0.19	0.13	0.23	0.22	0.16

Source: see previous figures.

periods. As mentioned earlier, democracy converged in the long term in our four countries (especially in the latter half of the 20th century), whereas public revenues at the general level remained very similar among them since our first data point (1965). GDP per capita also converged through most of the period but diverged considerably from the mid-1990s onward as a result of the Norwegian natural resources boost. At the end of the period, however, all of them attained high GDP levels and high standards of living. Despite this economic and political convergence, social spending diverged during the post–World War II period, mainly as a result of the 1970s' Swedish surge. Convergence took place only in the last period, at the same time when the economic differences were at their highest. These patterns suggest that the growth of social spending came along with a process of economic growth and democratization, but economic and political convergence was not matched with convergence in welfare policies. Specific conditions to each country determined the short and mid-term spending decisions within an upward long-term trend. Public revenues at the central level, on the other hand, converged to a certain extent until the late 20th century, with the notable exception of the interwar period (when the two World Wars set their military spending levels apart). Differences, however, bounced back in the 2000s.

Welfare policies and social fragmentation

Welfare states have been associated with a variety of social and economic outcomes, from lower levels of poverty to better protection of social rights, although the literature is not free of controversy and opposing views. In this final section, we specifically look at the historical evolution of welfare states vis-à-vis a set of indicators of social fragmentation, namely, internal violence, labor disputes, inequality, literacy rates, and women's political rights. Even if these indicators do not exhaust all the possible factors that belong to the realm of social fragmentation, they provide a persuasive picture of the historical evolution of social cohesion. With this brief revision, we intend to highlight some general patterns toward social peace among the Nordic countries in the long run and how they relate to the welfare state.

The presence of internal violence or the lack thereof constitutes a key indicator of the degree of cohesion in contemporary societies. In this regard, it is noteworthy that the Nordic region has been free from internal wars since well before the development of welfare policies. No major domestic military conflicts erupted during the last two centuries, except for the Finnish Civil War, a harsh internal strife initiated after the collapse of the Russian Empire at the end of World War I. The country emerged as an independent republic in the aftermath of the war, but the consequences of the conflict lasted for decades. For example, one of the factors that led to the war was the stark social and economic divisions among the landowners and crofters, which were addressed with several statutes immediately after the war.[39] The overall absence of internal wars within the Nordic states mirrored the lack of external military conflicts. The Nordic countries had become much less prone to participate in international military conflicts since the early 19th century. Up until this point, wars were almost a constant occurrence, which was similar to other European states at the time.[40] These constant flows of conflict – together with crop failures and famines – also hindered the possibilities of economic growth in other parts of Europe, as Stephen Broadberry et al. have argued.[41] After the Napoleonic conflicts were over, war became a rare state of affairs, with some minor exceptions. Of course, the World Wars did involve the Nordic countries to varying degrees, with only Sweden remaining outside of fighting entirely in World War II, but afterward, the Nordic countries have only participated in a few military operations as minor parties.[42]

Other aspects of internal violence that fell short of civil war did change significantly in the Nordic region throughout this period, such as the degree of freedom from political killings and torture. These two variables are coded by the V-Dem Institute based on country expert surveys and measure the extent to which torture and political killings were practiced by state authorities or their agents. Even if the data needs to be taken with a grain of salt (these phenomena are obviously difficult to put together in a quantitative long-term fashion), Figure 2.7 suggests that most Nordic countries remained consistently above the European averages for most of the period. Denmark stood ahead of the rest during the 19th and early 20th centuries, when Sweden attained similar levels. Finland and Norway lagged until the 1950s and 1980s, respectively (with Norway suffering a serious fallback during World War II as a result of the Nazi invasion). As with the other political indicators discussed in the previous section, the 20th century was a period of steady (albeit interrupted) progress, and virtually full convergence in the region was reached in the 1990s and 2000s.

To have a broader picture of internal violence, Figure 2.7 presents the evolution of interpersonal violence proxied by the number of homicides per 100,000 inhabitants – although interpersonal violence is, as a whole, more complex and multifaceted phenomenon, including both threat and actual use of physical force or power.[43] Once again, Finland stands out above the rest. The causes of interpersonal violence are, of course, complicated, but we can conjecture that Finish homicide rates increased substantially in the early 20th century due

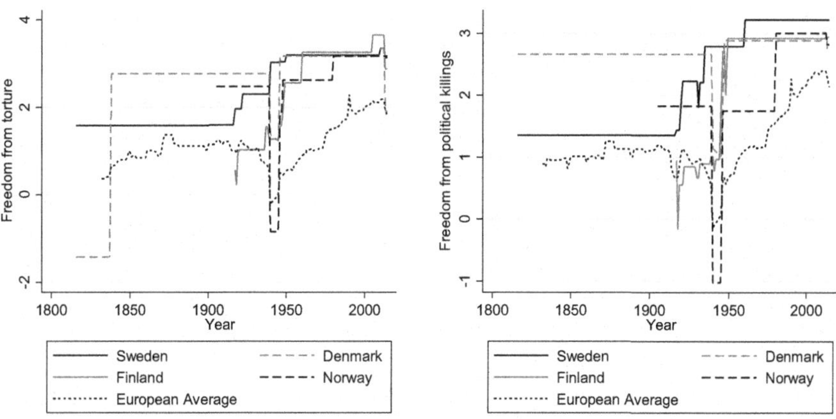

Figure 2.7 Freedom from torture (left) and political killings (right) in the Nordic societies, 1800–2015

Source: Pemstein et al. (2019).

Note: The two variables range from 0 (low freedom) to 4 (high freedom).

to societal unrest and the civil war. The rates stayed high during the interwar period and declined substantially by the 1960s. Since then, the homicide rates in Finland have remained fairly stable, although clearly above the Nordic levels overall.[44] The patterns of interpersonal violence among the other three Nordic countries, by contrast, were remarkably similar, with a slightly declining trend throughout the late 19th century and the first half of the 20th century. This decline went along with the implementation of some of the first welfare policies and the development of more inclusive political institutions. Interpersonal violence, however, increased again in the 1970s up until the mid-1990s, at a time when social spending in the region rose to its peak.

All in all, the rise of the welfare state seems to be only partially related to changing patterns in violence. On the one hand, internal and external wars were largely absent from the region even before the emergence of contemporary social policies. The World Wars shaped the political agenda in the Western Hemisphere, even for those who did not engage in direct combat, but the growth of welfare states did not change a long-term pattern of neutrality in the international arena. On the other hand, we do observe a declining trend in interpersonal violence at the time when social spending took off, but the opposite was true during the consolidation of welfare policies in the 1970s. Very high levels of internal violence in the first half of the 20th century did not prevent the Finnish governments from laying the foundations of a welfare state agenda either. The clearest link between the welfare state and social peace can be found in the case of state violence against its own citizens; in this case, the surge in social policies went along with decreasing levels of repression against dissidents.

Another way to examine internal turmoil is to look at labor unrest, which can be also considered an outcome of social fragmentation (albeit this time directly related to class and the labor market). Table 2.4 shows the number of workers involved in labor disputes as a percentage of the population (unfortunately, labor disputes as a share of the aggregate numbers of workers because are not available). Along the same lines as before, we see fairly low shares of labor disputes until the 1970s, when Finland became an exception to the Nordic pattern due to its high numbers. These disputes were not, however, very violent encounters like those in the earlier periods – rather most of them were short ones to immediately higher the wages, usually at the factory level.[45] Sweden attained similar levels than Finland in the 1980s, whereas Denmark featured a fair number of such disputes in the 1990s and early 2000s. Especially harsh were the Danish large conflicts connected to collective agreements in 1998 that were, in turn, related to various labor market reforms.[46] Despite the rise of welfare state policies in the 1970s and the 1980s, labor unrest rocketed in Finland and Sweden, and to a lesser extent in Denmark. Labor disputes could actually be seen as an outcome of welfare states, with labor having more freedom to protest over wages or conditions at the workplace. In any case, the data have to be taken with due caution given the large variety of labor unrest measured here.

Despite the mixed evidence that the analysis of internal unrest and welfare state renders, other indicators of social fragmentation and well-being should show clearer signs of being affected by the social policies that were implemented in the region. Income inequality is an obvious candidate and an important source of social strife. As shown in Figure 2.8, Nordic Gini indices decreased

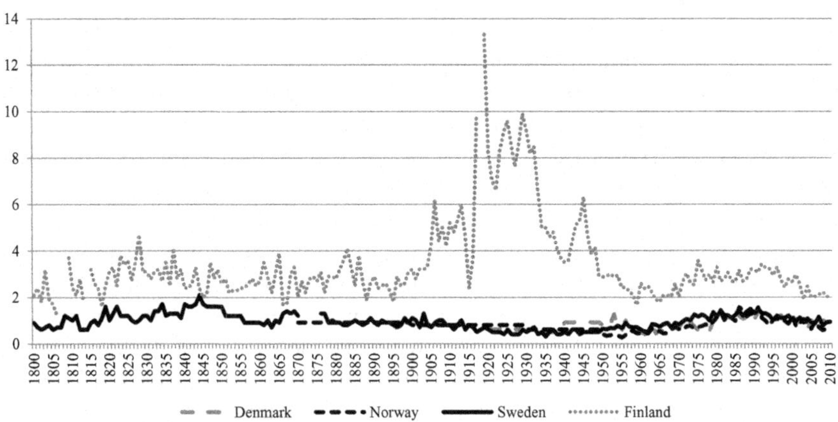

Figure 2.8 Number of homicides per 100,000 inhabitants, 1800–2010

Source: Fink-Jensen (2015).

Note: The data set uses as a geographical reference the current existing countries.

Table 2.5 Number of workers involved with labor disputes relative of total population, 1930–2010

Country	*1930*	*1940*	*1950*	*1960*	*1970*	*1980*	*1990*	*2000*	*2010*
Denmark	0.14	0.01	0.07	0.43	1.13	1.21	0.73	1.42	1.67
Finland	0.05	0.17	2.94	0.44	4.38	8.52	4.91	1.63	0.30
Norway	0.17	0.53	0.13	0.02	0.08	0.46	1.43	2.09	0.27
Sweden	0.37	0.04	0.03	0.02	0.33	8.98	0.85	0.00	0.14

Source: https://clio-infra.eu/Indicators/NumberofWorkersInvolvedinLabourDisputes.html.

significantly during the 20th century, and their evolution has been associated with progressive social and fiscal policies. For instance, top marginal tax rates have been found to affect negatively the concentration of income and wealth in the hands of top earners.[47] Even if Nordic countries were not the ones that taxed the rich more heavily, top rates increased significantly during the first half of the 20th century (especially during the interwar period).[48] Similarly, fiscal studies have considered social spending in social democratic welfare states to be the main source of income redistribution (rather than taxation).[49]

Another sign of the Nordic welfare states and societies becoming more egalitarian is the increasing recognition of women in the workforce and in prominent positions. As we can observe in Table 2.5, for example, women have become a much more prominent political presence in Nordic societies. In terms of gender inequality, the Nordic countries were about three times more equal than the more developed parts of the world by the end of the 20th century (although full equality is still a pending subject). Moreover, they were very similar to each other, and they improved further and converged toward similar levels of gender equality by today.[50]

Part of the reduction of inequality and societal unrest has come via the creation of more inclusive societies, especially via more egalitarian and robust societal institutions (including justice system and democracy on the aggregate) that have emerged via the creation of social and human capital.[51] The Nordic countries have, indeed, been at the forefront of creating very extensive and effective schooling systems. We can observe those efforts in Table 2.6, with steady increases in the average length of education. Finland was far behind the other Nordic countries still in the 19th century, but it began to catch up in the post–World War II period, especially after the school reforms of the 1960s and 1970s. By the 21st century, the Nordic countries look very similar. These systems have produced excellent results in international testing, for example, in the Programme for International Student Assessment tests.[52] Another common measure to gauge the human capital formation, besides literacy, is to estimate numeracy skills, which have enabled economic historians to estimate human capital in the long run.[53] As seen in Figure 2.9, Nordic numeracy skills varied quite a bit in the 19th century but converged after 1870, with Norway lagging the rest. This highlights the fact that the Finnish education system produced

Table 2.6 Number of women (as a percentage) in the Nordic parliaments, 1995–2010

Country	*1995*	*2000*	*2005*	*2010*	*2015*	*2018*
Denmark	33.0	37.4	36.9	38.0	37.4	37.4
Finland	33.5	36.5	37.5	40.0	41.5	42.0
Norway	36.4	36.4	37.9	39.6	39.6	41.4
Sweden	40.4	42.7	45.3	45.0	43.6	46.1
Very high human development	14.0	16.5	18.9	21.4	24.6	27.2
Low human development	10.1	9.7	15.4	17.7	21.2	21.5
Developing Countries	9.6	12.1	14.7	17.7	21.3	22.5
Oganisation for Economic and Development and Co-operation	14.9	17.6	20.2	23.0	27.6	30.1
World	11.5	13.9	16.3	19.1	22.7	24.2

Source: Human Development Reports (HDR) (2019). Available from: http://hdr.undp.org/en/content/gender-inequality-index-gii (retrieved December 20, 2019).

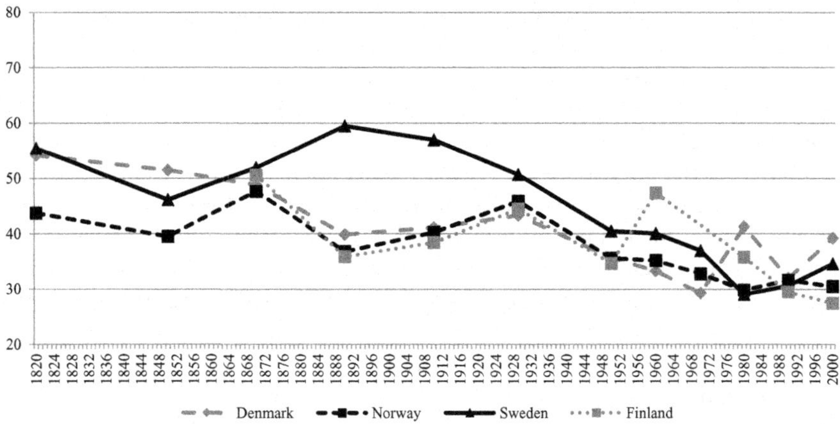

Figure 2.9 Nordic income inequality (gini index), 1820–2000

Source: Moatsos et al. (2015).

more human capital in the pre–World War II period than those of the other Nordic countries, given the lower average years of schooling. After the 1950s and 1960s, the Nordic countries, more or less, had the highest numeracy scores possible (=100).

Other indicators of well-being improved in a similar fashion during this period. For instance, life expectancy at birth (which depends on many of the underlying inputs into societies, for example, nutrition, medical care, technological development, schooling, and so on) exhibited a steady growth trend among the Nordic societies, especially from the 1860s onward. Finland lagged the other three for a long time, until it converged to the Nordic pattern in the late 20th century. The only dips in the process were caused by major crises, such as the World Wars. Overall, the investments in the society via the increases in democracy provided clear benefits for the Nordic societies as a whole, although

Table 2.7 Primary school enrollment among the Nordic countries, 1820–2010

Year	*Denmark*	*Finland*	*Norway*	*Sweden*	*UK*	*USA*
1820	84.9	..	48.5	80.7	..	41.4
1850	92.0	4.0	64.8	89.4	..	80.1
1880	100.0	16.0	78.3	100.0	77.2	100.0
1910	100.0	64.9	98.2	100.0	100.0	100.0
1940	100.0	100.0	100.0	100.0	92.4	100.0
1970	96.0	100.0	89.0	92.7	98.0	95.9
1990	96.0	99.0	99.0	99.0	97.0	98.0
2000	100.0	100.0	100.0	100.0	100.0	100.0
2010	100.0	99.0	99.0	100.0	..	99.0

Source: Lee and Lee (2016).

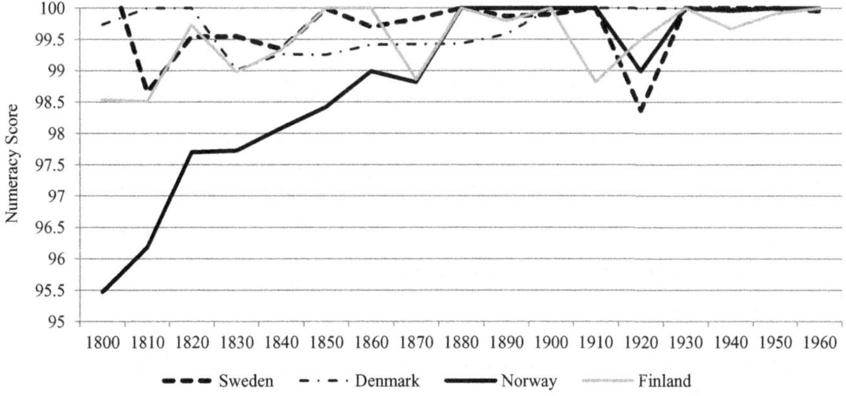

Figure 2.10 Nordic numeracy scores, 1800–1960

Source: https://clio-infra.eu/Indicators/NumeracyTotal.html.

in some cases, the path toward social cohesion had been already initiated in previous decades and varied among them.[54] In any case, it is quite clear that some of the most important changes, including the convergence between the Nordic countries and the most advanced economies on the globe, occurred in the post–World War II period. While economic convergence may have already started, in fits and starts, already in the 19th century, the various forms of institutional development were not uniform among the Nordic countries. The main thrust, however, of the institutional convergence toward less fragmentation also occurred quite fast after World War II.

Conclusion and further challenges

Democracies can be unstable in many ways, depending on how mature they are, the external and internal threats, the impact of economic and political crises, and so on. Typically, they, however, are more responsive to the needs of the majority of the population, given that policymakers will attempt to maintain their hold on positions of power. An essential part of an inclusive democracy is that citizens are free to express themselves in elections and in the public arena, as well as to engage in other forms of social participation (including freedom of assembly and the right to protest). Today these elements might seem self-evident in all Nordic countries. However, they have certainly experienced the rocky road, that is, not "smooth sailing", from fragmented societies to more inclusive and stable democracies in the 19th and 20th centuries. This chapter aimed at contributing to the understanding of the complex structural influences that have brought these changes about. To do so, we have had a look at the linkages between democratic institutions, economic and fiscal developments, and social policies. In particular, we have focused on the long-term coevolution of these factors and the processes of convergence among the Nordic countries toward less fragmented societies.

What did we find through our descriptive long-run analysis? First, economic development among the Nordic countries began later than in some of the early industrializers, but they caught up fast in the latter half of the 20th century. They also converged toward one another to a great extent, with high living standards, although Norway has set itself apart as the leader of the region in recent decades. Second, democratization in these countries occurred slightly earlier than in most European nations, that is, before World War I. After that, it progressed in steps, and it converged among the Nordic countries by the end of the 20th century. The country that democratized first, Denmark, also took the first steps in increasing social spending during the early 20th century. Sweden, on its part, took firmly the lead in the late 1960s and 1970s, while Norway and Finland did catch up thereafter. These countries also had bumps along the road; for example, the Second World War was harmful for Norway's democratization due to the societal divisions brought on by the occupation. In some sense, also the Finnish Civil War both delayed a more conscious policy toward welfare provision as well as hastened certain social policy dimensions, for example, more egalitarian landownership. Even if all countries increased their social spending effort in the post–World War II period, the convergence process toward a "Nordic model" progressed unevenly via the various dimensions of welfare, based on our examination of a large variety of indicators.

Social fragmentation levels also converged and decreased to a large extent among the four countries during the 20th century, although with some relevant differences. To begin with, all of them made the move from a warfare state to a welfare state latest in the 20th century, and they remained largely free from internal and external wars during the period (with the notable exceptions of the Finnish Civil War and, of course, the two World Wars). Other indicators of internal violence, such as freedom from political killings and torture, improved along the way; interpersonal violence at its extreme (homicides), on the other hand, decreased at a time when social spending took off, but it bounced back (albeit temporarily) during the consolidation of welfare policies in the 1970s. Labor disputes also varied considerably across countries. Finland and Sweden, in particular, had a much higher share of such conflicts in the 1970s and 1980s;

these strikes, though, can also be seen as an essential part of the maturing of a democracy and a welfare state. Despite the mixed evidence of a coevolution between internal unrest and welfare state, other indicators of social fragmentation and well-being showed clearer signs of being affected by the social policies implemented in the region. In this chapter, we have focused on income inequality, women political participation, and schooling, but we also point to others (such as life expectancy) that would render similar results.

All in all, we conclude that the postwar convergence in welfare and social cohesion was undeniable, strong, and fast, albeit it differed significantly across policy domains. Clearly, all the various forces acted in conjunction with one another, along with welfare state creation, and contributed to the emergence of more peaceful Nordic societies, with remarkably similar institutional setups. There were relatively small differences between the Nordic countries at the end of the 20th century, although differences were quite pronounced only a hundred years ago (with Finland occasionally lagging the others in the 19th and early 20th centuries). On the other hand, we can already observe remarkable connections between economic and social factors that need to be explored further. This is still, however, very much an initial stab at examining these complicated forces, and a quantitative in-depth analysis of the long-run linkages between some of the main variables is still pending. Moreover, there are clear signs of polarization among the Nordic populations nowadays, despite the high living standards and development toward more social cohesion. The populations of these countries are not immune to the same dynamics that are propelling populist parties in other parts of the world, namely, around issues such as migration, conflicts, globalization, and the future of the welfare state. The challenges for the Nordic societies, despite high levels of well-being, are linked to their ability to solve the perceived societal challenges in the political arenas. Social fragmentation is not a problem of the past, even if its impact has been lessened by the creation of some of the most egalitarian societies on the globe.

Notes

1 See esp. Esping-Andersen (1990). Social spending, however, might increase even in the context of authoritarian regimes See, for instance, Cutler and Johnson (2004); Segura-Ubiergo (2007). For an overview on the literature on Nordic Model, see especially Koivunen et al. (2021).

2 See, however, Przeworkski and Limongi (1993).

3 See Bergh (2006) and Lindert (2006a, 2006b). Bergh and Karlsson (2010) expanded on the harmful tax impacts to counter Lindert (2004).

4 OECD (2019).

5 World Happiness Report (2020). Available from: https://worldhappiness.report/ed/2020. (Cited December 6, 202+). The top spots are occupied by Finland (1st) and Denmark (2nd), while Iceland is ranked as fourth, Norway fifth, and Sweden seventh on the global list.

6 See, for instance, Christiansen and Markkola (2009); Koivunen et al. (2021).

7 These debates are indeed rooted to classic discussions in economics and social sciences since the writings of Adam Smith and, especially, Schumpeter (1942).

8 On the definition of institutions, see North (1990). On corporatist interests and interest-group influence, see, for example, Olson (1986). For a broader discussion, see Robinson and Acemoglu (2012); Acemoglu and Robinson (2005, 2019) and, for example, Rodrik et al. (2004). For a history of the field, see, for example, Coase (1984) and Hodgson (1998). For example, the Finnish scholarly debates on this, see especially Ojala (2017).
9 See especially Przeworski (1986, 1991, 2004). For a discussion on the role of economic growth to democratization, see especially Karvonen (1997), 28–46, or the classical account by Lipset (1959).
10 For example, Gat et al. (2009); Inglehart and Welzel (2009). For a discussion on the impact of democracy on economic growth, see also Przeworski and Limong (1993).
11 Teorell (2012). See also Acemoglu and Robinson (2000, 2005); Acemoglu et al. (2005).
12 According to Lindert (2003), the long-run analyses with multiple country cases can give us a richer understanding of these dynamics.
13 See also Lindert (2004); Espuelas (2012).
14 See, for instance, Mulligan et al. (2010).
15 See especially the discussion in Lindert (2003); Acemoglu and Robinson (2000). For a broader discussion, see Kettunen (2001, 2006), Petersen and Kettunen (2011), Robson (1976), and Esping-Andersen (1990).
16 The literature studying these topics has grown significantly in recent years. See, for instance, Dincecco and Katz (2016); Dincecco (2015); Besley and Persson (2009); Stasavage (2011); Hoffman (2017).
17 See, for instance, Grafe (2012). Economists have also studied the impact of state capacity on the economy (e.g., Besley and Persson, 2011, 2013).
18 See for a good summary of the literature, Hegre (2014). A compelling argument in favor of this proposition can be found in Doyle (1986).
19 A good review of the debate can be found in Levy and Thompson (2010).
20 See, for example, Moore (1966); Skocpol and Theda (1979); Osinsky and Eloranta (2014).
21 Mann (2012); Osinsky (2010).
22 See Christopher Lloyd's discussion on this earlier in the book. On the development of a social fragmentation index, see, for example, Okediji (2005). These types of efforts typically focus on combining elements of political, social, and ethnic fractions into a single measure.
23 See, for example, Casanova (2000); Kissane (2004); Archer and Joenniemi (2017).
24 Iceland is excluded in the analysis, because the data are less abundant, especially for some of the indicators we are using here.
25 Mokyr (2006).
26 Fukuyama (2014).
27 Porter (1990).
28 See, for example, Fellman et al. (2008), Kettunen (2001), and Meinander et al. (2018); Koivunen et al. (2021).
29 See especially Karonen et al. (2018).
30 On the Finnish convergence patterns, see, for example, Kokkinen et al. (2007).
31 See, for example, Ville and Wicken (2012); Mjøset and Cappelen (2011).
32 Teorell et al. (2019). The index takes into account the level of suffrage, of freedom of association and expression, the extent to which elections are free and fair, and the way in which officials are elected.
33 For the long-run roles of women in Nordic politics, see especially Haavio-Mannila and Skard (2013).
34 See, for instance, Putnam (1995). Concerning democratic breakdown, see, for example, Bernhard et al. (2020).
35 Similar results are found when looking at political participation defined as the share of population that cast a ballot in elections.
36 See, for example, Eloranta et al. (2014).

37 Eloranta and Kauppila (2006).
38 Hannikainen and Eloranta (2019). See also Kettunen (2001).
39 A number of studies have shown, however, that the division between crofters and landowners was not the major cause for the conflict; rather, it has been perhaps overemphasized in more popular writings. See especially Alapuro (1994).
40 Tilly (1990); Wiberg (2000).
41 Broadberry et al. (2015).
42 See also Ferguson (2002).
43 Husso et al. (2017), 1.
44 On discussion see especially Lehti and Kivivuori (2005, 2012); Savolainen et al. (2008); Kivivuori and Lehti (2006), Ylikangas et al. (2001).
45 Bergholm (2017), 189–190; Bergholm (2012), 209–233, 264–274, 308–317, 448–465.
46 Jørgensen (2004), 263; Lind and Knudsen (2018), 588, 590.
47 See, for instance, Roine et al. (2009).
48 Long-term series on top marginal income tax rates for our four countries can be found in the SSDS Social Science Data Collection.
49 See, for instance, Steinmo (1993); Lindert (2004); Pasad and Deng (2009); Henreksen & Stenkula (2015).
50 On overall trends, see especially Dorius and Firebaugh (2010). For a critique of the gender inequality index, see, for example, Permanyer (2013).
51 These types of processes have been suggested, for example, by Acemoglu et al. (2005). Education also can increase political participation and civic engagement in a given polity, see especially Glaeser et al. (2007).
52 Kjærnsli and Lie (2004). Some perspective on, for example, the Finnish results can be found in McIntosh (2019).
53 A review of the cliometric analyses of human capital can be found in Goldin (2016). See also Becker (2018).
54 On, for example, Finland, see especially recent analyses, such as Eloranta and Ojala (2018); Haapala and Lloyd (2018); Laine et al. (2019); Koponen and Saaritsa (2019).

References

Acemoglu, D., Johnson, S., Robinson, J. A., & Yared, P. (2005). From Education to Democracy? *American Economic Review, 95*(2), 44–49.

Acemoglu, D., & Robinson, J. A. (2000). Why Did the West Extend the Franchise? Democracy, Inequality, and Growth in Historical Perspective. *The Quarterly Journal of Economics, 115*(4), 1167–1199.

Acemoglu, D., & Robinson, J. A. (2005). *Economic Origins of Dictatorship and Democracy*. Cambridge: Cambridge University Press.

Acemoglu, D., & Robinson, J. A. (2019). *The Narrow Corridor: States, Societies, and the Fate of Liberty*. New York: Penguin Press.

Alapuro, R. (1994). *Suomen synty paikallisena ilmiönä 1890–1933*. Helsinki: Hanki ja jää.

Andersson, P., & Brambor, T. (2019). *Financing the State: Government Tax Revenue from 1800 to 2012*. Dataset. www.perfandersson.com/data.html.

Archer, C., & Joenniemi, P. (eds.). (2017). *The Nordic Peace*. Abingdon: Routledge.

Becker, S. O. (2018). Education and Human Capital. In M. Blum & C. L. Colvin (eds.), *An Economist's Guide to Economic History* (pp. 121–131). Cham: Palgrave Macmillan.

Bergh, A. (2006). Is the Swedish Welfare State a Free Lunch? *Econ Journal Watch, 3*(2), 210–235.

Bergh, A., & Karlsson, M. (2010). Government Size and Growth: Accounting for Economic Freedom and Globalization. *Public Choice, 142*(1–2), 195–213.

Bergholm, T. (2012). *Kohti tasa-arvoa: Tulopolitiikan aika I: Suomen Ammattiliittojen Keskusjärjestö 1969–1977*. Keuruu: Otava.

Bergholm, T. (2017). Ovatko työtaistelut vakava yhteiskunnallinen ongelma? In P. Pyöriä (ed.), *Työelämän myytit ja todellisuus* (pp. 184–196). Helsinki: Gaudeamus.

Bernhard, M., Hicken, A., Reenock, C., & Lindberg, S. I. (2020). Parties, Civil Society, and the Deterrence of Democratic Defection. *Studies in Comparative International Development, 55*(1), 1–26.

Besley, T., & Persson, T. (2009). The Origins of State Capacity: Property Rights, Taxation, and Politics. *American Economic Review, 99*(4), 1218–1244.

Besley, T., & Persson, T. (2011). *The Pillars of Prosperity*. Princeton: Princeton University Press.

Besley, T., & Persson, T. (2013). Taxation and Development. In A. Auerbach, R. Chetty, M. Feldstein, & E. Saez (eds.), *Handbook of Public Economics*. Amsterdam: Elsevier.

Boix, C. (2001). Democracy, Development, and the Public Sector. *American Journal of Political Science, 45*(1), 1–17.

Bolt, J., & van Zanden, J. L. (2020). *Maddison Style Estimates of the Evolution of the WORLD Economy. A New 2020 Update*. Maddison Project Database, version 2020.

Broadberry, S., Campbell, B. M., Klein, A., Overton, M., & Van Leeuwen, B. (2015). *British Economic Growth, 1270–1870*. Cambridge: Cambridge University Press.

Casanova, J. (2000). Civil Wars, Revolutions and Counterrevolutions in Finland, Spain, and Greece (1918–1949): A Comparative Analysis. *International Journal of Politics, Culture, and Society*, 515–537.

Christiansen, N. F., & Markkola, P. (2009). Introduction. In N. F. Christiansen & P. Markkola (eds.), *The Nordic Model of Welfare: A Historical Reappraisal*. Copenhagen: Museum Tusculanum Press.

Coase, R. H. (1984). The New Institutional Economics. *Zeitschrift für die gesamte Staatswissenschaft/Journal of Institutional and Theoretical Economics, 140*(1), 229–231.

Coppedge, M., Gerring, J., Knutsen, C. H., Lindberg, S. I., Skaaning, S-E., Teorell, J., Altman, D., Bernhard, M., Cornell, A., Fish, M. S., Gjerløw, H., Glynn, A., Hicken, A., Krusell, J., Lührmann, A., Marquardt, K. L., McMann, K., Mechkova, V., Olin, M., Paxton, P., Pemstein, D., Seim, B., Sigman, R., Staton, J., Sundtröm, A., Tzelgov, E., Uberti, L., Wang, Y., Wig, T., & Ziblatt, D. (2018). *V-Dem Codebook v8. Varieties of Democracy (V-Dem) Project*. Gotherburg: V-Dem Institute.

Cutler, D., & Johnson, R. (2004). The Birth and Growth of the Social Insurance State: Explaining Old Age and Medical Insurance Across Countries. *Public Choice, 120*, 87–121.

Dahl, R. A. (1998). *On Democracy*. New Haven: Yale University Press.

Dincecco, M. (2015). The Rise of Effective States in Europe. *The Journal of Economic History, 75*(3), 901–918.

Dincecco, M., & Katz, G. (2016). State Capacity and Long-Run Economic Performance. *The Economic Journal, 126*(590), 189–218.

Dorius, S. F., & Firebaugh, G. (2010). Trends in Global Gender Inequality. *Social Forces, 88*(5), 1941–1968.

Doyle, M. W. (1986). Liberalism and World Politics. *American Political Science Review, 80*(4), 1151–1169.

Eloranta, J., Andreev, S., & Osinsky, P. (2014). Democratization and Central Government Spending, 1870–1938: Emergence of the Leviathan? In *Research in Economic History* (pp. 1–46). Bingley: Emerald Group Publishing Limited.

Eloranta, J., & Kauppila, J. (2006). Guns and Butter-Finnish Central Government Spending in the 20th Century. In J. Ojala, J. Eloranta, & J. Jalava (eds.), *The Road to Prosperity: An Economic History of Finland*. Helsinki: Suomalaisen Kirjallisuuden Seura.

Eloranta, J., & Ojala, J. (2018). Suomi kansainvälisessä taloudessa 1600–2000. In P. Haapala (ed.), *Suomen rakennehistoria: Näkökulmia muutokseen ja jatkuvuuteen (1400–2000)* (pp. 143–169). Tampere: Vastapaino.

Eloranta, J., Voutilainen, M., & Nummela, I. (2016). *Estimating Finnish Economic Growth Before 1860.* Mimeo.

Esping-Andersen, G. (1990). *The Three Worlds of Welfare Capitalism.* Princeton, NJ: Princeton University Press.

Espuelas, S. (2012). Are Dictatorships Less Redistributive? A Comparative Analysis of Social Spending in Europe (1950–1980). *European Review of Economic History, 16*(2), 211–232.

Fellman, S., Iversen, M., Sjögren, H., & Thue, L. (eds.) (2008). *Creating Nordic Capitalism: The Business History of a Competitive Periphery.* Basingstoke: Palgrave Macmillan.

Ferguson, N. (2002). *The Cash Nexus: Economics and Politics from the Age of Warfare Through the Age of Welfare, 1700–2000.* New York: Basic Books.

Fink-Jensen, J. (2015). *Homicide Rates.* IISH Dataverse. http://hdl.handle.net/10622/FMI6L9hdl/10622/FMI6L9.

Fukuyama, F. (2014). *Political Order and Political Decay. From the Industrial Revolution to the Globalisation of Democracy.* London: Profile Books.

Gat, A., Deudney, D., Ikenberry, G. J., Inglehart, R., & Welzel, C. (2009). Which Way Is History Marching? Debating the Authoritarian Revival. *Foreign Affairs, 88*(4), 150–159.

Glaeser, E. L., Ponzetto, G. A., & Shleifer, A. (2007). Why Does Democracy Need Education? *Journal of Economic Growth, 12*(2), 77–99.

Goldin, C. (2016). Human Capital. In C. Diebolt & M. Haupert (eds.), *Handbook of Cliometrics* (pp. 55–86). Berlin: Springer.

Grafe, R. (2012). *Market Tyranny.* Princeton: Princeton University Press.

Grytten, O. H. (2015). Norwegian Gross Domestic Product by Industry 1830–1930. *Norges Bank Working paper 19/2015.*

Haapala, P., & Lloyd, C. (2018). Johdanto: Rakennehistoria ja historian rakenteet. In P. Haapala (ed.), *Suomen rakennehistoria: Näkökulmia muutokseen ja jatkuvuuteen (1400–2000).* Tampere: Vastapaino.

Haavio-Mannila, E., & Skard, T. (eds.). (2013). *Unfinished Democracy: Women in Nordic Politics.* Amsterdam: Elsevier.

Hannikainen, M., & Eloranta, J. (2019). Palveluiden ja tulonsiirtojen yhteiskunta. In J. Laine, S. Fellman, M. Hannikainen, & J. Ojala (eds.), *Vaurastumisen vuodet: Suomen taloushistoria teollistumisen jälkeen.* Helsinki: Gaudeamus.

Hegre, H. (2014). Democracy and Armed Conflict. *Journal of Peace Research, 51*(2), 159–172.

Henrekson, M., & Stenkula, M. (eds.). (2015). *Swedish Taxation: Developments Since 1862.* Dordrecht: Springer.

Hodgson, G. M. (1998). The Approach of Institutional Economics. *Journal of Economic Literature, 36*(1), 166–192.

Hoffman, P. T. (2017). *Why Did Europe Conquer the World?* Princeton, NJ: Princeton University Press.

Husso, M., Virkki, T., Notko, M., Hirvonen, H., Eilola, J., & Norko, M. (2017). A Spatial-Temporal, Intersectional and Institutional Approach to Interpersonal Violence. In M. Husso, T. Virkki, M. Notko, H. Hirvonen, & J. Eilola (eds.), *Interpersonal Violence: Differences and Connections* (pp. 1–13). New York: Routledge.

Inglehart, R., & Welzel, C. (2009). How Development Leads to Democracy. *Foreign Affairs, 88*(2), 33–48.

Jørgensen, H. (2004). Make Contacts – Not Contracts! Better Development of Labour Markets Through Corporatist Steering and Accountability, Illustrated by Danish Labour Market and Employment Policies. In J. Lind, H. Knudsen, & H. Jörgensen (eds.), *Labour and Employment Regulation in Europe* (pp. 254–283). Berlin: Peter Lang.

Karonen, P., Roitto, M., & Ojala, J. (2018). Politiska kulturer 1430–1930. In H. Meinander, P. Karonen, & K. Östberg (eds.), *Demokratins drivskrafter. Kontext och särdrag i Finlands och*

Sveriges demokratier 1890–2020 (pp. 65–97). Helsingfors/Stockholm: Svenska litteratursällskatet i Finland/Appel Förlag.

Karvonen, L. (1997). *Demokratisering*. Lund: Studentlitteratur.

Kettunen, P. (2001). The Nordic Welfare State in Finland. *Scandinavian Journal of History*, *26*(3), 225–247.

Kettunen, P. (2006). The Tension Between the Social and the Economic. A Historical Perspective on a Welfare State. In J. Ojala, J. Eloranta, & J. Jalava (eds.), *The Road to Prosperity: An Economic History of Finland* (pp. 284–312). Helsinki: Suomalaisen Kirjallisuuden Seura.

Kissane, B. (2004). Democratization, State Formation, and Civil War in Finland and Ireland: A Reflection on the Democratic Peace Hypothesis. *Comparative Political Studies*, *37*(8), 969–985.

Kivivuori, J., & Lehti, M. (2006). The Social Composition of Homicide in Finland, 1960–2000. *Acta Sociologica*, *49*(1), 67–82.

Kjærnsli, M., & Lie, S. (2004). PISA and Scientific Literacy: Similarities and Differences Between the Nordic Countries. *Scandinavian Journal of Educational Research*, *48*(3), 271–286.

Koivunen, A., Ojala, J., & Holmén, J. (2021). Always in Crisis, Always a Solution? The Nordic Model as a Political and Scholarly Concept. In A. Koivunen, J. Ojala, & J. Holmén (eds.), *The Nordic Economic, Social and Political Model: Challenges in the 21st century* (pp. 1–19). Abingdon: Routledge. DOI: 10.4324/9780429026690-1.

Kokkinen, A., Jalava, J., Hjerppe, R., & Hannikainen, M. (2007). Catching Up in Europe: Finland's Convergence with Sweden and the EU15. *Scandinavian Economic History Review*, *55*(2), 153–171.

Koponen, J., & Saaritsa, S. (eds.) (2019). *Nälkämaasta Hyvinvointivaltioon: Suomi kehityksen kiinniottajana*. Helsinki: Gaudeamus.

Laine, J., Fellman, S., Hannikainen, M., & Ojala, J. (eds.). (2019). *Vaurastumisen vuodet: Suomen taloushistoria teollistumisen jälkeen*. Helsinki: Gaudeamus.

Lee, J. W., & Lee, H. (2016). Human Capital in the Long Run. *Journal of Development Economics*, *122*, 147–169.

Lehti, M., & Kivivuori, J. (2005). Alcohol-Related Violence as an Explanation for the Difference Between Homicide Rates in Finland and the Other Nordic Countries. *Nordic Studies on Alcohol and Drugs*, *22*(1), 7–24.

Lehti, M., & Kivivuori, J. (2012). Homicide in Finland. In M. Liem & W. Pridemore (eds.), *Handbook of European Homicide Research* (pp. 391–404). New York, NY: Springer.

Levy, J. S., & Thompson, W. R. (2010). *Causes of War*. West Sussex: Wiley-Blackwell.

Lind, J., & Knudsen, H. (2018). Denmark: The Long-Lasting Class Compromise. *Employee Relations*, *40*(4), 580–599.

Lindert, P. H. (2003). Voice and Growth: Was Churchill Right? *The Journal of Economic History*, *63*(2), 315–350.

Lindert, P. H. (2004). *Growing Public: Volume 1, the Story: Social Spending and Economic Growth Since the Eighteenth Century*. Cambridge: Cambridge University Press.

Lindert, P. H. (2006a). The Welfare State Is the Wrong Target: A Reply to Bergh. *Econ Journal Watch*, *3*(2), 236.

Lindert, P. H. (2006b). Second Reply to Bergh. *Econ Journal Watch*, *3*(3), 461–465.

Lipset, S. M. (1959). Some Social Requisites of Democracy: Economic Development and Political Legitimacy. *American Political Science Review*, *53*(1), 69–105.

Mann, M. (2012). *The Sources of Social Power: Volume 3, Global Empires and Revolution, 1890–1945*. Cambridge: Cambridge University Press.

McIntosh, J. (2019). PISA Country Rankings Valid? Results for Canada and Finland. *Scandinavian Journal of Educational Research*, *63*(5), 670–678.

Meinander, H., Karonen, P., & Östberg, K. (eds.). (2018). *Demokratins drivskrafter. Kontext och särdrag i Finlands och Sveriges demokratier 1890–2020*. Helsingfors/Stockholm: Svenska litteratursälskatet i Finland/Appel Förlag.

Mjøset, L., & Cappelen, Å. (2011). The Integration of the Norwegian Oil Economy into the World Economy. In *The Nordic Varieties of Capitalism* (pp. 167–263). Bingley: Emerald Group Publishing Limited.

Moatsos, M., van Zanden, J. L., Baten, J., et al. (2015). *Income Inequality*. http://hdl.handle.net/10622/6OHMDS, accessed via the Clio Infra website.

Mokyr, J. (2006). Preface: Successful Small Open Economies and the Importance of Good Institutions. In J. Ojala, J. Eloranta, & J. Jalava (eds.), *The Road to Prosperity. An Economic History of Finland* (pp. 8–12). Helsinki: Suomalaisen Kirjallisuuden Seura.

Moore, B. (1966). *Social Origins of Dictatorship and Democracy: Lord and Peasant in the Making of the Modern World*. Boston, MA: Beacon Press.

Mulligan, C. B., Gil, R., y Sala-i-Martin, X. (2010). Social Security and Democracy. *The B.E. Journal of Economic Analysis and Policy, 10*, 1, article 18.

North, D. C. (1990). *Institutions, Institutional Change and Economic Performance*. Cambridge and New York: Cambridge University Press.

O'Brien, P. (2011). The Nature and Historical Evolution of an Exceptional Fiscal State and Its Possible Significance for the Precocious Commercialization and Industrialization of the British Economy from Cromwell to Nelson. *Economic History Review, 64*(2), 357–713.

OECD (2019). *OECD Social Expenditure Database*. www.oecd.org/social/expenditure.htm.

Ojala, J. (2017). Taloushistorian paluu ja liiketoimintahistorian nousu. *Historiallinen aikakauskirja, 115*(4), 446–456.

Okediji, T. O. (2005). The Dynamics of Ethnic Fragmentation: A Proposal for an Expanded Measurement Index. *American Journal of Economics and Sociology, 64*(2), 637–662.

Olson, M. (1986). A Theory of the Incentives Facing Political Organizations: Neo-Corporatism and the Hegemonic State. *International Political Science Review*, 7(2), 165–189.

Osinsky, P. (2010). Modernization Interrupted? Total War, State Breakdown, and the Communist Conquest of China. *The Sociological Quarterly, 51*(4), 576–599.

Osinsky, P., & Eloranta, J. (2014). Why Did the Communists Win or Lose? A Comparative Analysis of the Revolutionary Civil Wars in Russia, Finland, Spain, and China. *Sociological Forum, 29*(2), 318–341.

Pasad, M., & Deng, Y. (2009). Taxation and the Worlds of Welfare. *Socio-Economic Review*, 7, 431–457.

Pemstein, D., Marquardt, K. L., Tzelgov, E., Wang, Y., Medzihorsky, J., Krusell, J., Miri, F., & von Römer, J. (2019). The V-Dem Measurement Model: Latent Variable Analysis for Cross-National and Cross-Temporal Expert-Coded Data. *V-Dem Working Paper Series 2019(21)*. http://www.ssrn.com/abstract=2704787.

Permanyer, I. (2013). A Critical Assessment of the UNDP's Gender Inequality Index. *Feminist Economics, 19*(2), 1–32.

Petersen, K., & Kettunen, P. (2011). Introduction: Rethinking Welfare State Models. In P. Kettunen & K. Petersen (eds.), *Beyond Welfare State Models* (pp. 1–15). Cheltenham: Edward Elgar Publishing.

Porter, M. E. (1990). *The Competitive Advantage of Nations: With a New Introduction*. New York: Free Press.

Przeworski, A. (1986). *Capitalism and Social Democracy*. Cambridge: Cambridge University Press.

Przeworski, A. (1991). *Democracy and the Market: Political and Economic Reforms in Eastern Europe and Latin America*. Cambridge: Cambridge University Press.

Przeworski, A. (2004). Democracy and Economic Development. In E. D. Mansfield & R. Sisson (eds.), *The Evolution of Political Knowledge. Democracy, Autonomy, and Conflict in Comparative and International Politics* (pp. 300–324). Columbus: Ohio State University Press.

Przeworski, A., & Limongi, F. (1993). Political Regimes. *The Journal of Economic Perspectives, 7*(3), 51–69.

Putnam, R. D. (1995). Bowling Alone: America's Declining Social Capital. *Journal of Democracy, 6*(1), 65–78.

Rasumussen, M. B., & Pontusson, J. (2017). Working-Class Strength by Institutional Design? Unionization, Partisan Politics, and Unemployment Insurance Systems, 1870 to 2010. *Comparative Politics Studies, 51*(6), 793–828.

Robinson, J. A., & Acemoglu, D. (2012). *Why Nations Fail: The Origins of Power, Prosperity, and Poverty*. New York: Crown Business.

Robson, W. A. (1976). *Welfare State and Welfare Society: Illusion and Reality*. Crows Nest: Allen and Unwin.

Rodrik, D., Subramanian, A., & Trebbi, F. (2004). Institutions Rule: The Primacy of Institutions Over Geography and Integration in Economic Development. *Journal of Economic Growth, 9*(2), 131–165.

Roine, J., Vlachos, J., & Waldenström, D. (2009). The Long-Run Determinants of Inequality: What Can We Learn from Top Income Data? *Journal of Public Economics, 93*, 974–988.

Romero-Ávila, D., & Strauch, R. (2008). Public Finances and Long-Term Growth in Europe: Evidence from a Panel Data Analysis. *European Journal of Political Economy, 24*, 172–191.

Savolainen, J., Lehti, M., & Kivivuori, J. (2008). Historical Origins of a Cross-National Puzzle: Homicide in Finland, 1750 to 2000. *Homicide Studies, 12*(1), 67–89.

Schön, L., & Krantz, O. (2015). New Swedish historical National Accounts Since the 16th Century in Constant and Current Prices. *Lund Papers in Economic History no. 140*.

Schumpeter, J. A. (1942). *Capitalism, Socialism and Democracy*. Abingdon: Routledge.

Segura-Ubiergo, A. (2007). *The Political Economy of the Welfare State in Latin America. Globalization, Democracy and Development*. Cambridge: Cambridge University Press.

Skocpol, T., & Theda, S. (1979). *States and Social Revolutions: A Comparative Analysis of France, Russia and China*. Cambridge: Cambridge University Press.

Stasavage, D. (2011). *States of Credit: Size, Power, and the Development of European Polities*. Princeton, NJ: Princeton University Press.

Steinmo, S. (1993). *Taxation and Democracy: Swedish, British and American Approaches to Financing the Modern State*. New Haven and London: Yale University Press.

Sutch, R. (2006). National Income and Product. In S. B. Carter, S. S. Gartner, M. R. Haines et al. (eds.), *Historical Statistics of the United States: Earliest Time to the Present* (III, pp. 23–25). New York: Cambridge University Press.

Teorell, J. (2012). *Determinants of Democratization. Explaining Regime Change in the World, 1972–2006*. Cambridge: Cambridge University Press.

Teorell, J., Coppedge, M., Lindberg, S., & Skaaning, S. E. (2019). Measuring Polyarchy Across the Globe, 1900–2017. *Studies in Comparative International Development, 54*(1), 71–95.

Tilly, C. (1990). *Capital, Coercion, and European States*. Cambridge, MA: Basil Blackwell.

Ville, S., & Wicken, O. (2012). The Dynamics of Resource-Based Economic Development: Evidence from Australia and Norway. *Industrial and Corporate Change, 22*(5), 1341–1371.

Wiberg, H. (2000). *The Nordic Security Community: Past, Present, Future. Danish Foreign Policy Yearbook*. Copenhagen: Danish Institute for International Studies.

Ylikangas, H., Karonen, P., Lehti, M., & Monkkonen, E. H. (2001). *Five Centuries of Violence in Finland and the Baltic Area*. Columbus, OH: Ohio State University Press.

3 Public-sector growth in Finland before the welfare state

Central and local government perspectives

Matti Hannikainen, Sakari Heikkinen and Jarmo Peltola

Introduction

The Finnish welfare state has come into bloom during the last half a century. The public sector has doubled in size: the ratio of public expenditure to gross domestic product (GDP) was 27.7% in 1960, 47.9% in 2008 and rose in 2014 to the record figure of 57.3%, which was highest among European countries.[1] The latest surge resulted from the Great Recession, which hit Finland exceptionally hard. By 2019, the ratio of general government expenditure to GDP had decreased to 53.2% – still second-highest figure after France. The high percentage has given ammunition to the more fundamental criticism of the large public sector: public spending is more and more often viewed as a burden on the economy. Part of the criticism on the 'too big size' of the Finnish public sector is related to a more general discussion on the future of the Nordic welfare state model.[2]

In this chapter, we approach the problematics of the public sector from a historical angle by exploring the growth of the public sector in Finland before the welfare state era, from 1890 to 1960. Because during these years there were practically no social security funds in Finland, the general government consisted of central and local (municipal) governments.[3] Our aim is to measure the size of the general (central plus local) government sector in Finland from 1890 to 1960 and discuss the drivers and obstacles of public-sector growth before the welfare state era. Moreover, we analyze more deeply the growth mechanisms of local government development, which has not usually been in focus in previous research. In this, we concentrate on three aspects: the effects of urbanization and the institutional development of education and healthcare.

Finland, along with the other Nordic countries, caught up between 1890 and 1960 with the more developed economies. Figure 3.1 plots the growth rate of GDP per capita from 1890 to 1960 against the starting level of 1890 for 46 countries.[4] This commonly used measure of 'beta-convergence' shows great variation between the countries with no trend whatsoever as the horizontal regression line indicates. Yet all the Nordic countries were well above

DOI: 10.4324/9780429503870-4

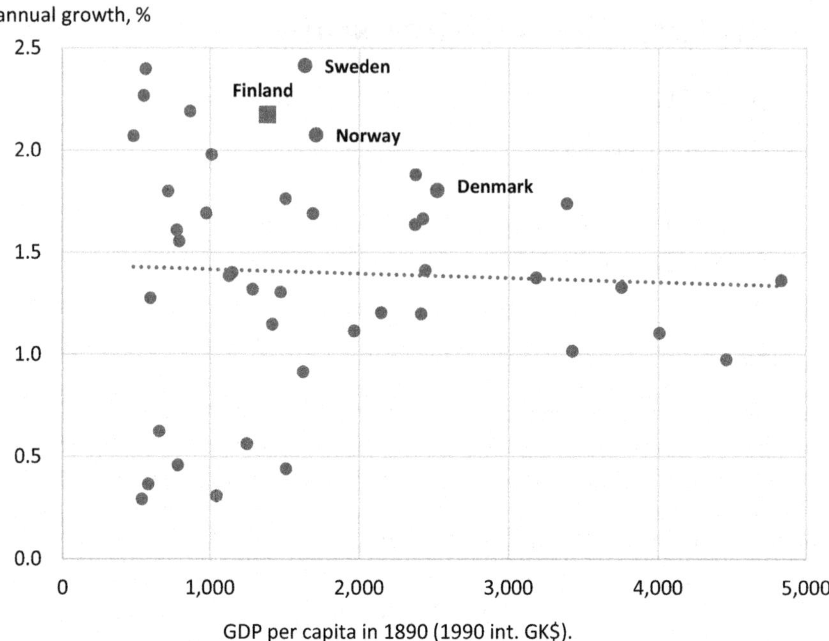

Figure 3.1 The average annual growth of real gross domestic product per capita from 1890 to 1960 in relation to gross domestic product per capita level in 1890 (in percentages)

Source: Maddison Project Database.

the regression line, implying that they succeeded in the economic catch-up converging with the leading economies.

What was the role of the public sector in the Finnish catch-up? Was its growth a consequence or a cause of the catch-up – or both? These questions are related to classical and recent debates on economic development. According to Gerschenkron's (1962) classic thesis, early industrialized countries and the latecomer countries develop in different ways. He stressed the importance of manufacturing industries in the progress of backward countries and the role of the state in creating preconditions for development. It meant that backwardness was consciously utilized, and a proactive state played a more important role in the latecomers' development than especially in British or American industrialization. For Gerschenkron, Russia was the best example of remarkable state intervention by constructing railways and factories and through the creation of tariff protection from the late 19th century.[5]

The role of the state as a promoter of growth via institutional and political factors has recently been emphasized by Acemoglu and Robinson (2012), who have discussed connections between different kind of institutions and economic development and highlighted the significance of democratic (inclusive) institutions. Social spending increased inclusiveness in a society. According to Lindert (2004) democracy played an important role in growing social spending which was one of the most remarkable changes in Western societies after World War II. Before the 20th century, the amount of social spending was very limited because 'political voice was so restricted'. Espuelas (2012) showed that non-democratic governments were less generous in providing social protection. In his comparative analysis, Dincecco (2011) came up with the findings that in many countries in Europe, there occurred a political transformation from absolutist to parliamentary regimes and fiscal transformation from fragmented public sectors to more central ones. Tanzi (2011) summed up that 'the economic role of the state is determined largely by politics',[6] and Cusack and Fuchs (2002) argued that political forces were behind (in addition to economic developments) the huge expansion over the control of economic resources by the government. Moreover, Hoffman (2015) has also stressed the importance of the state and politics in explaining economic development and attached weight to gather data on taxation and spending by local and central governments.

This chapter proceeds in the following way: the first section presents the essential features of structural change in Finland and discusses the role of politics in the public-sector development before the welfare state era. Second, we examine a quantitative analysis of general government growth, that is both central and local government expenditures. The third section of the chapter analyzes more deeply local government institutional development, concentrating on three aspects: urbanization, education, and healthcare, which essentially explained the growth of the public-sector in towns and municipalities.

Late structural change, the beginning of social planning, and political fragmentation, 1890–1940s

The Finnish society changed profoundly economically and politically from the late 19th century onwards when the country transformed from an agrarian industrializing country into an industrialized and modern wage-work society. In 1900, industrialization had already started, but the employment share of primary production was still 70%. From a comparative perspective, Finland remained an agricultural-dominated country. In 1950, almost half of the population still got their living from agriculture, forestry, and fishing. Structural change clearly accelerated in the latter half of the 20th century. The culmination of employment in secondary production occurred relatively late, in the middle of the 1970s. At the turn of the millennium, two thirds of employees worked in services, in private or public sectors, and the share of primary employment in the economically active population was only 5%.[7]

GDP per capita grew in Finland 12-fold from 1900 to 2000 which meant a growth of 2.5% per year on average. As well as many other latecomers, Finland, too, experienced a rapid catch-up growth; that is the growth was higher than in leading countries. The growth was not steady, and especially both World

Wars were disruptions in the growth path. During the Great Depression of the 1930s, Finland belonged to the group of countries which left the gold standard in the early stage and where the macro-level effects of the worldwide crisis were relatively modest, partly because of the big agricultural self-sufficiency sector. The gradual structural change, which followed the crisis, was interrupted due to World War II. Most of the convergence to Western European countries took place after World War II.[8]

The development in Russia essentially affected Finland which was an autonomous Grand Duchy of Russia from 1809 to 1917. Political conditions were, however, more liberal in Finland than in Russia. In the political arena, there emerged two different development paths, which entwined with each other: national separation from Russia and increasing democracy in the Finnish society. Internal development in Russia and the turbulence in international politics – Russo-Japanese War in 1905 – led to the first major political break in Finland in 1907: universal suffrage with the Social Democratic Party (SDP) as the biggest party in the first election despite the strong agrarian character of the country.

From the social planning point of view, Finland was not a latecomer. Various state committees were, from the late 19th century onwards important institutions to prepare nation-wide reforms. The committee members wanted to avoid mistakes made elsewhere and adopt good practices from more developed countries. There was an attempt to turn backwardness into an advantage. The state committees suggested in the late 19th and early 20th centuries, however, a cautious start, and many societal reforms were not realized. According to the committees, the society must be reformed gradually, and benefits and new institutions could be increased when industrialization proceeded, and the society moved to the new stage of development.[9]

The political change and increasing democracy between 1905 and 1907 were reflected in the design of social security. The emergence of the social democrats in the political arena challenged the dominant form of society and forced the other political groups to change their attitude towards societal reforms. The organized labour movement elite took a relatively positive attitude towards education and gradual social reforms. The same kind of thinking was also visible in the conservative and nationalistic ideology of the state. The dissent of the political groups and the Russian administration's reluctance to introduce change prevented most major reforms in the early 20th century. The political connection to Russia was, therefore, one important obstacle to progress with nationwide social reforms in Finland in the early 20th century.

Another major political break occurred when Finland gained independence from Russia during World War I in December 1917. The new state needed an administration and army which increased public expenditure. Independence did not lead, however, to big nationwide social reforms, although one important obstacle, that is the Russian power, was removed. Political instability continued when Finland drifted into civil war in 1918. The political left and the blue-collar trade unions lost some of their strength when the workers' side ('the reds') was defeated in the war and the previously unified socialist SDP split into two factions: the social democrats and communists. From the increasing democracy point of view, it is important to notice that in local elections universal suffrage was implemented for the first time only half a year after the end of the civil war in December 1918.

The bourgeois hegemony resulting from the civil war even intensified when an extreme right-wing association, 'Lapua Movement', entered the Finnish political stage in the early 1930s. The trade unions' central organization was dissolved in the political turmoil, and the new central organization was weaker for many years than the previous organization. Political voice – and especially leftist argumentation at the national level – for extensive social reforms remained relatively weak during the inter-war years. A small change in direction happened in the latter part of the 1930s when the social democrats formed a coalition government with the agrarian and liberal centre parties. In the spirit of a 'Popular Front', most of the rank-and-file communists returned to the SDP and the trade unions.[10]

The end of World War II denoted the third major political break and the beginning of a new era in Finnish society. The Communist Party entered from the illegal status into the one of the most important political forces. The improved status of the left in society meant not only increasing bargaining power but also great rivalry between the communists and the social democrats in the labour force. The emergence of collective bargaining at the national level and increasing unionism were important features in the formation of Finnish corporatism which had an important effect on Finnish society in the latter half of the 1900s. The political change created favourable conditions for growing social spending. Child benefits in the late 1940s, the construction programs of hospitals from the 1950s onwards and the emergence of social insurance (unemployment insurance, earnings-related pensions, health insurance) in the 1960s were major first examples.

Measuring the growth of the public sector

As Middleton (1996) has shown for the British case, the examination of public-sector growth is not an easy task.[11] Similarly, several data and measurement problems arise when elaborating the development in Finland before the welfare state era. First, we have fewer solid data before World War II than we have especially from the 1960s onward when the Organisation for Economic Co-operation and Development (OECD) statistics include the reliable time series which gives opportunities to make a longitudinal analysis and compare different countries. Instead, in the case of the first half of the 20th century and even more the earlier times, we must use more scattered sources and collect data from different statistics. Second, we emphasize that in the analysis of the public sector, examination of the central government is not enough. This is a common problem in international comparisons. In addition to central government development, the examination of local government increases our understanding of the public-sector growth mechanisms. Finally, when analyzing the general government's development, the question of consolidation is important, that is eliminating transactions between central and local governments and within local governments and considering (as far as possible) only real (not financial) investments.

Central government expenditure, relative to GDP, grew from less than 10% before World War I to about 25% in the 1950s. However, as Figure 3.2 shows, the growth was far from even, since both World Wars caused big jumps in the public expenditure/GDP ratio, which then returned to a lower level. Yet in both cases, the level of public expenditure did not come back to the pre-war level but remained notably higher related to GDP. Measured by percentage points the change, during and after World War II was much bigger than in the aftermath of World War I.

Although Finland became a sovereign state only in 1917, it had, as an autonomous Grand Duchy of Russia, its own state finances already since 1809.[12] Before World War I, expenditure policy was rather cautious. Besides the costs of the central administration, the main item of expenditure since the 1860s was railway building, as Finland adopted a national communication strategy based on state ownership financed by foreign loans.[13] Together, railways and administration took almost half of the central government expenditure. Spending on education was very limited in the 19th century but rose a bit at the turn of the 20th century. Still, the central government resources directed to education remained modest compared with investments in physical infrastructure.

The peculiarity of Finland's semi-independent status was reflected in military spending.[14] After Finland got its own military in the beginning of the 1880s, its share of central government expenditure was about 14%. The Finnish army was dismantled in the beginning of the 20th century because Finnish–Russian political conflict as the rising Finnish state-building nationalism collided with the Russian modernizing pursuit of administrative-political centralization. As a result of the conflict, Finland had to pay compensation for the defence to Russia, but the share of military expenses diminished below one tenth of the total central government expenditure. After gaining independence, Finland constructed an army of its own, resulting in a doubling of the relative share of military expenditure to about a fifth of the central government budget.

Independence and the Great Depression of the 1930s affected the development of the public-sector during the inter-war years. Expenditure on education rose a bit (to less than a fifth), whereas agriculture gained gradually more resources reflecting the self-sufficiency endeavour of agricultural policy. During the Great Depression, the share of central government expenditure on GDP rose but that should not be interpreted as a sign of countercyclical policy. There was extra expenditure for alleviating unemployment, but the rise of expenditure/GDP ratio had probably more to do with the deflation (declining nominal GDP) and the 'stickiness' of the state budget.[15] During the rapid post-Depression recovery ratio, rising income was used to pay the public debt, as the difference of two lines of Figure 3.2 shows.

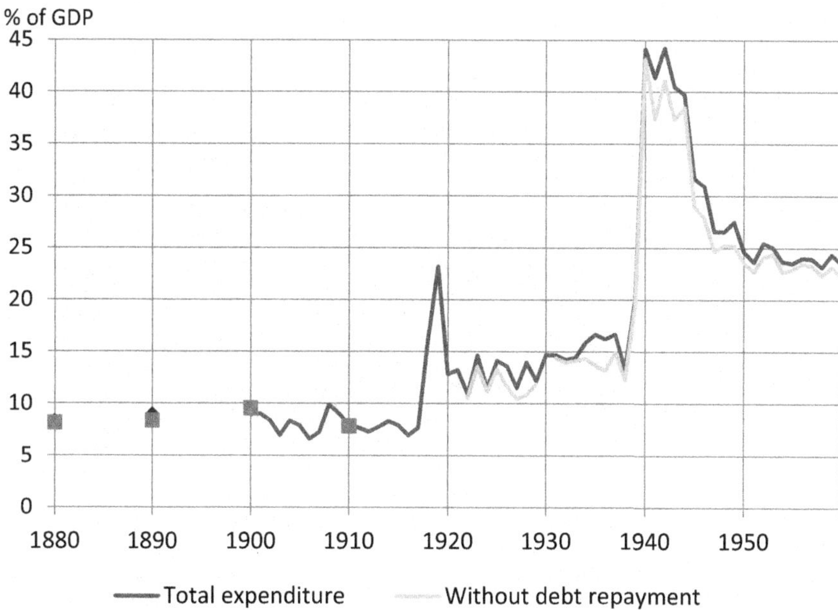

Figure 3.2 Central government expenditure (in percentages in relation to gross domestic product), 1880–1960

Source: Statistical Yearbook of Finland; Government Financial Statement; Tudeer (1931); Valvanne (1952); Pihkala (1977); Taimio (1986).

World War II caused the biggest surge in central government expenditure so far. All resources were mobilized for the war effort, which also took the lion share of the rising expenditure. After the war, the expenditure/GDP ratio remained high because the extra expenditure caused by the war: especially reparation payments to the USSR (1944–1952) and the costs of resettling the evacuees. The war was financed partly by (domestic) public debt and partly by taxation. There was a similar development as during World War I: as the state revenues declined because of shock, for example because of the declining tariff incomes, new taxes had to be imposed. During and after World War I, the novelty was income and property tax, during World War II, the turnover tax. After World War II, economic policy views differed on whether the tax rate should be lowered to the pre-war level or at least near it. The tax rate, however, remained on the notably higher level – as did the public expenditure.

Local government (towns and rural municipalities) constituted another important part of the public sector, although the central government was all the period significantly more important than local government. Local government expenditures were 12% in relation to GDP in 1960 (see Figure 3.3). It

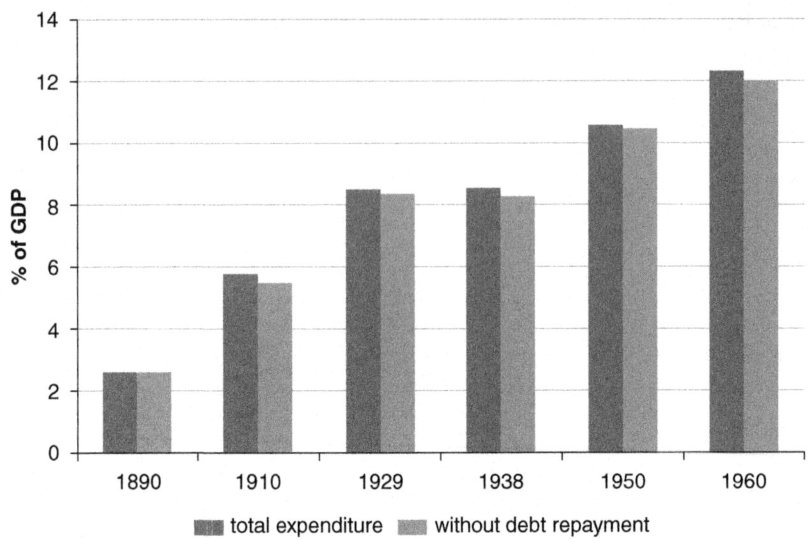

Figure 3.3 Local government expenditure (in percentages in relation to gross domestic product), 1890–1960

Source: Local Government Financial Statistics; Statistical Yearbook of Finland.

was almost five times higher than in 1890 (2.6%). The growth of local government was particularly rapid in the early 20th century when the growth of local governments' spending was significantly faster than in central government. The expansion of local government was linked to urbanization and growing social spending (see next chapter). Because Finland was a latecomer in structural change, the first phase of urbanization and the formation of new social institution, especially education and health care, entangled with each other in the early 20th century. The Great Depression of the 1930s stopped the growth which further continued after World War II.

Considering local governments' expenditure, the question of consolidation arises. This is not an easy task because of definition problems and inadequate data in the statistics. Consolidation means that we analyze central and local governments as if they were a single unit. The aim is to avoid double counting, that is eliminating transactions between central and local governments and within local governments. A typical example of the early 20th-century Finland was that state subsidies for the construction of schools are not counted twice, both in the central and the local government's expenditure. Because of state subsidies, the share of local government of all public expenditure (and relation to GDP) is smaller than without consolidation. Repayments of debt are not included, but interest payments are included, and real capital investments

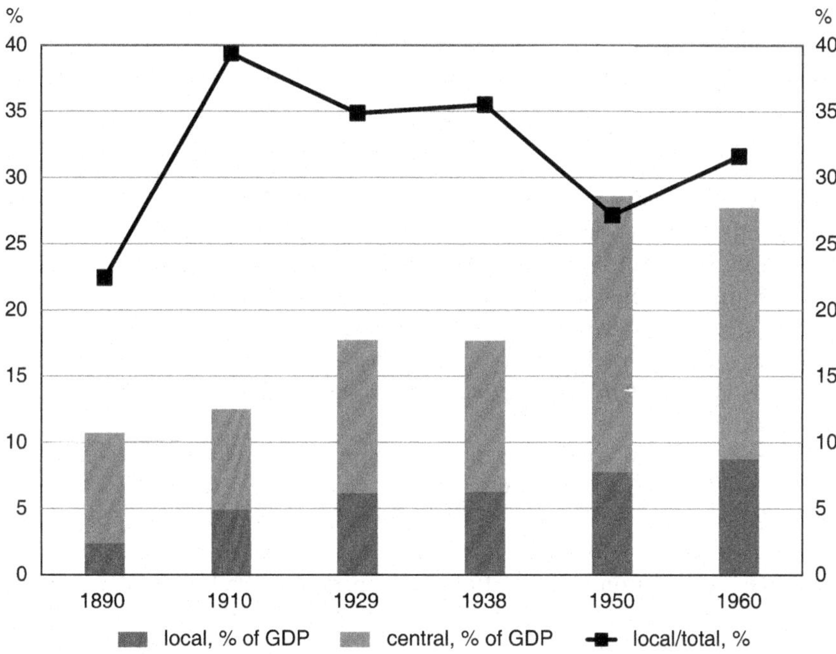

Figure 3.4 Consolidated public expenditure in Finland (central and local governments), 1890–1960

Source: See Figures 3.2 and 3.3.

Table 3.1 General government expenditure (in relation to gross domestic product, in percentages), 1890–1960

	1890	*1910*	*1930*	*1938*	*1950*	*1960*
Austria	12.9	17.6	19.8	20.6[a]	25.1	30.4
Denmark	10.6	12.3	13.5	16.7	19.6	25.2
Finland	**10.7**	**12.5**	**17.7**[b]	**17.7**	**28.6**	**27.7**
France	14.3	15.1	29.4	29.4	29.3	34.0
Germany	12.9	16.0	29.4	36.9	29.2	32.2
Italy	18.4	17.3	22.0	29.2	23.0	29.7
Netherlands	..	9.0	14.0	23.2	27.1	34.6
Norway	7.4	9.3	19.1	20.3	24.2	31.3
Sweden	..	10.4	19.1	20.3	26.3	31.3
United Kingdom	9.2	12.7	24.7	28.6	32.0	32.1
United States	6.5	8.2	12.2	19.7	22.4	28.4
AVERAGE	**11.4**	**12.8**	**20.1**	**23.4**	**26.1**	**30.6**

Source: Finland our calculations; Austria 1937 Tanzi & Schuknecht (2000); other countries Cusack & Fuchs (2002).

[a] 1937.

[b] 1929.

are included, but financial investments are excluded in our calculations. The expenditure of public enterprises is calculated as net expenditure.

In Finland, the pattern of public expenditure growth was quite similar to other countries. Somewhat surprisingly, Finland was not behind the other Nordic countries before World War I. It is, however, unclear whether local government's expenditure is included to the figures in the same way. Finland fell behind in public expenditure, especially during the inter-war years. Probably, it was not only a question about that public expenditure increased slowly in Finland, but economic growth was relatively rapid in Finland. In 1950, the high figure in Finland can be partly explained by the exceptional war-related expenditure. Without war reparations to the Soviet Union and resettling the evacuees, general government spending was in Finland 25.1%, that is approximately at the same level as in Austria, Norway, and Sweden. Overall, it seems that Finland was clearly lagging many other Western European countries than Denmark in 1960.

However, Finland's development looks even more average, if we relate the ratio of public expenditure to GDP to the logarithmic level of real GDP per capita (1990 int. GK$). Figure 3.5 displays this comparison for the eleven countries reported in Table 3.2. It shows that Finland followed very closely the regression line from 1890 to 1938 but departed in 1950 – partly because of the war-related extra expenditure. Perhaps a bit against the received wisdom, Finland had a bigger public sector than Sweden during the whole era[16] when related to the GDP/capita level. Sweden's development was exceptionally even, and the public sector gained size at a quicker pace than in the sample countries in average. The US, again, had the smallest public sector when compared to its (high) GDP/capita level.

The dynamics of local government growth

Next, we analyzed more exactly some phenomena which can be linked to the growth of local government: urbanization, education, and healthcare.[17] These phenomena caused investments to infrastructure which were often produced by local governments. Urbanization especially increased local government expenditure, because of construction of transport systems, sanitation, power plants and the like, and many forms of social spending first developed in municipalities. However, the central government often subsidized local government, for example in the construction of schools or hiring doctors, and moreover, even the division of public and private sector is not clear. Moreover, by analyzing local governments' development, it is possible to examine how these phenomena entangled with each other and what kind of regional differences were involved in the growth of public expenditure.

Social spending (education, healthcare, poor relief, and social benefits) was the largest group of local government's expenditure the entire period between 1910 and 1960: 42% in 1910, 52% in 1938 and 57% in 1960. The structure of public expenditure, however, remarkably differed regionally. In rural areas, social spending was clearly the most important part of public expenditure

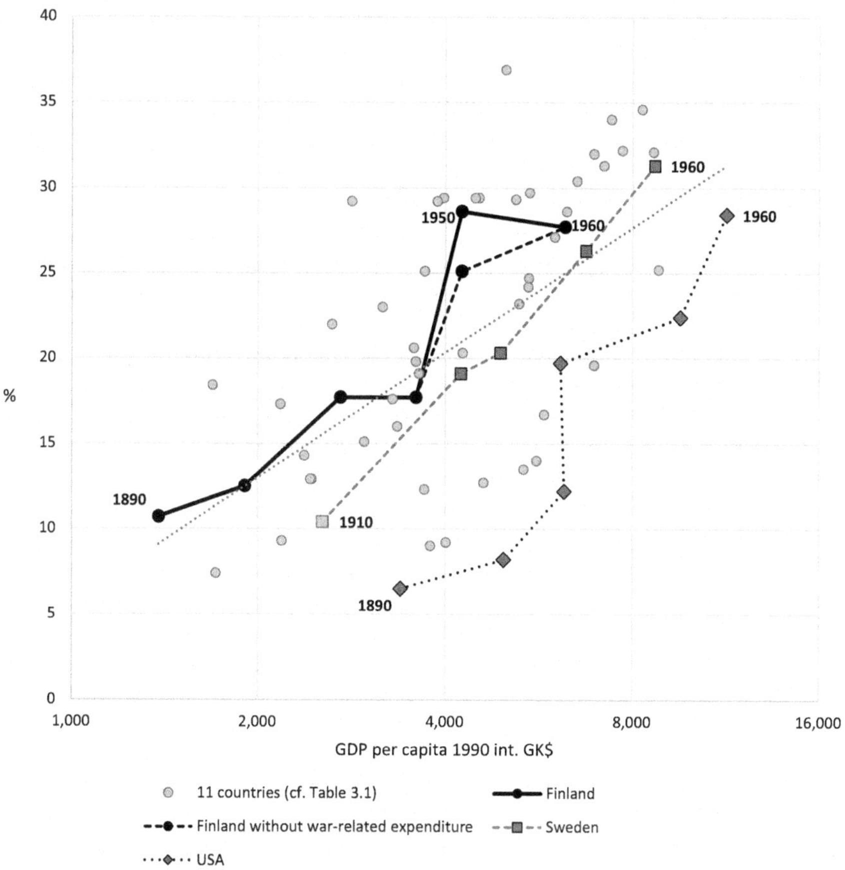

Figure 3.5 General government expenditure/gross domestic product (GDP; %) in relation to real GDP/capita, 1890–1960

Source: Table 3.2 and Maddison database.

Table 3.2 The shares of urban and rural population in Finland (in percentages), 1890–1960

	Cities and towns	*Rural areas*	*Total*
1880	8.5	91.5	100.0
1890	9.9	90.1	100.0
1900	12.5	87.5	100.0
1910	14.7	85.3	100.0
1920	16.1	83.9	100.0
1930	20.6	79.4	100.0
1940	26.8	73.2	100.0
1950	32.3	67.7	100.0
1960	38.4	61.6	100.0

Source: Statistical Yearbook of Finland.

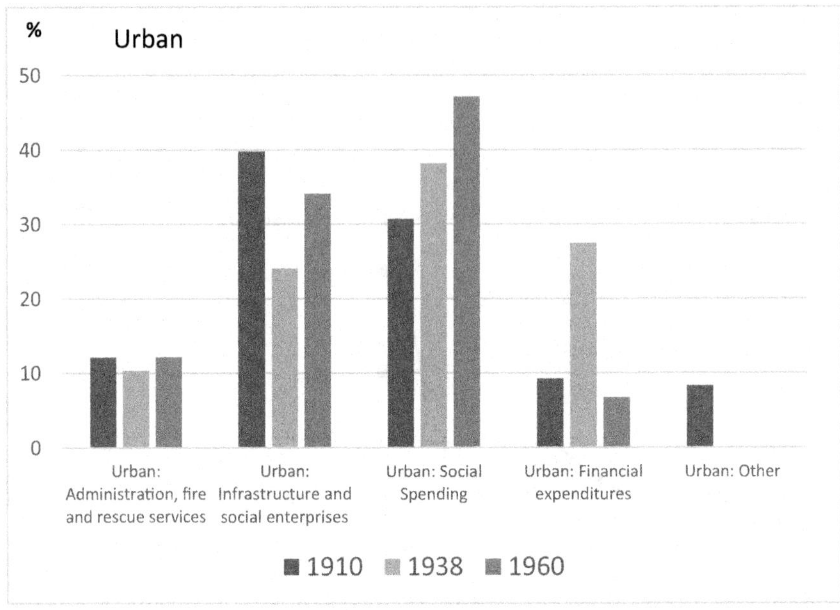

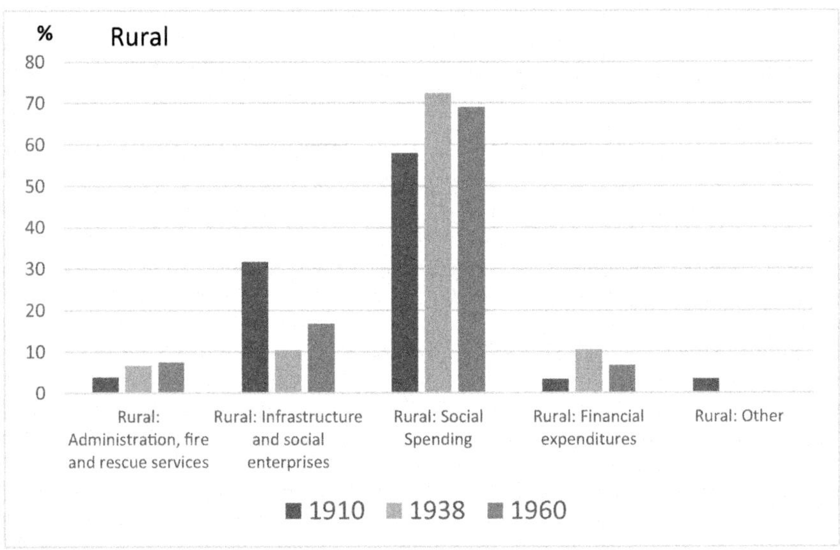

Figure 3.6 Local government expenditure (urban–rural division), 1910, 1938, 1960

Source: Local Government Financial Statistics.

(varied between 58%–73%), whereas the main difference between urban and rural municipalities was that the expenditure for infrastructure and social enterprises were much higher in towns. The construction of streets, harbours, and traffic and energy systems in towns explained this difference. Financial expenditure was at first higher in towns than in rural municipalities, but after World War II, this expenditure was relatively at the same level. Financial expenditure mainly included debt interests (repayment of debt excluded) which also linked to infrastructure investments. Administration costs including fire and rescue services were higher in urban than rural municipalities but even those differences were diminishing.

Slow pace of urbanization

Finland was sparsely populated country, and its towns and cities were small in a comparative perspective. In 1890, only 10% lived in urban areas. During the first decades of 20th century, the relative urbanization pace was faster than before: 16% of people lived in the cities and towns in 1920. Especially the capital Helsinki, the old capital Turku, the coastal harbour and trade city Viipuri and inland industrial city Tampere began to grow relatively rapidly. During the inter-war era, the growth accelerated. After World War II, urbanization continued despite the settlement of evacuees in rural areas. However, the share of urban population remained in the European context relatively small, and despite the growing share of urban population, the number of people living in the countryside also increased until the 1950s. In 1960, 38% of the population lived in urban areas in Finland. The urbanization turn linked to simultaneous changes in agriculture when the absolute number of people employed in agriculture and forestry work began to decrease.

Structural change and urbanization increased public expenditures but also regional differences. Many aspects of public sector growth occurred in urban areas. Local investments to roads and streets, harbours, public city traffic systems, energy, electric, water and sewer systems concentrated mainly on cities and towns. Because Finland was a latecomer in structural change, this expenditure was initially low but grew especially in the 20th century. Without old infrastructure, it was possible to use modern technology which was an important advantage to later development and rapid catch-up growth. State-financed public railway and road investments were also directed to rural areas.[18]

Cities and towns were the centres of public administration and services. It was a question of not only local administration but also state administration concentrated mainly in cities. Moreover, it was quite natural that cities also developed as the centres of education and healthcare (hospitals). These urban services were used also by rural population. Linkages of different public-sector investments increased further urbanization and public-sector growth. For instance, because of better education it was easier find livelihood outside agriculture and because of better traffic systems, it was easier to move to urban areas.

From unequal towards universal education

Compared to other Nordic countries, Finland was a latecomer in organizing popular education. The percentage of children who were in the folk schools or secondary schools from 1890 to 1960 developed as follows (percentage of 7- to 15-year-old population):[19]

1890	13.9
1900	24.2
1910	33.8
1920	41.8
1930	69.6
1940	77.5
1950	98.6
1960	100.0

Primary schools were organized according to the imperial act in 1866.[20] It made it possible to establish local folk schools. The new act treated urban and rural inhabitants in a different way. In towns, the school system was more extensive than in rural municipalities, where teaching of 6- to 9-year-old children occurred at their own homes and for 10- to 16-year-olds, it was organized in folk schools. The development was uneven in the different parts of the country. For local governments establishing primary schools was voluntary for many decades. Schooling advanced earlier in towns than in rural municipalities, but there was variation also between the towns and within the towns – between wealthier centres and working-class suburbs. The uneven development also occurred within rural municipalities. Every municipality had its own centre and periphery.

The uneven regional development can be partly explained by the fact that new educational reforms denoted new public expenditure: the construction of new school buildings, training of teaching staff and paying their salaries. Although the central government financially supported the construction of school buildings, voluntariness and different resources to implement reforms increased regional divergence. Education reforms progressed more rapidly in economically more prosperous southern and western Finland whereas educational conditions were the worst in the remote and poorest areas. Differences between the regions grew because of positive and negative path-dependent developments. If local decision-makers were aware of social problems, favoured educational activities and were eager to social reforms, after building a school in one village, inhabitants of the municipality required more school buildings in other villages. Instead, without this kind of positive experience, the peasantry and poorer people could resist new ideas and institutions because they were afraid of new costs and obligations.[21]

Compulsory education law in 1921 (six-year compulsory education) was another important but, in a comparative perspective, a belated milestone in the institutional formation of the education system. It clearly obliged municipalities to organize schools. As a result, older 'ambulant' schools were finally replaced by permanent schools. After the compulsory law, the educational system started to develop regionally and socially to a more equal direction.

The post–World War II period denoted the expansion of education and an increasing regional equality. The size of the school-age cohorts grew because of the baby boom after the war. The number of children at primary and secondary schools increased at the same time, when the awareness of the importance of higher education grew. Secondary schools were established in relatively small, rural population centres which increased regional and societal schooling equalities and the possibilities to continue higher education studies. Many secondary schools were originally privately funded but state-regulated and -subsidized. There were about 77,000 pupils in secondary schools in 1945/46. Fifteen years later, the number was almost three times higher. In 1960, almost 100% of school-aged children sat on the school bench, either in folk schools or in secondary schools. The next big reform was carried out in the 1970s (Act 1968), when a new comprehensive school replaced the old system.

Slowly developing healthcare

In healthcare, the role of the public is different from in education, and even the concept of public is more difficult to define than in education. For instance, in 1890, 23% of doctors in Finland worked in the local government, 35% in the central government and 42% in the private sector. In 1928, the corresponding figures were 36%, 29% and 35%. In 1954, 59% of doctors worked in the public sector and 41% in the private sector. Some larger mills had a doctor, and sickness funds were established in factories as of the mid-19th century. They were usually financed through employer and employee contributions. In addition, many doctors worked in both the public and private sectors. Moreover, public healthcare was not free, but fees varied according to the client's wealth. Municipal poor relief was the last form to get healthcare and medicine costs.[22]

Finland was a latecomer in public health. In 1890, there was only 236 legalized doctors in Finland. It denoted one doctor per 10 085 persons. The corresponding figures for Sweden were 6 357 (1889) and Norway 3 011 (1899).[23] The situation was the best in towns, but especially in remote areas, it was often difficult to get a doctor. Comparing Norway and Sweden, the mortality rate was in the late 19th century significantly higher in Finland and in rural areas higher than in towns. Epidemics, tuberculosis, and a high infant mortality rate were particular problems.[24]

Healthcare services increased in the early 20th century. In 1920, there was 657 legalized doctors in the country, and 20 years later, the number had doubled. The number of dentists more than tripled during the inter-war years. Other medical staff and the number of beds in hospitals also increased during the same period. Like in education, regional differences in healthcare were still remarkable: people in southern and western Finland had better access to doctors and other healthcare services than in eastern and northern Finland, and urban–rural division was also evident in healthcare. More demanding medical

Table 3.3 Institutionalization of healthcare in Finland, 1890–1960

	Doctors	*Dentists*	*Midwives*	*Officially assisted births, %*	*Births in hospitals, %*
1890	236		452	7.3	1.3
1900	373	28	650	26.4	3.8
1910	523	90	781	39.3	7.5
1920	657	250	777	43.9	10.2
1930	1 000	496	977	66.6	19.1
1940	1 378	879	882	80.0	30.6
1950	1 999	1 303	1 410	95.4	58.4
1960	2 961	1 778	1 841	99.8	92.5

Source: Statistical Yearbook of Finland.

Note: Including public and private sector.

treatments were carried out in larger hospitals in the provincial centres, and the best experts were in the capital, Helsinki.

Birth was a risk for both child and mother. Before 1850, there were only a few educated midwives in towns in Finland, and some towns did not have any educated midwives. The situation was even worse in rural areas. Local governments started to hire midwives after the new state order in 1859.[25] The development was initially slow, but the importance of midwives grew later: in 1890, less than one in ten; in 1930, already two thirds; and in 1960, almost every childbirth was assisted by midwives. Births in hospitals became more common at a much slower rate: in 1890, only 1%; in 1920, 19%; but in 1960, already 93% of all children were born in a hospital. However, inequality between urban and rural remained high for long. When in the towns almost all children were born in hospitals already in the 1920s, for the rural population, it was rare for a long time. Moreover, the birth rate was higher in the countryside and midwives had large working areas. Problems increased in winter due to the poor transport links.

As well as in education, the gradual growth of healthcare volumes denoted more equal opportunities for urban and rural population. Public health and healthcare systems were, however, completely inadequate and were lagging, compared to other Nordic countries, still in 1960: it was one doctor per 1 502 persons in Finland, 1 054 in Sweden and 842 in Norway.[26] The most acute public investments were required in remote areas of the country where public healthcare providers were rare. The situation was better in bigger towns, where there were also more private practitioners but there was also a remarkable economic inequality between different social classes in access to healthcare services. The construction of a comprehensive hospital network was in public sector's focus in the 1950s and 1960s. At least as important was health insurance (Act 1963) – daily allowances, medical expenses, maternity allowances, and doctors' expenses – which was carried out in two stages in the

1960s. Healthcare centres for municipalities (Act 1972) improved significantly regional and social equality.[27]

Conclusion

The development in Finland can, to some extent, be described as an example of the relative 'Gerschenkronian type of backwardness'. Finland was an agrarian-dominated society until the 20th century. Structural change gradually increased the need for new forms of social spending, and economic growth increased resources for public expenditure. When the size of public sector is (synchronically) related to the level of real GDP per capita, Finland, perhaps surprisingly, was not lagging that followed the average trend or was even ahead of it. However, because of the lower income level, Finland was in a diachronic comparison behind the most developed European economies in the size of its public sector.

According to our new consolidated general government figures, the public expenditure/GDP ratio increased from 11% in 1890 to 28% in 1960. Both World Wars are clear breaks in the development. The share of central government was the entire period much higher than local government. The picture is, however, somewhat different when the scope is changed from the state what happened in municipalities. The effect of urbanization and the first steps of education and healthcare gives an interesting perspective to the growth of the public sector at the local level. The late structural change partially explained the low level of public expenditure in Finland until the early 20th century. Urbanization increased government spending because of the construction of infrastructure and because of agrarian social security was not suitable and sufficient for people getting their living from manufacturing and service. Local governments provided many of the new services. Most of the actual tasks were implemented voluntarily in municipalities for a long time but subsidized by the central government. The state also tried to speed up the development. Many reforms were first realized in urban areas, but they were later implemented also in rural municipalities.

Public education, healthcare and pensions became the cornerstones of modern welfare states in the latter half of the 20th century. Backwardness was especially visible in social insurance in which many of the most significant reforms were only realized from the 1960s onwards. In social planning point of view Finland was, however, not a latecomer but in addition to late structural change political factors – the Russian influence, the civil war and right-wing hegemony during the inter-war years – essentially explained the development until World War II. Increasing economic resources and democracy removed the obstacles to public-sector growth in latter part of the 20th century. The development was reflected in the compromise between the left-wing parties and the agrarian party. The goal was more equal society with universal benefits and services which was built through the growth of public sector.

Notes

1 AMECO-database. The percentage was even higher during the depression of the early 1990s peaking at 64.2% in 1993.
2 Andersen et al. (2007); Valkonen and Vihriälä (2014).
3 Finland has no financially independent state level between central and local governments.
4 Of them Western Europe 16, Eastern Europe 7, "Western Offshoots" 4, Latin America 10, Asia 6 and Africa 1.
5 Schön (2010).
6 Tanzi (2011), 307; Tanzi and Schuknecht (2000).
7 Hjerppe (1989); Heikkinen (1997); Häkkinen and Peltola (2001); Hannikainen and Heikkinen (2006); Haapala (2018).
8 Eichengreen and Sachs (1985); Feinstein et al. (1997); Hjerppe (1989); Kokkinen et al. (2007).
9 Kettunen (2006); Hannikainen (2013).
10 Peltola (2008).
11 "Many of the most interesting aspects of public sector growth do not involve direct financial transactions which can be captured in the conventional indicators of the public sector". Middleton (1996), 88.
12 Heikkinen and Tiihonen (2009a).
13 Arola (2006).
14 Eloranta et al. (2016).
15 Heikkinen and Tiihonen (2009b).
16 Sweden's public expenditure figures for 1890 are lacking.
17 Jetter and Parmeter (2012); Cain (1997).
18 Hietala (1987); Turpeinen (1995); Peltola (1998).
19 Statistical Yearbook of Finland 1900–1962; own calculations.
20 Heikkinen and Leino-Kaukiainen (2011).
21 Peltola (2006a, 2006b).
22 Suomenmaan virallinen tilasto (II), Katsaus Suomen taloudelliseen tilaan vuosina 1886–1890; Saaritsa (2014); Harjula (2015); Peltola (2015).
23 Suomenmaan virallinen tilasto (II), Katsaus Suomen taloudelliseen tilaan vuosina 1886–1890, 178.
24 Harjula (2007).
25 Harjula (2015); Peltola (2015).
26 Statistical Yearbook of Finland 1962; Official Statistics of Sweden, Public Health in Sweden 1960, Stockholm 1962, 59–65; Statistical Yearbook of Norway 1962, Oslo 1962, 31.
27 Kuusi (1961); Alestalo and Uusitalo (1986); Harjula (2015).

References

Acemoglu, D., & Robinson, J. (2012). *Why Nations Fail: The Origins Power, Prosperity, and Poverty*. New York: Crown Publishing Group.

Alestalo, M., & Uusitalo, H. (1986). Finland. In P. Flora (ed.), *Growth to Limits: The Western European Welfare States Since World War II*. Berlin, New York: Walter de Gruyter.

Andersen, T. M. et al. (2007). *The Nordic Model: Embracing Globalization and Sharing Risks*. Helsinki: Taloustieto.

Arola, M. (2006). *Foreign Capital and Finland: Central Government's First Period of Reliance on International Financial Markets, 1862–1938*. Helsinki: Bank of Finland.

Cain, L. P. (1997). Historical Perspective on Infrastructure and US Economic Development. *Regional Science and Urban Economics*, *27*, 117–138.

Cusack, T. R., & Fuchs S. (2002). *Ideology, Institutions, and Public Spending*. Discussion Paper, Wissenschaftszentrum Berlin für Sozialforschung.

Dincecco, M. (2011). *Political Transformations and Public Finances: Europe, 1650–1913*. Cambridge: Cambridge University Press.

Eichengreen, B., & Sachs J. (1985). Exchange Rates and Economic Recovery in the 1930s. *The Journal of Economic History, 45*(4), 925–946.

Eloranta, J., Golson, E., Markevich A., & Wolf N. (eds.) (2016). *Economic History of Warfare and State Formation*. Berlin & Heidelberg: Springer.

Espuelas, S. (2012). Are Dictatorships Less Redistributive? A Comparative Analysis of Social Spending in Europe, 1950–1980. *European Review of Economic History, 16*, 211–232.

Feinstein, C. H., Temin P., & Toniolo G. (1997). *The European Economy Between the Wars*. Oxford: Oxford University Press.

Gerschenkron, A. (1962). *Economic Backwardness in Historical Perspective: A Book of Essays*. Cambridge, MA: Belknap Press of Harvard University Press.

Haapala, P. (ed.) (2018). *Suomen rakennehistoria: Näkökulmia muutokseen ja jatkuvuuteen (1400–2000)*. Tampere: Vastapaino.

Haapala, P., & Peltola J. (2018). Elinkeinorakenne 1750–2000. In P. Haapala (ed.), *Suomen rakennehistoria: Näkökulmia muutokseen ja jatkuvuuteen (1400–2000)* (pp. 170–209). Tampere: Vastapaino.

Häkkinen, A., & Peltola J. (2001). On the Social History of Employment, Unemployment and Poverty in Finland 1860–2000. In J. Kalela, J. Kiander, U. Kivikuru, H. A. Loikkanen, & J. Simpura (eds.), *Down from the Heavens, Up from the Ashes: The Finnish Economic Crisis in the Light of Economic and Social Research* (pp. 309–345). Helsinki: Valtion taloudellinen tutkimuskeskus.

Hannikainen, M. (2013). Comparison, Measurement, and Economization: The Origin of the Retirement Age of 65 in Finland. In H. Haggrén, J. Rainio-Niemi, & J. Vauhkonen (eds.), *Multi-layered Historicity of the Present: Approaches to Social Science History* (pp. 297–311). Publications of the Department of Political and Economic Studies 8. Helsinki: Unigrafia.

Hannikainen, M. & Heikkinen S. (2006). The Labour Market, 1850–2000. In J. Ojala, J. Eloranta, & J. Jalava (eds.), *The Road to Prosperity: An Economic History of Finland* (pp. 165–186). Helsinki: Suomalaisen Kirjallisuuden Seura.

Hannikainen, M. & Vauhkonen J. (2012). *Ansioiden mukaan: Yksityisalojen työeläkkeiden historia* [Earning Your Keep: The History of Finnish Earnings-Related Pension in the Private Sector]. Helsinki: Suomalaisen Kirjallisuuden Seura.

Harjula, M. (2007). *Terveyden jäljillä: suomalainen terveyspolitiikka 1900-luvulla*. Tampere: Tampere University Press.

Harjula, M. (2015). *Hoitoonpääsyn hierarkiat: Terveyskansalaisuus ja terveyspalvelut Suomessa 1900-luvulla*. Tampere: Tampere University Press.

Heikkinen, A., & Leino-Kaukiainen P. (2011). Yhteiskunta ja koulutus. In A. Heikkinen, & P. Leino-Kaukiainen (eds.), *Valistus ja koulunpenkki: Kasvatus ja koulutus Suomessa 1860-luvulta 1960-luvulle* (pp. 16–33). Helsinki: Suomalaisen Kirjallisuuden Seura.

Heikkinen, S. (1997). *Labour and the Market: Workers, Wages and Living Standards in Finland, 1850–1913*. Helsinki: The Finnish Society of Sciences and Letters.

Heikkinen, S., & Tiihonen S. (2009a). *Valtionrakentaja: Valtiovarainministeriön historia 1, 1809–1917* [The History of Finnish Ministry of Finance 1809–1917]. Helsinki: Edita.

Heikkinen, S., & Tiihonen S. (2009b). *Kriisinselvittäjä: Valtiovarainministeriön historia 2, 1917–1966* [The History of Finnish Ministry of Finance 1917–1956]. Helsinki: Edita.

Hietala, M. (1987). *Services and Urbanization at the Turn of the Century: The Diffusion of Innovations*. Helsinki: Finnish Historical Society.

Hjerppe, R. (1989). *The Finnish Economy 1860–1985: Growth and Structural Change*. Studies on Finland's Economic Growth XIII. Helsinki: Bank of Finland Publications, Government Printing Office.

Hjerppe, R., & Jalava J. (2006). Economic Growth and Structural Change. In J. Ojala, J. Eloranta, & J. Jalava (eds.), *The Road to Prosperity: An Economic History of Finland* (pp. 33–64). Helsinki: Suomalaisen Kirjallisuuden Seura.

Hoffman, P. T. (2015). What Do States Do? Politics and Economic History. *The Journal of Economic History*, *75*(2), 303–332.

Jetter, M., & Parmeter, C. F. (2012). *Does Urbanization Mean More Government?* www.michaeljetter.com/Urban_November_2012.pdf.

Kettunen, P. (1994). *Suojelu, suoritus, subjekti: Työsuojelu teollistuvan Suomen yhteiskunnallisissa ajattelu- ja toimintatavoissa*. Helsinki: Suomen Historiallinen Seura.

Kettunen, P. (2006). The Tension between the Social and the Economic: A Historical Perspective on a Welfare State. In J. Ojala, J. Eloranta, & J. Jalava (eds.), *The Road to Prosperity: An Economic History of Finland* (pp. 285–313). Helsinki: Suomalaisen Kirjallisuuden Seura.

Kokkinen, A., Jalava, J., Hjerppe R., & Hannikainen M. (2007). Catching-up in Europe: Finland's Convergence to Sweden and EU15. *Scandinavian Economic History Review*, *55*(2), 153–171.

Kuusi, P. (1961). *60-luvun sosiaalipolitiikka*. Helsinki: WSOY.

Lindert, P. H. (2004). *Growing Public: Social Spending and Economic Growth Since the Eighteenth Century*. Cambridge: Cambridge University Press.

Middleton, R. (1996). *Government versus the Market: Growth of the Public Sector, Economic Management and British Economic Performance, 1890–1979*. Cheltenham, UK: Edward Elgar Publishing.

Peltola, J. (1998). *Onnikoita ja Rollikoita: Viisi vuosikymmentä (1948–1998) kunnallista joukkoliikennettä Tampereella* [Buses and Trolleys: History of Public Transport in City of Tampere 1948–1998]. Tampere: Tampereen kaupungin liikennelaitos.

Peltola, J. (2006a). Leveämpi leipä: Elinkeinojen murros. In *Nouseva maakunta 1870–1939: Satakunnan historia VII* (pp. 49–145). Pori: Satakuntaliitto – Satakunnan museo.

Peltola, J. (2006b). Satakunta ja sen ihmiset. In *Nouseva maakunta 1870–1939: Satakunnan historia VII* (pp. 3–45). Pori: Satakuntaliitto – Satakunnan museo.

Peltola, J. (2008). *Työmailla, kabineteissa ja kaduilla: Valta ja lamapolitiikka Tampereella 1928–1938: 1930-luvun lama teollisuuskaupungissa III* [At the Sites, in the Cabinets, in the Streets: Power and Unemployment Policy in Tampere in 1928–1938. The Depression of the 1930s in an Industrial City III]. Tampere: Tampere University Press.

Peltola, J. (2015). *Pääradan ja kolmostien kunta: Janakkalan historia 1866–2014* [History of Janakkala Municipal]. Janakkala: Janakkalan kunta.

Pihkala, E. (1977). *Valtion tulojen ja menojen rakenne 1800-luvun jälkipuoliskolla*. Helsinki: Helsingin kauppakorkeakoulu.

Saaritsa, S. (2014). Koska lääkäriin? Sosiaalinen kerrostuneisuus ja sairaanhoidon kulutus maailmansotien välisen ajan Suomessa. In M. Hannikainen (ed.), *Työväestö ja hyvinvointi* (pp. 105–144). Tampere: Työväen historian ja perinteen tutkimuksen seura.

Schön, L. (2010). *Vår världs ekonomiska historia, Del 2: Den industriella tiden*. Stockholm: SNS Förlag.

Taimio, H. (1986). *Valtion menojen ja valtion julkisten palvelujen kasvu Suomessa 1900-luvun alkupuoliskolla*. Helsinki: Bank of Finland.

Tanzi, V. (2011). *Government versus Markets: The Changing Economic Role of the State*. Cambridge: Cambridge University Press.

Tanzi, V., & Schuknecht, L. (2000). *Public Spending in the 20th Century: A Global Perspective*. Cambridge: Cambridge University Press.

Tudeer, A. E. (1931). *Suomen valtiontalous vuosina 1922–192: Vertaileva katsaus valtion tuloihin ja menoihin*. Helsinki: Taloudellisen neuvottelukunnan julkaisuja.

Turpeinen, O. (1995). *Kunnallistekniikkaa Suomessa keskiajalta 1990-luvulle*. Jyväskylä: Suomen kuntatekniikan yhdistys.

Valkonen, T., & Vihriälä V. (eds.) (2014). *The Nordic Model: Challenged but Capable of Reform*. Copenhagen: Nordic Council of Ministers.

Valvanne, H. (1952). Valtiontalous vuosina 1938–1951. In *Taloudellisia selvityksiä 1952* (pp. 5–26). Helsinki: Bank of Finland.

4 The (strong) state, the welfare state and social cohesion

Finland in comparison

Susanna Fellman, Reino Hjerppe and Riitta Hjerppe

Introduction

It is often thought that the construction of the modern Finnish welfare state was important not only in the fight against poverty, inequality and social problems but also for advancing economic development and strengthening social cohesion and therefore social peace. Finland was at the beginning of the 20th century lagging economically most countries in Western Europe, and the country was politically unequal, socially fragmented and marked by both open and underlying tensions and conflicts, ending up in a civil war in 1918. In the inter-war period, the heritage from 1918 left a long shadow on social development. However, industrial progress was fast, which paved the way to social development as well.

In the post–World War II decades, swift economic growth and policies to support skill formation, improvements in health and social well-being and the advancement of equal opportunities and social inclusion changed the society profoundly. In the new millennium, the country can be counted as one of the top in living standards and equality, combined with a competitive business sector, a generous welfare state, a broad range of public services renowned for their quality (educational system and health care), while social and political tensions were, if not eradicated, clearly tapered. How did this development occur?

To answer this question and understand the development trends require us to take a look further back in history. In this chapter, we will study the development of the Finnish welfare system from the end of the 19th century until today, with a particular focus on the post-war period and on which role the welfare state development played in economic development and in the process of creating social cohesion (for the earlier period, see Hannikainen et al. in this volume). The debate concerning the relationship between the welfare state and economic development has raised a lot of interest both in economics and economic history. Is the welfare state a consequence or precondition of economic development? Which factors actually led to the emergence of the welfare state? And, in particular, what role has the welfare state project played in creating 'modern' Finland and in overcoming fragmentation and reaching social cohesion?

DOI: 10.4324/9780429503870-5

This chapter is primarily a synthetization of recent debates about the history and the future of the welfare state and its role in the previously mentioned transition process. Our focus is on the Finnish case, but the questions and results will be put within a broader Nordic comparative perspective. The Nordic countries are often cited as examples of countries with highly elaborate welfare states, and Finland has, to a large extent, followed a Nordic development path.

When discussing the Nordic model, the active role of the state and a large public sector are factors usually seen as characterizing this model. This is also an issue we address here. It is evident that state policies often actively promoted economic and social development by managing in the economic and social spheres. The large public sector, the allegedly strong and active state, the high level of taxation and the extensive welfare system in combination with the successful economic development of the Nordic countries have often been considered something of a paradox. According to some views, high taxation connected with a large public sector leads to a loss of economic efficiency and are, thus, harmful for economic growth. The Nordic countries have not fitted to this 'textbook model' of best practices for furthering economic development. These countries have been both economically successful and competitive. They have even been labelled the 'bumblebee', which was not supposed to be able to fly but, in spite of that, continues to do so![1]

However, we also recognize that this transition path from social fragmentation and conflict to social cohesion and peace might be broken or take a new turn. In many Western societies, growing cleavages and increasing polarization have re-emerged, which cause concerns for a new era of instability. Occasionally, these trends are even claimed to form a threat to Western liberal democracies. One reason for the growing polarization and political instabilities was the global financial crisis which started in 2008, but other factors have also furthered such sentiments. Forces emerging from globalization, especially the global relocation of work to new economic areas, threats from climate change and the large migration waves, combined with demands for austerity policies and cuts in welfare provision, have put strains on the political systems and on the social peace. Populist parties and groups both on the left and the right are on the rise. These questions are also on the agenda in Finland, where especially the economic recessions both in the early 1990s and again after the financial crisis put the public finances in front of severe challenges leading to cuts in the welfare provision and welfare services. Also a rapidly ageing population has made the outlook for the future bleak from an economic perspective.

Moreover, the fundamental outlook on the Nordic (universal) welfare state system has become challenged. The welfare state project during the post-war decades was largely based on a perception of a common 'us',[2] in which the advancement of economic growth and social cohesion was a core goal and also an important part of nation building. The idea of a welfare state as a basis for something common for all Finns – and thus a tool to strengthen social cohesion – is experiencing threats also from within. There are debates about how much can be directed via market forces and what is the responsibility of the state. And what is the responsibility of the individual? The transformation from a country whose history as an independent nation started with a civil war, to a country with high social cohesion and social capital, has been remarkable, but the situation cannot be taken for granted.

Frame of analysis and the structure of the chapter

In this chapter, we first present the general development of the size and expenditure structure of the public sector and show how the focus of activities has shifted between various expenditure categories. Next, we consider the relationship between the development of the welfare state and the economy as a whole. We explore briefly from a historical perspective the question of whether the welfare state precedes and supports economic development or whether it only follows the general development of the economy and enlarges because there are more resources available for the use of public-sector purposes. In the second half of the chapter, we discuss how the welfare state development supported the creation of social cohesion and what role in particular the 'state' (understood as the government) played in this development and, especially, in relation to other groups in society. We discuss the main compromises in the development of the public activities in the political context, including the roles of the state, of interest groups, such as labour market organizations, and of the civil society. What role has the state and various groups played in this process and how has this affected the process towards social cohesion. We focus especially on the post-war period, but occasionally we go further back in history to put the development in a longer time perspective (for the time prior to World War II, see also Hannikainen et al. in this volume).

The role of the state and the public sector has often been somewhat superficially dealt with within the context of economic development. There has been a tendency to classify the state and public sector according to simple lines of axes, for example of 'active' versus 'passive' or 'strong' versus 'weak' or of 'large' versus 'small'. The role and significance of the state and the public sector have been, however, both complex and multifaceted. We do not go into detail about these complex discussions but instead focus on the concrete role of the state and public sector in the welfare state development and in the path to social cohesion. However, some issues have to be emphasized. First, it is evident that the state and the public sector have played a significant part in Nordic societies and in the development of the 'Nordic model', but the size, role and activities of the state and the public sector have varied between the individual countries. The public sector and its activities have also transformed significantly over time; for example, the 'division of labour' between central and local government have shifted. Second, the state or the public sector cannot be seen as entities with necessarily common goals and interests, but instead, they should be grasped as arenas for various competing interests, for example between strong interest groups and political parties, between civil servants and politicians, within the political decision-making and within state bureaucracy and between local and central government.

To analyze the development, we have developed a frame of analysis, which is presented in Figure 4.1. In the background, we see the long-term economic growth and development, which has emerged in both a national and an international (now rather global) context. The welfare system has been generated in the framework of this larger national economic system. Different actors or forces have been influencing the development. These forces can be divided into three groups. First, there is a structural change in the economy, driven mainly by profit-seeking enterprises and other actors on the market. We claim that a change from an agrarian society to an industrial (manufacturing) society and then, more recently, towards an economy dominated by services has been a fundamental factor influencing welfare state development. Other important factors are the state itself, with political groups, state bureaucrats and civil servants, and the civil society, with various interest and pressure groups, which drive for or are against welfare state reforms. These groups have varying and to some extent conflicting goals with respect to welfare reforms. Moreover, both the roles and goals of different actors in welfare state development can change over time. In the Nordic context, welfare services have mainly been developed within the public sphere, although there have existed private parallel systems, for example in health care and day care.

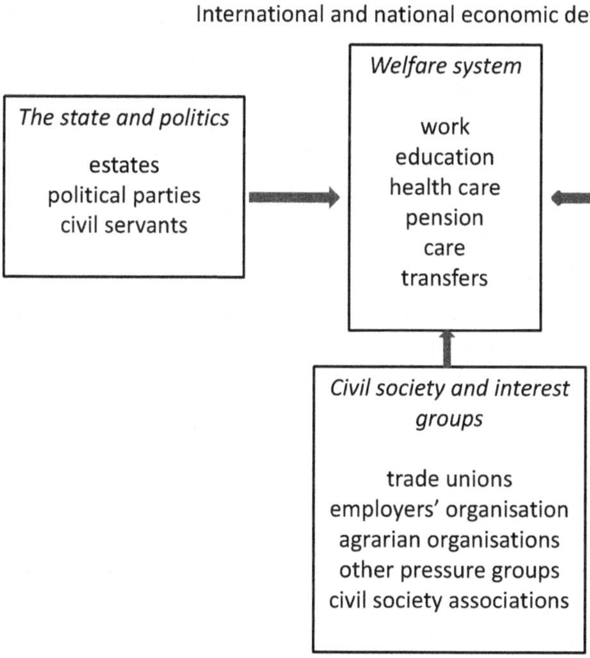

International and national economic development

The state and politics
estates
political parties
civil servants

Welfare system
work
education
health care
pension
care
transfers

Structural change
agriculture
industry
services

Civil society and interest groups
trade unions
employers' organisation
agrarian organisations
other pressure groups
civil society associations

Figure 4.1 Factors influencing welfare state development

The overall development of the public sector in Finland

To define exactly what is meant by the 'welfare state' so that it is not unambiguous, we adopt a broad definition; besides public social and health expenditures, public educational expenditures are also considered part of the welfare state. The size of the welfare state is measured by these expenditures in relation to the gross domestic product (GDP). We stress the difference between the 'welfare state' and the 'public sector'. The present-day public activities consist of general administration, maintenance of public order and defense, construction and upkeep of infrastructure, provision of education, health and other social services and paying of transfers and subsidies, as well as interests on the public debt. Outlays for these purposes form total public expenditure.[3] Therefore, the size of the public sector does not necessarily tell us much about the size or structure of the welfare state. Instead, we have to disaggregate the public expenditures. In Finland, the government produces most of the services itself on either a central or a local level.[4]

Providing education, health and other social services is the basic activity of a welfare state. Another important and growing part of government welfare activities has been transfers to households. Table 4.1 shows some basic indicators of the size of the Finnish public sector in relation to the GDP from 1900 (see also Hannikainen et al. in this volume).

During the 20th century, the Finnish public sector has grown faster than the GDP and, accordingly, increased its share in the economy. The relative size of the total public sector, that is total government expenditure, has almost quadrupled from 13 to 47 per cent of GDP, and public consumption has relatively tripled from 7 to 21 per cent. Central government consumption was slightly larger than the local government share until the Second World War. Since then, the local government consumption has grown almost twice as fast. This is due to the expansion of existing local services and the creation of new services, but many services previously produced by the central government have been transferred to be a responsibility of the local government. The public sector is also nowadays a significant employer with about a quarter of total employment.

At the end of the 19th century, roughly 40 per cent of central government public expenditures went to consumption and another ample 40 per cent to investments, 10 per cent consisted of transfers and subsidies – one third of those to the local government. Within the overall small public sector of the late 19th century, general administration and the construction of infrastructure were the core of these expenditures. Interests on public debt required a few percentage points. The largest investments were in railways, but the government invested also into administrative buildings and schools.[5] In public consumption, general administration and defence were the major expenditures.[6] One quarter was spent on education, health and other social services, education taking by far the largest share and growing fastest during the last decades of the 19th century. Health and social services received only a few percentages of the outlays.[7]

Local governments had the main responsibility of poor relief, health care and primary education; education was, however, subsidized by the central government. Until the law of primary education, which was passed in 1921, it was, in reality, mainly the church and occasionally paternalistic companies in mill communities which provided primary education in rural areas. The poor financial situation of local governments made the number of schools remain low.[8] In cities and towns, the school system developed more rapidly. Health care was modest. Rural municipalities often had only one doctor and one midwife, while towns had small hospitals for infectious diseases. Other tasks of the local governments during this period were the maintenance and construction of local roads, bridges and harbours, as well as local government buildings.

Local governments and town and rural community councils had initially a relatively autonomic position in local administration and could quite freely choose what social services to produce. Local independence has decreased gradually over the last 100 years, as more and more public activities, particularly the welfare services, are today based on national legislation. Nevertheless, the services are still produced largely by the local governments and primarily funded by municipal taxes and by central government transfers to municipalities.

Approximately the same responsibilities and the same structure of public spending continued in the inter-war period although all items in Table 4.1 grew. A rough estimate based on the central government accounts from 1937 shows that about one quarter of the expenditures went into education, health and social services. Social policy measures consisted, however, still mainly of poor relief by the local governments. In an International Labour Organization comparison from 1930, Finland was the only member country, where poor relief was larger than state social insurance expenditures. In spite of the rudimental

Table 4.1 The size of the public sector in Finland, 1900–2018*

	1900	*1938*	*1960*	*1990*	*2018*
Total general govt. expenditures, % of GDP	11	22	28	45	53
Public consumption expenditures, % of GDP	7	11	12	20	23
Central government consumption, % of GDP	4	6	5	8	8**
Local government consumption, % of GDP	3	5	7	14	15
Value added of the public sector, % of GDP	5	8	9	19	27
The public sector employment, 1,000 persons	19	89	167	585	631
The public sector employment, % of total employment	2	6	9	24	24

Source: Hjerppe and Hjerppe (1992, p. 77); Official Statistics of Finland, Kansantalouden tilinpito 1998–2007 (National Accounts 1998–2007).

Note: GDP = gross domestic product.

* Without debt payments.

** Includes social security funds, 1.6% of GDP.

Table 4.2 Finland's total public expenditures in relation to the gross domestic product (in percentages), 1960–2018

	1960	*1980*	*1990*	*2018*
Public consumption	11.9	18.1	21.1	22.7
Gross capital formation	4.5	3.8	3.6	4.2
Subsidies	2.9	3.2	2.8	1.2
Transfers	5.5	8.3	10.5	20.8
Other	1.8	3.2	3.3	4.1
Total	26.6	36.6	41.2	53.4

Source: Statistical Yearbooks of Finland 1960–2018; Hjerppe and Hjerppe 1992, 79.

level, social care took the highest share, about a quarter, of all expenditures in rural municipalities.[9] Nevertheless, both central and local government continued to be basically a "night watch" state and not an active welfare provider.[10]

The post–World War II development directed the public sector on to a very different path (Table 4.2). From the 1960s to 1980s, public consumption and transfers were the fastest growing items. Since the 1980s, transfers to households have continued to grow swiftly. Gross capital formation has been relatively stable. Transfers mainly include pensions for old age and disability, family allowances and unemployment benefits. The growth of this item shows that the tasks of the public sector are very different today compared to the first half of the 20th century. The years from about 1960 to 1990 can be called the welfare state construction period, with many new welfare programs and extended benefit levels. Also the attitudes towards the role of the public sector in the society experienced a substantial change during this period; the majority of the inhabitants came to accept at least some provision of tax-financed welfare services, as well as publicly funded education and health care. However, the level of benefits and form and extent of services have continuously been debated. Since the severe economic crises of the early 1990s, some welfare retrenchment have occurred, but mainly by cutting down on the generosity of transfers and pushing through reforms to promote labour supply, while the system is mainly intact. At the same time, also the debates about the responsibilities of the public sector and of the individual grew.

Finland in an international comparison

If we look at Finland in international comparison, the structures of public consumption and gross capital formation or investments are quite similar (Table 4.3). This is also discussed in the chapter by Hannikainen et al. in this volume. In all countries, the share of public consumption has shown a rising trend. In the post–World War II period, the fastest growing category in total public expenditures has been income transfers. The share of government investments has decreased, while the share of public transfers has grown.

Table 4.3 Final consumption expenditure and gross capital formation of total government expenditure, in relation to gross domestic product (in percentages), 1952–2007

	Consumption expenditure				*Gross capital formation*		
	1952	*1963*	*1980*	*2007*	*1963*	*1980*	*2005*
Finland	11	14	19	21	4	4	3
France	15	13	15	23	4	3	3
Germany	15	16	20	18	4	4	1
Holland	14	16	18	25	5	3	3
Norway	10	14	19	20	4	4	3
Sweden	13	17	29	26	5	4	3
U.K.	19	17	21	21	4	2	1
U.S.A.	16	18	18	16	3	2	2
Japan	11	9	10	18	4	6	4

Source: OECD National Accounts, 1951–2007.

Unfortunately, they cannot be shown separately over a long period because of lacking comparable statistical data, but in principle, the difference between total public expenditures and government consumption and investments consists mainly of transfers. Some comparisons are possible.

In Table 4.4, we compare the structure of public consumption in relation to GDP in three Nordic countries since the 1960s. Also in this case we can observe some striking similarities but also a few differences. The overall trend was a rising relation of the public consumption to the GDP from the 1960s to the 1980s. After that, the relative growth stagnated in Norway and slowed in Finland, while a small decrease occurred in Sweden. Sweden has had the largest public consumption between 1960 and 2005. The fastest growing and constantly growing category in all three countries was social security. The shares of education and health expenditures grew between 1960 and 1980 but decreased then by 2005. The shares of education outlays have actually decreased considerable.

The overall developments of the welfare state expenditures in Finland seem to have followed the patterns in the other developed countries and particularly the Nordic ones. The early development of the welfare state was a slow, gradual and stepwise process. The big expansion of education and health care were carried out mostly in the post-war period (pension system, sickness insurance, maternity allowances, unemployment benefits, etc.), while transfer payments developed and expanded since the 1980s meaning a maturing of the system.

The Finnish development lagged the forerunner countries, especially in the early 20th century. This is often considered to have stemmed primarily from the low economic level in the 1900s; the Finnish GDP per capita was less than half of that of the United Kingdom and the United States, and it was behind the other Nordic countries by 30 to 40 per cent. However, during the 20th century, Finland caught up with the most advanced Western European

Table 4.4 Government final consumption expenditure by function in relation to gross domestic product (in percentages) in Finland, Sweden and Norway, 1960–2005

	Finland			*Sweden*			*Norway*		
	1960	1980	2005	1963	1979	2005	1963	1980	2005
General administration	3.0	4.1	3.6	2.3	3.7	4.2	2.0	2.3	2.4
Defence	1.4	1.4	0.7	4.3	3.1	0.8	3.4	2.8	0.8
Education	4.0	5.4	2.7	4.3	6.0	3.4	3.9	5.1	2.8
Health	2.2	3.9	3.1	3.1	6.8	3.2	1.6	4.1	3.4
Social security	1.1	2.3	9.3	1.4	4.8	11.1	0.9	1.5	7.8
Other	0.9	1.0	2.9	1.9	4.0	3.7	2.6	3.0	2.8
Total	12.6	18.1	22.2	17.3	28.4	26.4	14.3	18.8	19.9

Source: Hjerppe and Hjerppe (1992), p. 78; OECD National Accounts 1951–2007; Nordic Statistical Yearbook (2007), table 128.

countries. Currently, the GDP per capita is about ten per cent higher in Sweden than in Finland and the UK. During this period, the Finnish welfare state also caught up with the other Western European countries. Therefore, in case the welfare state is studied in relation to economic development, it can be claimed that the Finnish welfare development did not emerge especially late.[11]

The supply and demand for public services and social security

In all industrialized countries, public spending increased with growing economic development, although the developments were not uniform. One reason was economic development, but also institutional and cultural factors, as well as political struggles, affected the development patterns.[12]

A stylized picture of the public sector and welfare state growth could be described as follows: in the traditional pre-capitalist economy the public sector was minimal. During the early industrialization the dominant ideology was that everyone should support themselves or rely on family and relatives. Moreover, the public finances were weak and would not have allowed for any extensive public reforms. Besides the few services that the local municipalities were compelled to provide, the church, some philanthropic organizations and, occasionally, paternalistic employers engaged in welfare activities.

With industrial progress, entrepreneurs started to demand more public services: law and order (intangible infrastructure) and physical infrastructure (public capital like roads, railways, harbours). As the technological development progressed, the demand for a more skilled workforce grew as well. The emergence of wage labour and the pitfalls of the working conditions contributed to some early labour protection legislation and the emergence of labour unions, which, in turn, aimed to raise the wage level of their members but gradually also began to demand other services and benefits and later other social security measures. In the early 1900s, the demands for welfare initiatives became more prevalent. Social political associations were formed, social insurances were propagated by insurance industry and state committees pondered on social issues. However, in the Finnish case, efforts were mostly unsuccessful, especially as they were as a rule blocked by the Russian administration (see Hannikainen et al. in this volume).

In spite of political fragmentation in the 1920s and 1930s, health care and education reforms were passed but the weakened left, combined with insufficient public finances in the still poor country stalled any significant welfare state reforms. A national old-age pension system was passed in 1937 but implemented only in the post-war period. In the Finnish case, the questions of the limited public finances and if the country can afford such reforms have been common arguments through history.[13] This continued into the post-war period. Conservatives, employers and various business lobbies continuously stressed that the tax burden was 'too high'.[14] On the other hand, also many of those who were in principle against reforms, were aware that welfare efforts could counteract revolutionary tendencies. Possible reforms should, however, preferably be private and voluntary systems based on insurances with individual contributions. In the paternalist era, big business also developed their own welfare programs, which could be quite elaborate and advanced, but concerned their own employees. Overall, the discussions of more general social insurance reforms became more frequent but lead only to a few legislations.

In the post-war period, the demands for reforms became swift. The changing political landscape with increasing support for the political left and growing unionization made new and more pronounced demands emerge. As economic development became swift, new opportunities to invest in welfare evolved; economic growth increased the public sector's tax revenue. In a fairly short period in the late 1950s and early 1960s some big social reforms were carried through (e.g. a reformation of the old-age pension system in 1956, the work-pension system 1961, a general health insurance in 1964). During the following decades, the level of social benefits was raised. Government policies also supported these efforts. For example, during periods of high inflation, the Finnish government made deliberate decisions not to adjust tax progression scales according to inflation, which made a de facto increase in the tax burden, which increased these resources.

In spite of objection from some political groups against new reforms, there has been, since World War II, overall a fairly wide acceptance for tax-financed basic services in Finland, as in the other Nordic countries. The idea of paying for something that extends to the whole population has been assumed to lead to trust in the system and one of the strengths of the Nordic system. Also conservatives have been able to accept quite high taxes as the business sector, and higher income groups have received 'pieces of the common cake' or could control the system.[15] Other policy areas (industrial policy, monetary policy competition policy) benefitted from the expanding manufacturing sectors.

Also, infrastructural and educational investments supported the corporate sector. During this period, compromise-seeking policies emerged, and it was also in the interest of the employers to create trust and peace on the labour market. As the left had gained more power, businesses and employers could not be too confrontational. We turn to this later in the chapter.

An interesting question in this context is whether the public sector was somehow leading the economic development or whether it was only following the development, making necessary adjustments in the system when needed or when there were demands for such services. By looking at the expansion of the welfare state in various countries, a general observation is that demands for such services appeared hand in hand with economic and industrial development. In case there is a positive causality between investments in welfare services and economic growth, it is evident that a slow welfare state development can, in principle, retard economic development. Scholars have also asked whether public-sector development follows or leads the development of the GDP. According to one early study for the period from 1900 to 1962 in Finland using causality tests, no causality in either way was found; that is it seems that both the public-sector expansion and economic growth occur simultaneously.[16] Another study in which the contribution of public capital to economic growth was tested by using a time-series cross-country regression over the 1960–2002 period shows some interesting results.[17] The authors developed a concept of 'enlarged public capital', which included not only the physical capital but also human capital based on the expenditures of health and education. According to this study, the public capital stock has a positive impact on private-sector productivity. The results of the study suggest that in addition to traditional infrastructure, public health and education expenditures (i.e. intangible public investments in human capital) have also contributed positively to private-sector productivity in almost all countries included in the study. Although the causalities are difficult, it seems that the public sector plays an important part in economic growth and that welfare reform is important for growth. However, this depends on what the state (and the public sector) does with its resources.

State as an arena for organized interest

As mentioned, demands for public sector growth come from both the supply and the demand side. *One political issue has been who is to decide what will be produced and how can these decisions be efficiently carried out.* With these questions, we study how the other factors in Figure 4.1 – political parties, state bureaucracy and interest groups – have influenced the development of the welfare state. If we look at European – and especially Nordic – countries, interest groups, civil servants and political parties have all put their distinct marks on the welfare state development.[18] As the welfare state – and the public sector – expanded, the power relations between the various groups and actors and between the local and central government changed (see Hannikainen et al. in this volume). This makes the issue tricky.

In the introduction, we entered the question of the weak and the strong state. One of the characteristics of the Nordic model has often been considered a strong and centralized state, and this has been a prerequisite for the welfare state development. In Sweden – and thus also in Finland – this state model is seen as having a long history, going back to the 17th century.[19] However, the ability of the state to influence the development varies according to, for example, the quality of its civil servants and ability to raise taxes – so-called state capacity – an issue often seen as a strong point in the Nordic countries. Strong bureaucratic rules and quite high competence requirements for civil servants have safeguarded this. There has also been relatively little corruption in the public sector in the Nordic countries and have been a reason for the high social trust in the public sector.[20] Overall, there is a long history for a legally based social order, which has enjoyed a high legitimacy by its citizens. Nonetheless, Finland has also had both open and underlying tensions. The country experienced a civil war in 1918, when the legitimacy of the prevailing system was challenged. Also during the post-war decades, political tensions, short-term governments and restlessness on the labour market were prevalent. Mutual trust between social groups, especially the workers and employers, is often considered to have taken a longer time to construct than in the other Nordic countries.

We acknowledge that the role of the state in the process, and if it is has been strong or weak, is a complex question; already, the concept of the 'state' is ambiguous. Does it consist of the parliament, the government or the civil servants and bureaucracy or semi-independent government bodies as well? Empirical research dealing with the state has often been looking at elected governments and/or departments of states, but there are a variety of organizations, which could claim to be part of the state.[21] In practice, it acts under the influence of different political forces, at the same time as the views and influence of civil servants – claimed to be non-political actors – can be significant. A democratic state forms an arena for various groups and agents, all with their own goals to shape the policies. States should be considered as entities, whose internal and external boundaries are shifting over time and who are subject to negotiation and change. For example, the state system in Finland at the end of the 19th century consisted of estates and a few civil servants. The democratic parliamentary reform in the early 20th century replaced the estates with political parties. However, it does exist and has the capacity to act autonomously.[22] In most democratic countries, the state can rather be viewed as a palette; in some policy areas, it can be strong, in some weak, or in some interventionist and in some at arm's length. State strategies can also vary between policy areas. The state can rather be viewed as a palette.[23]

We are not interested here to discuss what the state is, or the limits of the state, but want to look at what its role has been in welfare state formation and in transition from a fragmented society to social cohesion. The state, understood as the central government, creates and maintains the legal foundation of the society. Both the state and the political system are important for economic growth, structural transformation and for the development path of the welfare regimes. For example, in the fragmented and federalist political system in the US, the welfare system took a different path from the Nordic one, which has been based on a unified, centralized political system. In the US, the welfare system has primarily been based on the state, not the federal, level.[24] In Finland, the expansion of the welfare state meant a system from local variation to centralization with similar services and benefits for everyone, although local governments have been important as producers of welfare services. This has occasionally caused tensions.

An active state is not always a strong one, nor is a strong one always active. A big public sector does not either mean that the state is strong, although the state has more abilities to act when the public sector is of considerable size and the tax revenues are substantial. An active state can be weak towards and captured by sector interest, for example. This was the case in the inter-war period in Finland, when the state was fairly weak with respect to especially business interests, whose influence in economic policy agenda setting was extensive. At the same time, the state became more active, which was marked by the development of the first state companies, while public expenditures on education and health increased.

After the Second World War, Finland entered a corporatist era, when the unions' influence grew. Also employers and the agrarian interest groups were part of this system. A willingness to involve interest groups and/or civil society into policymaking is not always a sign of weakness, however, but can be a deliberate strategy.[25] In the post-war period, the state in Finland – as also in for example Sweden – must be considered quite strong, but it gave power to labour market parties, as part of consensus building.

During this era of neo-corporatism, it was also common with semi-independent government and expert organizations, especially within the social policy area (e.g. so-called sector institutes such as STAKES – today the Institute for Health and Welfare) but also within economic and industrial policy, many platforms for policy formulation existed. Formal and semi-formal councils, boards and *ad hoc* committees played an important role both in preparatory work for legislative and political reforms and formed platforms for discussions, consultations and even for the implementation of policies.[26] For example, the influential and permanent Economic Council (Talousneuvosto) received a formal position through legislation in 1954.[27] These councils, advisory boards and ad hoc committees consisted of a mix of policy-makers, civil servants, experts and interest group representatives received important roles. Such groups were especially common when compromise thinking was at its height and was considered to give legitimacy to the decisions among broad groups in society.[28] This was intended to smooth out conflicts and policy reforms supported by large groups. However, tensions could not always be avoided and compromise seeking made policy reforms slow as strong groups were occasionally able to delay the process.

In particular, labour market organizations (trade unions, agrarian interest groups and employer organizations) played an important role in shaping the systems of the welfare state. For instance, the unemployment insurance system and the work pension system strengthened the position of the labour market parties, as their role in the administration. They were influential enough to mould the system in a direction they preferred.[29] In the Finnish system, the agrarian interest also had significant influence.

Nevertheless, the state (i.e. civil servants, the parliament, the government and the political parties) has been important. For example, civil servants were prominent for sketching the reforms and carrying out plans as part of the expertise work. It is also important not to neglect the political system. In the end, the politically elected parliament gave the last acceptance and was overall important as an arena for both political debate and decision-making.[30] Social legislation is a parliamentary process. Sometimes, the parliament accepted the negotiated contract concluded by the labour market parties, but at other times, the parliament raised the voice that its role not only to accept negotiated results.

The state was important also as a balancing factor. With respect to the welfare state, there have been several conflicting interests to balance, not only 'labour' and 'capital' but also between the goals of the Social Democratic Party/trade unions and the agrarian/Centre Party. Tensions between the agrarian interests and the working-class population was for long a prominent feature affecting the Finnish welfare state, where the division line was between income-related and flat-rate compensations. Moreover, there were also diverging views about the structure of welfare reforms between various left-wing fractions (mainly between communists and social democrats). Balancing between these interests was important in the search for compromises. Overall, the corporatist system blurred the limits of the state.

The government occasionally also interfered in the corporatist bargaining. Within the income policy system, the state used social-political reforms and/or taxations as trump cards in the negotiations in order to make the employers and employees agree. Even the president occasionally interfered, especially while Urho Kekkonen was president, when the constitution gave the president extensive power also in domestic politics. For example, he declined to affirm a legislative bill concerning additional benefits to old-age pensions in 1972, due to unclear funding.[31] The constitution changed in the 1990s decreasing the presidential powers in domestic politics.

Interference from politics into what the labour market parties considered their domain did not always occur without conflict. For example, when the future of the Finnish pension system was debated in the early 2000s, both the prime minister of Finland and the civil servants within the Ministry of Health and Social Affairs met with resistance from the labour market parties. As Olli Kangas has stressed, it has been easier to complete reforms pension system in Sweden as the system there is governed within the political process.[32] Also the Finnish pension system went through changes during the last decades, but the process was perhaps slower and more troublesome. On the other hand, a compromise model usually enjoys more legitimacy. For example, the effects of the Swedish pension reform of the 1990s is heatedly debated currently, when the baby boomers retire and find their pension level disappointing after a long working life.

The role of councils, and overall interest-group influence, has decreased since the 1990s. For example, in Finland, the political administration has abandoned the committee work and moved towards a system with "one-man" committees. This has been part not only of the demands for more efficient public governance but also as a consequence of the weakening of the corporatist model.

However, the boundaries of the state are still difficult to define but partly for other reasons, especially a tendency towards increasing public–private networks, agents and projects. For example, the expanding 'third sector' often carries out services in close cooperation with the local or state authorities. Some of these agents can receive considerable public or semi-public funding, for instance in Finland from the state gambling monopoly.[33] In many countries, for example Sweden, which for long relied heavily on public provision of welfare services, the significance of private actors has increased dramatically, especially in health care and education. In Finland, similar developments were planned to occur with the extensive reform of the organization of public healthcare and social welfare (SOTE), which nonetheless failed in early 2019. A reformed legislation was passed in 2021.[34]

Civil society, inclusion and social cohesion

An important force in the 'Nordic model' and in Finnish welfare development comes from civil society associations; they are 'countries of associations'. Therefore, it can be claimed that Nordic societies have been characterized by a public–private mix, rather than a split.[35] The strong state–strong civil society has formed something of a puzzle, however.[36] The prominent role of the civil society is obviously linked to the prominent interest groups, but the civil society consists of a much broader range of voluntary associations than just interest groups.[37]

Civil society association can be considered important for economic and social development from different aspects. First, civil associations spread useful information amongst their members. This information is often consistent with the creation of human capital, which is crucial for economic development. Second, civil associations can enhance the solidarity amongst their members and therefore promote trust amongst them. This can 'spill over' to society more broadly. Interest groups or civil associations can obviously work as hindrances for development if their role is mainly to distribute benefits and form strong insider–outsider features. Nevertheless, it is believed that the quite varied and extensive civil society in the Nordic countries has predominantly been a positive force in economic and social development and especially for trust creation.

According to the World Value Survey, the amount of trust is large in the Nordic countries, and in Finland, it is among the highest.[38]

In the area of social policy, one important early association was for example the Social Policy Association – a common forum for academics, business leaders within the insurance businesses and reform-oriented civil servants – established in 1908. It formed a forum for discussion of social policy reforms and even prepared proposals for reform laws to parliament.[39] In the social policy areas also many other associations have been important to channel information and give voice to decision-makers, for example patient groups and associations of social and medical professions. As already mentioned, the committee institution was an arena for such a meeting between the civil society and the state in Finland and Sweden.[40]

The reason behind the vitality and strength of the civil society, with its wide range of grass-root and voluntary associations is interesting. Why did they gain the political capacity to influence the development? According to historian Henrik Stenius, the strength of the early voluntary associations (especially cooperatives, temperance movement) stemmed from the fact that they involved the middle class.[41] Due to the late industrialization, the first civil societies were not the trade unions, and the associations could therefore be embraced also by the middle class. This was for example the case of the Social Policy Association mentioned earlier attracting social reformers over the political spectrum. Another important explanation is that local governments were sometimes collaborating with and supporting the civil movements and therefore gave them a stronger voice. The close relation between local authorities and voluntary associations can be observed if we look at the local level: private–public partnerships between voluntary associations, occasionally private companies and municipalities were common in welfare provision, especially health care and education.[42] Local government and civil societies formed a counterforce to the strong and central state.[43] On the other hand, it has been emphasized that the state in the Nordic countries was also quite open and inclusive towards these associations, and in this way, they provided a link for citizens into the state.[44]

In fact, the perception that the low degree of inequality in the Nordic countries since the post-war period, and especially in Sweden, is rooted in a historically egalitarian society with a large share of independent farmers making Sweden (and the other Nordic countries) somewhat exceptional ('egalitarian exceptionalism'), has lately been challenged.[45] According to economic and political historian Erik Bengtsson, Sweden was not particularly egalitarian until significantly later. The policies to reduce the large income differences and towards an egalitarian and inclusive society was a result of the strong civil society groups emerging in the late 19th century and, later, the labour movement pursuing egalitarianism and inclusion. Social cohesion, trust and egalitarian societies do not emerge automatically but require active efforts. In the Nordic countries, the state has been open towards these groups and therefore important also in trust building and for the increasing equal societies historically.

The state in the small state and social cohesion

As mentioned, welfare provision and, in particular, educational and other public infrastructure investments have enjoyed a broad legitimacy in the Nordic countries. The smallness of Finland and the other Nordic countries, in conjunction with a centralized state structure and aims for social cohesion, has probably made it easier to develop the universal welfare system. These two features are connected. The openness and export dependence of these small economies have fostered the conception that the state has an important role as an enabler of economic growth and catching-up, swift structural transformation and adaptability to changes in market conditions.[46]

In Finland, the growth-oriented economic policy, mainly promoting exports and investments in fixed and human capital by various economic-political measures, gave the state a particularly strong role during the post-war decades. In this environment also welfare reforms became a tool to enhance development. Substantial welfare services and egalitarian policies, equal opportunities to education, efforts to lower income differentials and gender equality were not perceived as *per se* in conflict with growth and productivity. As political historian Pauli Kettunen has emphasized, there was a shared belief in a 'virtuous circle' between social and economic advancement.[47] This view stemmed from the strong focus on human capital formation as a source of economic growth during this period. The idea of a virtuous circle was overall strong in the Nordic countries; as these small open economies were dependent on foreign trade, they were especially vulnerable to economic fluctuations.

In Finland, the role to overbridge outside (i.e. Soviet) and inside (primarily communists) threats made national unity not only economically beneficial but also important for safeguarding stability and security. According to Kettunen, the Finnish welfare state project was considered in the 1960s a common project to which many groups were to be committed. The social reforms enhanced this commitment. The policy was quite pragmatic and aimed at balancing between – and eradicating – various conflicting interests. As the government often did not correct the progressive taxation scales for inflation, the possibilities to advance actively social reforms and improve the levels of welfare benefits in a quite short time, which expanded the system further. The deep rupture after the civil war delayed the birth of a compromise model of a Nordic type, but Finland caught up rapidly in the post-war period.

In the post-war period, the state was both strong and active, but it was so in many other countries as well. It appears however that the Finnish state-led, economic policy model was particularly elaborate.[48] Compromise policies, a shared perception of the importance of peace on labour market for economic growth, of the importance of human capital formation in economic development, but also of a country under threat made the government respond to demands by the strong groups in the society and worked as a balancing factor between the interest groups in a society. The particularly active involvement of the state in Finland in promoting growth originated also in the economic backwardness, in combination with nationalistic overtones due to the recent independence. Nevertheless, in all Nordic countries, welfare reforms had economic motivations. Overall, these small, late-coming open economies have mobilized and made efficient use of their scarce resources.[49]

The history of the Finnish welfare state was not a smooth path, the power balance varied and conflicts occurred. Some welfare reforms were fairly easy to accept by most groups and parties over the vast political spectrum; some were less so. There has also been a considerable change in the dominant ideologies with respect to the role of state. The country moved from liberal ideologies of the 19th century to progressive Beveridgian–Keynesian view of the role of the public sector after the Second World War. After a long period of deepening involvement of the state in economic matters, the tide has changed during the past couple of decades towards tendencies with more market-based solutions and a withdrawal of the state. This is a phenomenon observed in many other countries and is a reflection of prevailing ideologies. On the other hand, especially emerging market economies seem to move towards what could be called social democratic welfare systems.[50] Furthermore, after the 2008 financial crisis, calls for more and stricter regulation and even a turn towards more active state interference have emerged also in liberal market economies. The perception of the state as enhancing growth is still important. While the emphasis was mainly on infrastructural investments in the late 19th century and early 20th century and human capital and fixed investments during the decades after World War II, today the role of support for research and development and innovations are seen as crucial for future development.

It has often been assumed that the state has become weaker during the 'neoliberal' regime of the last decades, which meant de- or re-regulation, more market-based solutions, fostering increasing competition and an ideology of non-interference from the state in the economic sphere. Although a rapid liberalization, an opening up of the economy to globalization, and an active promotion of the working of the market forces occurred in Finland since the 1980s, it does not necessarily mean that the state has become 'weak'. It can still be seen strong, although perhaps more withdrawn ('at arm's length') by, for example, monitoring and actively promoting the functioning of the market mechanism. The state, instead of interfering directly in the economy, plays in the new environment the role of a monitoring and controlling actor, enforcing the 'rules of the game' in the economy. That cannot be seen *a priori* as a sign of a weak state, but indicates a state not captured by the interest groups.

Discussion: welfare state development and transition from social fragmentation towards social cohesion

Together with the other Nordic countries, Finland has been able to combine a favourable long-term economic performance with a large welfare state. The country developed quite active policies to overcome fragmentation and tensions in society. In this chapter, we have focused on the emergence of the welfare state and the role(s) of the state in the economic development in this process. Finland indeed transitioned from a poor and unstable county to one marked with high income, solid governance and social cohesion: today, the country places high on most international comparisons of economic competitiveness based on a large variety of indicators.

At the beginning of the 20th century, the public sector was not exceptionally large in the other Nordic countries compared to other European countries, but in the post–World War II period the public sectors expanded. Although welfare state institutions and structures in Finland expanded somewhat later than in other Nordic countries, it caught up rapidly since the 1970s and 1980s. Public-sector programmes and activities have developed more or less simultaneously with the industrial development: industrialization puts new pressures for the development of the supply factors, such as education and infrastructure, while individuals demand security in an uncertain world.

The role of the state as an enabler of economic growth and development, as well as a mediator between various interests, has been important for social cohesion. One key factor was the process of centralization, that is that systems became more similar in all parts of the country when the large variation of services provided by private, church, philanthropic or voluntary was gradually replaced by compulsory services provided by the public sector, although the municipalities often were given tasks to fulfil. The centralized state played a key role in this process. This development aimed for equal standards on services irrespective of where an individual lived and was enabled by the state system of transfers from richer areas to poorer ones. These factors were indeed important for overbridging social cleavages, although this order tended to create new tensions, for example between local and central government.

Finland has followed the Nordic countries, although somewhat later. The formal and informal contacts to Sweden both among politicians, in civil service, among interest groups and associations, have been intense, long lasting and important for spreading ideas and 'models' amongst the Nordic countries. There was for example active searching for models and for cooperation on the Nordic level, for example in Nordic Social Meetings.[51] Coming a little after, Finland has perhaps avoided some of the pitfalls of social and welfare state reforms which 'first-movers' ran into.

Societies with strong corporatist features have been slower to reform, and occasionally, the system provided a hindrance, but at the same time, these countries have in the long run shown fewer swings and ruptures. The neo-corporatist era of the 1960s and 1970s created platforms for discussions and deliberation. Often the process was slow and the compromises weak, but the partners felt co-responsible. Such platforms are perhaps not effective in a globalized economy but were so during an era when there was an active aim to overcome societal cleavages. Olli Kangas emphasizes that social policy is about much more than the distribution of the welfare more evenly or about securing a decent living standard for the lowest income groups, the sick, the old and the disabled. It is (considered) important for creating a social sense of togetherness, a 'glue'.[52]

However, it can also divide – or at least make specific interests more pronounced and visible and therefore accentuate tensions. The effects depend on the structure of the system and its legitimacy. The idea of universalism in the welfare system have probably worked as a 'glue' and increased the legitimacy and trust in the system.[53]

So what does the future look like? The Nordic countries have generally favoured openness and benefitted from this. Globalization puts, however, pressure on structural changes in small countries. An interesting question is overall what happens to the welfare state and to the state as the promoter of both growth and social cohesion in the globalized world. Although the current view is that the state should not interfere in the market mechanism, it still is seen to have a significant role in providing a favourable working environment, and in this health care, education and decent social security continue to form important building blocks.

On the other hand, the new political movements have made politics come back in focus. As already stated in the introduction, there seems that the development has gone towards more fragmentation – social and political. The growing populist movements (both to the right and to the left) are increasingly putting traditionally stable Western countries against new and unforeseeable development scenarios. New groups are also on the rise, especially groups focusing on environmental problems and climate change. Discontent and polarization can lead to rapid shifts in politics.

In many traditional 'compromise' societies, the idea of a 'common us' is also rupturing. This originates partly from immigration, an ageing population, combined with the problems of staggering growth and environmental issues, but most likely other factors are also at work. As political scientist Kathrine Cramer discusses, a 'politics of resentment' is on the rise. Graham pinpoints to a rural–urban gap in this development in the US economy.[54] Similarly, in Finnish society, the social cleavages have not only been one between 'labour' and 'capital' or between left and right but also between the rural periphery and the urban growth areas. Although the share of population getting their livelihood from primary production is low today, this cleavage is still very visible when looking at political party support in elections. It is likely that rural–urban division will grow in the future due to a rapidly ageing population in the more remote areas, while the large cities grow and become increasingly diverse.

Acknowledgements

We wish to thank participants in the session "State and Socio-economic Change: The Nordic Model in the 'World of Models'" the World Economic History Congress in Utrecht in August 2009 for comments of an early draft of this paper. This paper has gone through several changes since that. We also thank Prof Chris Lloyd and Dr Matti Hannikainen for their extensive efforts to improve the paper.

Notes

1 Andersen et al. (2008).
2 For the idea of a common 'us', see Kettunen (2006, 2008).
3 Long-term quantitative descriptions of the public sector are difficult as there are not comparable data covering all the public activities. International comparisons are also difficult because of different budgetary and statistical practices.
4 It is typical in the Nordic countries that government itself produces most of the welfare services. In "non-Nordic" models of welfare state services (health and social) are often financed by transfers from the government budget or from social insurance systems and the producers may be private-sector entities. However, during the last decades, increasingly private providers are also allowed for in the Nordic countries. For example, in Sweden, since the 1990s, the system allows private providers, especially in health care and education, where the customer is quite free to choose among providers.
5 Pihkala (1977), 60–73, 91–115, Appendix table 2.
6 Finland under Russian rule had a small conscript army between 1878 and 1901. Pihkala (1977), 95–96.
7 This estimate is based on the distribution of wages and salaries in Pihkala (1977), 62; for discussion Hjerppe and Hjerppe (2007).
8 For example Rahikainen (2010).
9 Karisto et al. (1985), 278–280.
10 Taimio (1986), 50–51.
11 Kangas and Palme (2005).
12 See for example Baldwin (1990) on the variety of social and institutional factors behind European welfare state development.
13 Kangas (2006).
14 See Fellman (2019).
15 On how the employers accepted the work pension reform, see Vauhkonen (2016).
16 Hjerppe et al. (2007); Taimio (1986).
17 Hjerppe et al. (2007).
18 See for example Kangas (2006), 199.
19 For a recent discussion on the ability to – and need – to centralize the state in the 17th century in order to strengthen the dynastic right to the throne. Hallenberg et al. (2008).
20 See for example Rothstein (1998).
21 Flinders (2006).
22 Balogh (2003); Skocpol (1985); Hay and Lister (2006), 5.
23 See for example Baldwin (2005).
24 For the US model, see Fishback (2009).
25 Baccaro and Simoni (2008).
26 For example Paavonen (2006), 30–31; Rainio-Niemi (2010).
27 Paavonen (2006), 30.
28 See Rainio-Niemi (2010).
29 Vauhkonen (2016); Kangas (2006).
30 Kangas (2006), 199ff., for a discussion.
31 Paavonen (2006), 127.
32 Kangas (2006), 272–273; Kangas et al. (2010).
33 Flinders (2006).
34 The role of private actors appears to become more limited.
35 Hernes (1988).
36 For example Kettunen (2001).
37 Moreover, Kettunen (2019) emphasizes, that the 'state' is not to be conflated with 'society' although occasionally done so in the Nordic, and especially in the Swedish context (*stat* versus *samhälle*).

38 www.imd.org/centers/world-competitiveness-center/rankings/world-competitiveness/ Retrieved 12.9.2021.
39 Hellsten (2009).
40 Rainio-Niemi (2010).
41 Stenius (2010).
42 Enbom and Fellman (2019).
43 Stenius (2010).
44 Alapuro (2010).
45 Bengtsson (2019), 134.
46 According to Katzenstein (1985), several of the economically vulnerable, small, open economies in Western Europe managed to stay economically competitive while at the same time preserving their political institutions. This was done by creating a democratic corporatism. See also Fellman and Sjögren (2008).
47 Kettunen (2008), 162.
48 For a discussion, see for example Fellman (2008).
49 Fellman and Sjögren (2008).
50 Lloyd (2009).
51 Petersen (2006, 2011).
52 Kangas (2006), 195.
53 Kangas (2006), 272.
54 Cramer (2016).

References

Alapuro, R. (2010). Introduction: Nordic Associations and Civil Society in a Comparative Perspective. In R. Alapuro, & H. Stenius (eds.), *Nordic Associations and Civil Society in a Comparative Perspective* (pp. 11–28). Berlin: Nomos.

Andersen, T. et al. (2008). *The Nordic Model: Embracing Globalization and Sharing Risks*. The Research Institute of the Finnish Economy (ETLA). Helsinki: Taloustieto Oy.

Baccaro L. & Simoni M. (2008). Policy Concertation in Europe: Understanding Government Choice. *Comparative Political Studies, 41*(10), 1323–1348.

Baldwin, P. (1990). *The Politics of Social Solidarity: Class Bases of the European Welfare State, 1875–1975*. Cambridge: Cambridge University Press.

Baldwin, P. (2005). Beyond Weak and Strong: Rethinking the State in Comparative Policy History. *Journal of Policy History, 17*(1), 12–33.

Balogh, B. (2003). The State of the State among Historians. *Social Science History, 27*(3), 455–463.

Bengtsson, E. (2019). The Swedish Sonderweg in Question: Democratization and Inequality in Comparative Perspective, c.1750–1920. *Past and Present, 244*(1), 123–161.

Cramer, K. (2016). *The Politics of Resentment Rural Consciousness in Wisconsin and the Rise of Scott Walker*. Chicago Studies in American Politics. Chicago: University of Chicago Press.

Enbom, L., & Fellman S. (2019). Nödhjälp eller skapandet av ett idealsamhälle? Filantropisk verksamhet i lokalsamhället under mellankrigstiden. *Historisk Tidskrift för Finland, 105*(3), 353–392.

Fellman, S. (2008). Growth and Investment: Finnish Capitalism, 1850–2005. In S. Fellman, M. Iversen, H. Sjögren, & L. Thue (eds.), *Creating Nordic Capitalism: The Development of a Competitive Periphery* (pp. 139–217). Basingstoke: Palgrave Macmillan.

Fellman, S. (2019). Private or Public? Employer Attitudes and Strategies towards Early Welfare Reforms in Finland. In D. O. Nijhuis (ed.), *Business Interests and the Development of the Modern Welfare State*. Routledge Studies in the Political Economy of the Welfare State (pp. 136–159). London and New York: Routledge.

Fellman, S., & Sjögren, H. (2008). Conclusions. In S. Fellman, M. Iversen, H. Sjögren, & L. Thue (eds.), *Creating Nordic Capitalism: The Development of a Competitive Periphery*. (pp. 558–579). Basingstoke: Palgrave Macmillan.

Fishback, P. (2009). The Government and the Economy. In P. Fishback (ed.), *The Government and the Economy. A New History* (pp. 1–27). Chicago: University of Chicago Press.

Flinders, M. (2006). Public/Private: The Boundaries of the State. In C. Hay, M. Lister, & D. Marsh (eds.), *The State: Theories and Issues* (pp. 223-–247). Basingstoke: Palgrave Macmillan.

Hallenberg, M., Holm J., & Johansson D. (2008). Organization, Participation, Legitimization: State Formation as a Dynamic Process – the Swedish Example, c. 1523–1680. *Scandinavian Journal of History, 33*(3), 247–268.

Hay, C., & Lister M. (2006). Introduction: Theories of the State. In C. Hay, M. Michael, & D. Marsh (eds.), *The State: Theories and Issues* (pp. 1–20). Basingstoke: Palgrave Macmillan.

Hellsten, K. (2009). Työväensuojelus- ja sosiaalivakuutusyhdistyksen synty ja alkutaival. In R. Jaakkola, S. Kainulainen, & K. Rahkonen (eds.), *Työväensuojelusta sosiaalipolitiikkaan: Sosiaalipoliittinen yhdistys 1908–2008*. Helsinki: Edita.

Hernes, H. (1988). Scandinavian Citizenship. *Acta Sociologica, 31*(3), 199–215.

Hjerppe, R., Hämäläinen, P., Kiander, J., & Viren M. (2007). Do Government Expenditures Increase Private Sector Productivity? Cross-Country Evidence. *International Journal of Social Economics, 34*(5), 345–360.

Hjerppe, R., & Hjerppe R. (2007). Suomalainen hyvinvointivaltio: kehitys, kiistat ja tulevaisuus. In V. Heinonen, M. Jäntti, & J. Vartiainen (eds.), *Kansantaloustiede, talouspolitiikka ja hyvinvointivaltio: juhlakirja Jukka Pekkarisen kunniaksi* (pp. 68–78). Helsinki: Palkansaajien tutkimuslaitos.

Hjerppe, R., & Hjerppe R. (1992). Taloudellinen kasvu sosiaalipolitiikan edellytyksenä. Sosiaalipolitiikka 2017. In O. Riihinen (ed.), *Näkökulmia suomalaisen yhteiskunnan kehitykseen ja tulevaisuuteen*. Helsinki: WSOY.

Kangas, O. (2006). Politiikka ja sosiaaliturva Suomessa. In T. Paavonen, & O. Kangas (eds.), *Eduskunta hyvinvointivaltion rakentajana*. Helsinki: Edita.

Kangas, O., & Palme, J. (2005). Coming Late – Catching Up: The Formation of a 'Nordic Model. In O. Kangas, & J. Palme (eds.), *Social Policy and Economic Development in the Nordic Countries* (pp. 17–59). Basingstoke: Palgrave Macmillan.

Kangas, O., Lundberg, U., & Ploug N. (2010). Three Routes to Pension Reform: Politics and Institutions in Reforming Pensions in Denmark, Finland and Sweden. *Social Policy and Administration, 44*(3), 265–284.

Karisto, A., Haapola, I., & Takala, P. (1985). *Elintaso, elämäntapa, sosiaalipolitiikka: suomalaisen yhteiskunnan muutoksesta*. Porvoo: WSOY.

Katzenstein, P. (1985). *Small States in World Markets Industrial Policy in Europe*. Cornell Studies in Political Economy. Ithaca: Cornell University Press.

Kettunen, P. (2001). The Nordic Welfare State in Finland. *Scandinavian Journal of History, 26*, 225–247.

Kettunen, P. (2008). *Globalisaatio ja kansallinen me*. Tampere: Vastapaino.

Kettunen P. (2019). The Concept of Society in the Making of the Nordic Welfare State. In S. Kuhle et al. (eds.), *Globalizing Welfare: An Evolving Asian-European Dialogue* (pp. 143–161). Cheltenham: Edward Elgar.

Lloyd, C. (2009). *Social Democratic Welfare Capitalism since 1970: Crises, Responses, Divergences*. Paper presented at WEHC Utrecht, Session F6 – State and Socio-economic Change: The Nordic Model in the 'World of Models' (Presidential session).

Nordic Statistical Yearbook 2007. Copenhagen: Nordic Councils of Ministers. http://norden.diva-portal.org/smash/record.jsf?pid=diva2%3A700804&dswid=5977.

OECD Organisation for Economic Cooperation and Development, National Accounts, 1951–2007. Paris: Organisation for Economic Co-operation and Development, Statistics Directorate.

Official Statistics of Finland, Kansantalouden tilinpito 1998–2007 (National Accounts 1998–2007), 2009.

Paavonen T. (2006). Talouden kehitys ja talouspolitiikka hyvinvointivaltion kaudella. In T. Paavonen, & O. Kangas (eds.), *Eduskunta hyvinvointivaltion rakentajana*. Helsinki: Edita.

Petersen, K. (2006). Consturcting Nordic Welfare? Nordic Social Political Cooperation 1919–1955. In N. F. Christiansen, K. Petersen, N. Edling, & P. Haave (eds.), *The Nordic Model of Welfare: A Historical Reappraisal* (pp. 67–98). Copenhagen: Museum Tusculanum Press.

Petersen, K. (2011). National, Nordic and Trans-Nordic: Transnational Perspectives on the History of the Nordic Welfare States. In P. Kettunen, & K. Petersen (eds.), *Beyond Welfare State Models: Transnational Historical Perspectives on Social Policy* (pp. 41–64). Cheltenham: Edward Elgar.

Pihkala, E. (1977). *Valtion tulojen ja menojen rakenne 1800-luvun jälkipuoliskolla*. Helsinki: Helsingin kauppakorkeakoulu.

Rahikainen, M. (2010). School, Child Labour and Rationalization in Industrializing Europe. In G. K. Lieten, & E. N. Meerkerk (eds.), *Child Labor's Global Past*. Berlin: Peter Lang.

Rainio-Niemi, J. (2010). On Boarders of the State and Civil Society: The State's Committees in Finland in a European Perspective. In R. Alapuro & H. Stenius (eds.), *Nordic Associations and Civil Society in a Comparative Perspective* (pp. 241–268). Berlin: Nomos.

Rothstein, B. (1998). *Just Institutions Matter: The Moral and Political Logic of the Universal Welfare State*. Cambridge: Cambridge University Press.

Skocpol, T. (1985). Bringing the State Back in: Strategies of Analysis in Current Research. In P. Evans, D. Ruschmemeyer, & T. Skockpol (eds.), *Bringing the State Back in* (pp. 3–43). Cambridge: Cambridge University Press (repr.1999).

Stenius, H. (2010). Nordic Associations in a European Perspective. In R. Alapuro & H. Stenius (eds.), *Nordic Associations and Civil Society in a Comparative Perspective*. Berlin: Nomos.

Taimio, H. (1986). *Valtion menojen ja valtion julkisten palvelujen kasvu Suomessa 1900-luvun alkupuoliskolla*. Helsinki: Suomen Pankki.

Vauhkonen, J. (2016). *Elatuksesta eläkkeeseen: vanhuudenturva suomalaisessa työnantajapolitiikassa työeläkejärjestelmän rakentamiseen saakka*. Helsinki: Helsingin yliopisto.

5 Decades of disagreement

Rise of the coordinated welfare state in the Netherlands in the nineteenth and twentieth centuries

Jeroen Touwen

Introduction

How can we explain the trajectory from social fragmentation to socio-political consensus in the Netherlands? The Netherlands is an interesting case when we study the process of peaceful integration in fragmented societies. It has been famous for its consultation economy, sometimes called 'poldermodel', but in many regards, it was not a very homogeneous society. In this chapter, I review the development of the welfare state in the Netherlands through the lens of social fragmentation. After a brief survey of the nineteenth century, I focus on the introduction of formal consultation and of social laws during the inter-war period, analyzing three case studies.[1] As I show, the introduction of welfare state laws hinged on the introduction of formal cross-class consultation.

Fragmentation in spatial, social and religious terms was strongly influenced by the halcyon days of the Dutch Republic in the seventeenth century. Early urbanization created relatively autonomous cities. The Dutch Revolt and subsequent religious tolerance resulted in an influx of talented workforce that supported the Dutch Golden Age. In the tumultuous period between 1781 and 1794, patriots attempted to renew the political economy but did not succeed. After the Napoleonic era, in 1813, King Willem I became monarch. Since then, the Netherlands was a relatively quiet monarchy. Of course, there were numerous conflicts and discussions, but all in all the Low Countries were a relatively calm corner of Europe. It excelled in overseas trade and was creative with dykes and polders in the struggle against floods. Urbanization in this country full of rivers and lakes was made possible by high agricultural productivity.

Industrialization in the Netherlands came relatively late; it only gained momentum in the second half of the nineteenth century. In the late nineteenth century, Dutch society became organized and coordinated in a vertical structure with religious pillars. During the twentieth century, a welfare state system consolidated the transformation to an advanced economy. Welfare state expansion is often crucial to peaceful social integration, but how was it connected to and influenced by the strong division in religious pillars? What was the attitude of entrepreneurs and unions in the fragmented industrializing economy towards national social laws? And what was the effect of World War

DOI: 10.4324/9780429503870-6

I on this small, open economy that remained neutral but suffered the effects of worldwide stagnation in trade? I analyze three case studies from primary source material. These three examples are based on archival research of employer views on issues relating to labour relations and social protection: (1) collective labour agreements in the early 1920s (which opened the door to codetermination and the expansion of more elaborate welfare provisions), (2) the Sickness Act of 1913–1930, and (3) the Unemployment Act initiatives of 1921–1923.

All through this chapter, employer views are emphasized, because their voice was crucial in supporting or rejecting the introduction of social laws. My analysis builds on the institutionalist view that temporal processes generate and reinforce actor preferences.[2] This can be viewed as the effect of a logic of *membership* (of the interest group) on the logic of *influence* (on the consultative platform).[3] I show which concerns the stakeholders had and how consultation reduced fragmentation.

Societal commitment, local loyalties

In the nineteenth century, as in most industrializing economies, the gap between rich and poor in the Netherlands was large. Social fragmentation in classes and regions created tensions as it did elsewhere. But the Low Countries stood out with an affluent past, a rich bourgeois elite, and a large influence of religion on society. In the cities, there was an elaborate system constituting various types of social provisions and charities. Dutch citizens in the cities were conscious of their societal commitment, because of the struggle against the threat of the nearby sea and because of the desire to protect their urban autonomy. They organized meetings to adjust local agendas to national ambitions and displayed in their diversity a convincing unity.[4]

One may observe three types of fragmentation in Dutch society. First, in spatial terms, the economy was fragmented because the cities had their own institutions, including certain taxes and welfare arrangements.[5] Second, in income terms, the economy was fragmented in social classes. An increasing class of urban workers shared a low-income level with the poorer agricultural population in the rural areas. In particular, in the southern and eastern parts of the country, agriculture had modernized to a lesser extent than in the northern and western parts. Third, in religious terms, the economy and society were increasingly divided. The Protestants, who had the dominant position in society since the Dutch Revolt in the sixteenth century, had to accept a stronger position of the Catholics and were themselves increasingly divided into different groups.

There is a direct connection between nineteenth-century religious rivalry and twentieth-century consultation which is explored in this chapter. Competition between Protestants and Catholics accompanied industrialization and renewed the organization of civil society. In the early nineteenth century, about 38% of the population was Catholic. The Protestants, constituting about 62%, split into different groups in 1834 (when Hendrik de Cock organized a divergent group) and 1886 (when Abraham Kuyper led another separatist movement of orthodox Protestants). The constitution of 1848 had allowed the Catholics to organize themselves and pressure from Rome to do so created much unrest among the Protestants. Different religious views resulted in lengthy vehement discussions, for example on the right to organize private (Christian) schools and the way these should be financed (an issue that was only resolved in 1917).[6]

However, instead of disrupting social order, these conflicts were solved in a relatively peaceful way. Often, petitions were used to voice a broadly backed protest, as an instrument of social movement.[7]

Welfare state expansion

The expansion of social laws took place in conjunction with the development of a coordinated market economy. In this institutional type, drawn from the varieties of capitalism theory, non-market coordination plays a role in a number of institutional fields.[8]

The Netherlands were slow in introducing state-level social laws because welfare was organized locally, in the cities. During the late nineteenth and early twentieth centuries, elite democracies (where voting rights were given on the basis of property, such as the Netherlands, Sweden and Britain) were not exactly eager to install tax-financed pension or sickness programs. As can be observed in Figures 5.1a and 5.1b, the Nordic states together with the United Kingdom took a lead in organizing social transfers, while countries, such as the Netherlands, Belgium, Austria and France, caught up much later.

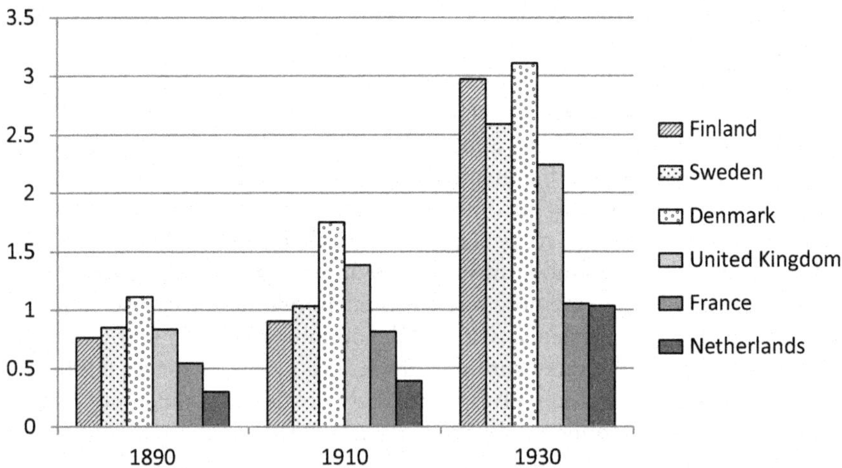

Figure 5.1a Nordics plus the United Kingdom in the lead, 1890–1930

Source: Lindert (2004), 12–13.

Note: Social transfers from 1890 to 1930 as a percentage of gross domestic product (GDP) at current prices. Welfare, unemployment, pensions, health and housing subsidies. Social transfers from 1960 to 1980 are given as a percentage of GDP at current prices. These are based on the Organisation for Economic Co-operation and Development (OECD) old series, from *OECD Social Expenditure 1960–1980* (Paris 1985).

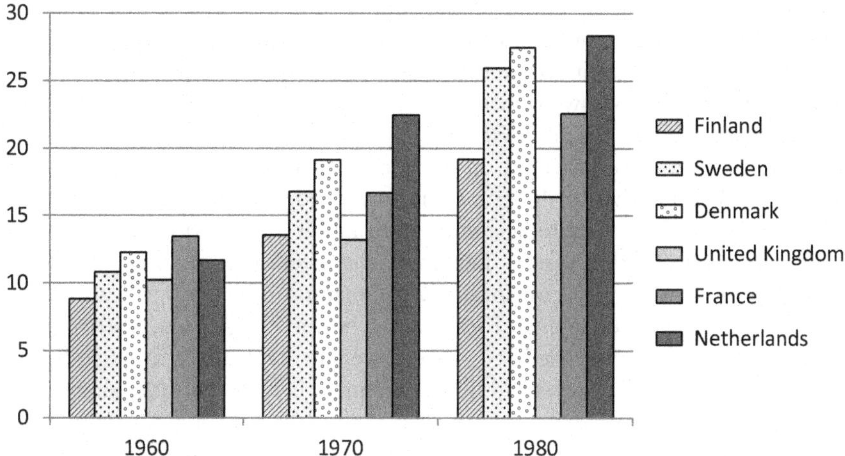

Figure 5.1b Western European catch-up in social transfers, 1960–1980

Source: Lindert (2004), 12–13.

Note: See Figure 5.1a.

During the course of the nineteenth century, the idea developed that the state should take care of the poor and had a role in organizing social protection for workers. The concept of a collective welfare state had far-reaching consequences for social stability and the diffusion of prosperity. Several explanations have been given for the fact that social laws made welfare from a gift into a right, consolidating democratic societies into robust welfare states with unprecedented high degrees of social spending. One is public pressure (mostly by lower classes) for social safety nets. Another explanation is that rising incomes supplied higher tax earnings (which facilitated social spending). In addition, Peter Lindert emphasizes that social affinity between middle-income voters and the perceived recipients encouraged social transfers. This was often fostered by ethnic or cultural homogeneity. If you realize something may happen to you, you may support measures to enlighten the burden of accident or sickness in your group.[9]

The Dutch catch-up in terms of social transfers took place after 1945. There were many reasons to introduce social laws after the war. The disastrous developments during the Great Depression had prepared the minds to provide more social protection. Objections to grant this role to the state had slowly eroded. In the post-war decades, Dutch stakeholders quickly, and almost unanimously, decided to introduce a generous welfare state. My claim is that this was facilitated by the Dutch system of consultation in the field of labour relations that had developed in the inter-war years and been formally installed by public law in 1950. In the pre-war consultative system, opposing parties got to know each other and expressed the intention to improve the common good. Frequent and institutionalized consultation generated new actor preferences by shifting priorities and creating new commitments. After the Second World War, Dutch labour relations were ready to embrace modernization – including a full-fletched modern welfare state.

Globalization also provided an incentive to organize safety nets. Peter Katzenstein shows that small open economies tend to develop neo-corporatist institutions that have a strategic argument to install social entitlements in order to buffer cyclical downturns.[10] This may have been an argument specifically reflected in business views on social laws. Finland can be viewed as a paradigmatic example of such a small European economy.[11] The post-1960 Netherlands welfare state resembled the Nordic welfare states in many regards, but the Dutch version had several different features. It matured more slowly and was more breadwinner-oriented for most of the century. Only during the late twentieth century can a convergence be observed toward a social-democratic model, albeit a slightly less generous one. In Esping-Andersen's taxonomy, the Netherland forms a cross-over between the social-democratic welfare regimes and the corporatist-conservative regimes that were less universalistic and more breadwinner-oriented.[12]

Fragmentation along religious lines was a major hindrance for state social laws in an otherwise quickly industrializing economy. During the nineteenth century, increasingly, the idea was voiced that the private initiatives of social protection, which were in the hands of churches, municipalities and charity, did not suffice. This feeling was intensified by increasing pressure from the socialist movement and by the example of Germany, where Bismarck had introduced laws that obliged employers to insure workers, and Denmark, where, in 1891, a pension law was passed. Several other groups in Dutch society rejected the introduction of social laws on the state level: Christian-democratic parties believed in decentralized solutions and preferred private charity with only a residual (municipal) public safety net. Churches and municipalities claimed the field of poverty protection. The religious groups slowed down central welfare state development for issues such as industrial injury, unemployment and sickness since they preferred their non-government welfare initiatives.[13] In addition, liberal businesspeople and politicians preferred private measures in insurance against industrial injury, since this gave the entrepreneur more autonomy.

At the turn of the century, the belief in laissez-faire gave way to an interventionist approach.[14] In the Netherlands, the desire to organize and coordinate was strengthened by the First World War and resulted in increasing support for consultative platforms. It did not yet result in extensive social laws, but many Christian employers were in favour of consultation, since they valued harmonious labour relations. Thus, fragmentation along religious lines explains the rise of consultation while welfare state development stalled.

In this setting, an increasing number of entrepreneurs, politicians and union leaders advocated the establishment of formal consultative institutions. Representatives of employers, unions and the government would discuss wages and working conditions. After experiments on the municipal level, it became accepted to organize these platforms nationally. Interestingly, although many entrepreneurs were in favour of economic coordination in the form of cartels (they found unbridled laissez-faire capitalism obsolete and had learned to appreciate coordinating measures during the war), they were only slowly won over to introduce codetermination, since they hardly trusted the unions. Regulation would serve their interest, preventing destructive foreign competition, labour unrest or volatile markets. But the introduction of consultative platforms also introduced that control had to be shared.[15]

The consultative system that developed as the consequence of the existence of religious 'pillars' was eventually beneficial to the development of a generous welfare state. The welfare state was not a prerequisite for social peace. Despite the occurrence of incidents such as the 'Palingoproer' in 1886 and the railway strikes of 1903, the pressure from the working class seemed manageable for the elites. Even while in 1918 there were hardly any general social laws issued by the state, the attempts by Troelstra to launch a socialist revolution hardly stood a chance.[16]

Increasing organization and new institutions

Centralizing tendencies towards a national economy can be observed from the Napoleonic era onward, but in the Netherlands, the introduction of national institutions gained momentum in the late nineteenth century.[17] Different types of institutions with specific functions developed, aiming at coordination, distribution of information, and interest representation on the national level, such as the Central Commission for Statistics (Centrale Commissie voor de Statistiek, 1892) and the Mining Council (Mijnraad, 1902). In the first decades of the twentieth century, several were added to this list: the Unemployment Council (Werkeloosheidsraad, 1914), the Commission for Economic Politics (Commissie voor de Economische Politiek, 1917), the Council for Industry (Nijverheidsraad, 1919) and the Council for Retailers (Middenstandsraad, 1919).[18] Clearly there was enthusiasm for coordinating and regulating institutions.

It is not surprising that labour relations were also increasingly coordinated. The High Council of Labour (Hoge Raad van Arbeid, 1919) was a landmark innovation: it formed the main platform for discussing state law proposals with employers and unions. This peak institution was preceded by an experiment on the local level, called the Chambers of Labour (Kamers van Arbeid, 1897–1923). These Chambers of Labour had been established in 1897 in order to formulate bipartite advice in labour conflicts and to investigate and improve local labour conditions. There were organized per sector on the municipal level. One can debate whether such local initiatives of consultation were either relatively unsuccessful or, in fact, essential forerunners of the national concertation platform. Although for a long time judged as a failure, they are increasingly viewed as the latter, signifying the transition towards consultation.[19] They seem to have been the municipal pioneers of the future neo-corporatist institutions, useful experiments that took away the antagonism and proved that deliberation could lead to practical solutions. In some sectors, in some cities, they functioned well, but in other sectors, they seemed to have been an instrument in the hands of dominant employers.

The build-up of the consultative system was analyzed by Nijhof and Van den Berg, who distinguish period between 1890 and 1912 as one of state-led development and between 1912 and 1939 as one that formed the heyday of Christian corporatism.[20] In a corporatist system, consultation takes place on labour relations in order to negotiate issues such as wages, working conditions, the duration of the working week and a degree of codetermination.[21] Welfare states introduce social protection that may include arrangements for industrial injury insurance, income protection, healthcare and pensions for all. At a time when poverty and bad living conditions of the workforce could form a threat to society, employers had to become 'social' in improving labour relations. They were hesitant in introducing social protection for the wider population. However, in the bargaining platforms, labour relations and social protection sometimes formed different angles of the same problem. For example, one could exchange a wage increase for social entitlements, but this required bargaining on the peak level with the government.

In the nineteenth century, the Christian parties were already heavily debating the principle of individual responsibility for social protection. In 1890 the Dutch government held surveys on labour conditions in a large number of firms: the '*Arbeidsenquete*' of 1887 and the '*Staatsenquete*' of 1890. Various kinds or abuse were reported, and new legislation was deemed necessary: the Labour Act of 1889 (Arbeidswet) can be viewed as a result, as well as the later proposal for a law on industrial injury (Ongevallenwet, 1899).[22]

Expansion and obstruction of social protection

But at the time, poor relief in the Netherlands was not organized by state law, and there were hardly any laws for the protection of workers against sickness, professional injury or old age.[23] Although in international comparison social spending was relatively generous in the nineteenth century (slightly below 'top spender' England), it was a system based on charity, not on rights. The liberal view dominant at the time was characterized by a strong belief in free trade and laissez-faire, symbolized by the abolition of the Cultivation System in 1870, with only a small 'night watchman' role for the state.[24] Self-reliance and incentives to engage in work were viewed as more important than social support.

It dawned slowly that more was needed to solve the 'social question'. Many younger Dutch liberals in the late nineteenth century advocated state intervention to strengthen the position of workers. In 1872, the organization of labour unions became legally permitted.[25] In this year a hybrid organization started, the General Dutch Worker Association (Algemeen Nederlands Werklieden Verbond, ANWV) that was a union and an employer organization at the same time, because workers and small entrepreneurs were members. Immediately after its establishment, it started to take action against child labour, resulting in the law on child labour of 1874. In 1896, it supported a proposal to widen the electoral base. Democracy, labour relations, and welfare state development were strongly interconnected.

Traditional private and church-related social provisions were thus merely supplemented by hesitant state-issued social laws. The 1874 law on child labour, the Kinderwetje by Samuel van Houten, prohibited hiring children younger than the age of 12 for factory work. But this can only be viewed as a precursor to state responsibility in social matters, because it was a weak initiative. At most, it was an attempt to mitigate ruthless economic competition between industries. There was no adequate inspection, so for many children the law had no effect. Only when in 1901 compulsory education between the ages of 6 and 12 was introduced (with a marginal majority of 50 against 49 votes!) could children not be sent to work in factories any longer.

In 1899 the Industrial Injuries Act (Ongevallenwet) was presented to Parliament. It took effect in 1901 and was an early example of state regulation of social protection, although it was still largely based on employer responsibility. Injured workers received a 70% pension (which did not stop at the age of 65, because there was not yet a pension law). In the following, I observe that an important effect of this law was that it stimulated entrepreneurs to organize themselves, in their resistance to this state intervention in their affairs. I focus on employer associations to the detriment of labour unions, of which the history can be found elsewhere.[26] In turn, business-interest organizations propelled the development of the consultation economy.

Weak pre-1945 welfare state initiatives

The starting point for the state seriously taking up responsibility for people's welfare can be placed about 1900. Around this time, industrial capitalism reached a higher degree of organization: workers' unions gained importance, confessional groups advocated a social agenda and state legislation increased. Firms began to organize themselves in associations partly in response to these initiatives. However, during the inter-war years, state-led welfare expansion was restricted to relatively small-scale initiatives in sickness laws and old-age pensions. As said before, civil society still debated the stronger role of the state. The confessional pillars rejected the tendency toward centralized state provisions and insurances. In addition, liberal employers were afraid of such commitments, fearing that state laws would be dominated by unions and that the entrepreneur would lose control and profits. Among employers, the protagonists for social laws could be found predominantly among Christian-democrat employers.

After the Industrial Injuries Act was passed in 1901, it took another 12 years before minister A.S. Talma introduced a law providing income in the case of industrial injury and old age in 1913. This law took effect after the war, in 1919. By way of pension, workers who were more than 70 years old obtained a small 'work invalidity' benefit (usually it was too small to live on). Meanwhile, a law for health insurance, the Sickness Act (Ziektewet), was passed in 1913, but it came into effect only in 1930 (see the following discussion). This law aimed at a regional provision of insurance against sickness.[27]

The sociologist Schuyt points out that the Dutch welfare state had both material and moral foundations.[28] We observe different early initiatives of social protection in which the modern welfare state was rooted: private charity, employer initiatives, state-led initiatives, and union-based initiatives. After the Depression, the Keynesian realization that consumptive demand needed to be supported in times of crisis formed a *material* foundation of the welfare state. Social provisions and social insurance programs sustained consumption by providing income to vulnerable groups, such as the unemployed, elderly, or injured (thus functioning as automatic stabilizers). The *moral* foundation was the ambition to provide an income for state citizens with disregard for their success in the labour market (a *decommodified* income, therefore). To some extent this constituted an agenda for a 'just' income distribution, correcting market failures in the distribution of economic and social goods.[29]

Organization against the chaos of industrial capitalism

Concertation was supported by the idea that nineteenth-century laissez-faire capitalism was outdated and the economy needed to be regulated – in the same vein that large companies needed professional managers to run smoothly. (In the later Cold War antagonism between the free market and the socialist command economy, this recognition of voluntary regulation of business has often been ignored.) The economy had become too complex to hand over all processes to the invisible hand; coordination was needed 'against the chaos of capitalism'. Economic actors, including entrepreneurs, increasingly became convinced that markets should be regulated and coordinated because of the complex nature of the modern industrialized economy.[30]

New coordinating institutions were inspired by an emergent organizing principle that was advocated by technologically advanced sectors. Their interests differed from the old liberal ideology that was cherished by landed gentry and handicraft trades. The nationalist industrial development ideology replaced liberalism as a hegemonic philosophy at the end of the nineteenth century.[31] 'Classic liberalism' was increasingly challenged by 'social' or 'progressive' liberalism. Interestingly, *neo-liberal* ideology has sketched an image of a long fight for free markets that lasted about a century (a 'long march' of neo-liberalism, guided by thinkers such as Von Hayek, a lengthy effort to break markets loose from the straps and bridles of the imposing state). In fact, the opposite happened: advocates of free markets were *not* afraid of a supportive state (although they rejected socialism!) and were increasingly convinced that markets should be regulated and coordinated, because of the complex nature of the modern industrialized economy.[32]

Thus, in many countries, emerging forms of corporatism were accepted. It provided a state-organized, legally bound structure in which employers were required to negotiate.

One may therefore wonder whether the Dutch case was exceptional, although it has frequently been advocated to be so. In 1968, Lijphart published his famous hypothesis on the *consociational* Dutch society, stating that the pillarized structure enhanced a stable and harmonious democracy. He explains that elite competition was replaced by elite cooperation and that there is a disciplining effect of vertical interaction within pillars, reducing class struggle. The drawback of this view is that it overemphasizes univocal solutions, whereas consultation in labour relations and among business networks included strong disagreement, long delays in sensitive issues and lengthy debates on policy alternatives. The horizontal interaction between different elites may have been more important than the disciplining effect of vertical interaction in the pillars. Indeed, non-market coordination found its shape in a system of industrial organization. But compromise did not entail consensus, and as we will see, disagreements abounded.

In due course, the practice of organized consultation had an effect on the bargaining culture. Dutch concertation became less conflict-oriented than for example bargaining practice in France, less formal than in Germany or Austria and less class-conscious than in the United Kingdom. The Dutch pillars did not constitute strong immobile blocs that influenced all aspects of society, and, moreover, there was a very unequal regional distribution of the influence of the various pillars. Nevertheless, the pillars were very influential in the public debate before 1914; the First World War led to a 'breakthrough' in national politics.[33]

The depression of the 1930s provided the coordinating institutions with a new function: Keynesian economic policy. Collective bargaining and minimum wage setting provided stabilizing effects and helped prevent deflation. For these reasons, John Maynard Keynes favoured a greater role of the trade unions: collective bargaining could regulate wages, set a wage floor and prevent cut-throat competition. This, according to Keynes, would prevent downward spirals of recession and benefit an economic growth that was more equally spread among the populace.[34] The acceptance of Keynesian economic policy also implied the acceptance of bargaining platforms. In the resulting system of organized consultation, employers and unions of the different pillars coordinated their policy decisions. The material foundations of the Dutch welfare state were observed in that vein after World War II. But in contrast with the views of Schuyt expressed earlier, before the war, this was not a widespread idea.

Employer organizations

But in order to consult each other, employers and workers need to organize themselves, so that they can send their representatives to the consultative meetings. How did the peak employer associations come about? The establishment in 1899 of the first modern employers' association, the Organization of Dutch Employers (Vereeniging van Nederlandsche Werknemers, VNW) was closely connected with the preparation of the Industrial Injuries Act (Ongevallenwet) that would take effect in 1901.[35] The government initiative to introduce such a law induced resistance among employers and made them realize that cooperation was desirable.[36]

The ambition of that particular Industrial Injuries Act was to make insurance of *risque professionnel* compulsory for employers of dangerous industries so that selfish employers could not rely on public provisions in this regard. The law was written by C. Lely, the famous minister of Waterworks, Trade, and Industry who also developed the plan to build the Afsluitdijk (which turned the Zuiderzee into the IJsselmeer). The proposal incited massive protests among employers and prompted them to set up an employers' organization. The campaign was initiated by D.W. Stork, owner of the machine manufacturing firm Stork in Hengelo. He claimed to have a good private factory fund for injuries and stated that a law stipulating compulsory insurance would damage free entrepreneurship.[37] The government did not budge and denied that the new law would be expensive for employers.

During the formative decades, a system developed with employer organizations for small and medium-sized firms, firms in agriculture and horticulture, and large firms (industry and big business), and in each group, there were Catholic, Protestant and non-confessional general associations. There were 'entrepreneurial' associations looking after the *economic* interests of their members, such as the Association of Dutch Employers (VNW) and employers' organizations taking care of *social* matters, such as the Central Social Employers Association (Centraal Sociaal Werkgevers Verbond, CSWV). Some similar associations took care of both economic and social affairs or merged after some time. Three pillars can be observed in the development of employer organizations: a general (or liberal) pillar (starting with VNW in 1899), a Catholic pillar (1915) and a Protestant pillar (1918).[38] In the postwar era, these organizations combined and consolidated into three peak organizations that represented about 800 to 1,200 smaller employer' associations and branch organizations. Of these three, in 2004 VNO-NCW had 160 associations totalling about 100,000 firms, MKB-Nederland (small and medium-sized firms) represented 500 associations and about 175,000 firms and LTO-Nederland (agriculture and horticulture) held 18 associations and represented about 55,000 firms.[39] In short, we observe a strong consolidation in employer associations.

In the period up to the late 1960s, membership of these employer associations tended to be more constant and more loyal than that of the unions, where free riders and high turnover caused some trouble. But internal disciplining and developing uniform employer policies was difficult. The central organizations of labour held more authority over the individual industry-level unions than employer central organizations over their affiliates. As Windmuller writes, 'employers only grudgingly surrendered a slice of independence to their associations'.[40] In the consultation process, firms looked after their interests rather than having the intention to develop better working conditions: one could say that continuity rather than change was on their agenda.

As we saw, during the First World War and during the 1930s' Depression, Dutch firms did not appreciate fierce competition or a race to the bottom in prices, because these would further destabilize their position. Cartels were widely found. The government complied and increasingly regulated and coached domestic competition. Industrial organization was accompanied among some groups by the idea of *state planning*. For example in 1935, the social-democratic 'Plan of Labour' (Plan van de Arbeid) of J. Tinbergen and H. Vos, took up the state responsibility for the macroeconomy. But this was met with much resistance. Harmonious labour relations formed an acceptable goal, but giving up autonomy was not a popular idea.

An accepted system of consultation

In this manner, in a gradual process, Dutch employers increasingly supported industrial organization. Industrialization inspired cooperation to regulate competition and implement standardization. The increasing complexity of economic activities made that these efforts were deemed necessary. It also corresponded with views on the organization of capitalism. Moreover, banks were increasingly involved with industrial finance: in the Netherlands, this came about in the 1910s. It meant that bankers took a seat in advisory boards, reinforcing directorship networks.[41]

All these new organizations formed extra-parliamentary institutions that at the time were also regarded as alternative avenues of political representation. They were perceived to be part of the solution to an alleged inter-war crisis of parliamentary government.[42] After the war, the system of industrial organization and organized consultation, in turn, supported the introduction of social provisions. In the successor of the High Council of Labour, the tripartite Socio-Economic Council (Sociaal-Economische Raad, SER, established in 1950), employers consented with ideas that came forward from the government and the unions. Once neo-corporatist bargaining had reached an agreement, the Christian-democratic parties, which broadly speaking had a left-wing and centre orientation, and the Dutch liberal party (Volkspartij voor Vrijheid en Democratie, People's Party for Freedom and Democracy) was willing to provide political support for the expansion in social spending between 1958 and 1982.

The system of coordination thus preceded the expansion of social laws in the prewar years. The social partners and the Raden van Arbeid favoured wage-earner laws and did not encourage the state to introduce universal provisions (a universal pension scheme for all elderly was only officially implemented in 1956). While the construction of a negotiating platform for employers and workers received much attention, the state did not superimpose central social policy before the war. The consequence was that the Dutch system became rather strongly breadwinner oriented – prewar social provisions were directed towards the wage earner and not universally to all the population. The main social provisions were added after the war.

Three examples of consultation

In order to show the opinions and concerns of the Dutch employers, I present three case studies dealing with social themes. We screened the archival sources of employer organizations, searching for discussions on social laws, in order to discover the strategic preferences of Dutch employers. How did entrepreneurs prepare for the bi- or tripartite discussions with unions and government representatives? And which arguments did they express during the tripartite meetings? In these preparatory meetings, only business colleagues were present, so we could examine genuine objections and concerns. We systematically examined sources of the negotiating platforms in the Netherlands from the 1910s onward – including both meetings with the unions and preparatory meetings with only employers. If business representatives would outline the advantages of social laws, this could show that employers were probably not *forced* to accept welfare state expansion as a result of union power. If they accepted additional social laws and expressed pragmatic second-best attitudes, this confirms that secondary preferences could be supportive of welfare state expansion.

The three case studies that follow were the only instances I found during the inter-war period in which employers explicitly voiced their opinions and standpoints on welfare state laws. Of course, employers may have discussed these issues in informal settings where no reports were made, or in meetings with different formal agenda's that we overlooked. However, I am convinced that these are representative examples, since consultation was increasingly institutionalized and the preparation of their position in the formal platforms was essential for the negotiations.

1 Collective Labour Agreements, 1920

Early 1920, the minister of labour, P.J.M. Aalberse, and the minister of justice, Th. Heemskerk, sent a proposal to the High Council of Labor for a law that facilitated collective labor agreements (Collectieve Arbeidsovereenkomsten, CAOs). A tripartite subcommittee of the council, the 'Committee on Industrial Organization' (Commissie voor de Bedrijfsorganisatie) discussed this proposal on 12 April 1920.[43] The view of the High Council of Labour was essential in the outcome of the discussions whether CAOs should be made binding for all employees in a branch of industry, whether union member or not.

Since 1907, collective labour agreements had had a small footing in Dutch Civil Law. The law said that if there were national labour agreements in specific industrial sectors, such as the graphic industry, individual employment contracts were not allowed to deviate from these.[44] The Christian Union (CNV) was in favour of a nation-wide system with collective labour contracts and wanted to expand their use. Since 1918, the CNV had also advocated equal treatment of union and non-union workers. A special jury committee should decide on labour conflicts, which abandoned the right for workers to launch a strike until the jury had spoken. In irony, they even called the collective labour agreement 'a contraceptive against open conflict'.[45] The CAO law of 1920 met this wish and constituted a major step in labour relations. It meant that employers could not individually decide on wages, labour conditions and individual social security arrangements such as sickness and pension payments. What did employers at the time think about this law?

To begin with, the discussions were chaired by a supporter: Professor J.A. Veraart (1886–1955). Veraart was a progressive Catholic and the intellectual architect of legislation that coordinated industrial organization. Several decades later he designed the 'PBO Act' (Publiekrechtelijke bedrijfsorganisatie, industrial organization under public law), the law that introduced a multilayered system of tripartite consultation in the Netherlands and came into force in 1950. Veraart was an ardent believer in the possibility of harmonious relations between employers and workers.[46]

In 1920, Veraart started by asking whether the Committee on Industrial Organization thought this issue had to be arranged by *civil law* or by *public law*. Surprisingly, the employers in the committee were not against such arrangements at all, because they thought it would reduce labour conflicts. They favoured collective labour agreements in the form of *civil law* (private law) contracts. They viewed an agreement as something that was as likely to restrict unions as employers and were even afraid that the unions would not comply. So they suggested that sanctions should be included to force unions to stick to the arrangement. This showed that they had a very pragmatic approach to such arrangements. Neither employers nor union representatives wanted to include regulations about strikes – that subject was obviously too sensitive.

Later on, it was decided to make this into *public law*. This turned out to be important, since it points at the perceived role of the state. Private law deals with the relationship (and conflicts) between individuals and companies among each other. By contrast, public law governs the relationship between individuals and the government and provides mandatory rules to which everyone should conform. It increases the coordinating role of the state.

In contrast with employers, the representatives of the workers' unions were generally *not* in favour of collective labour agreements. It is telling of this period that many of their representatives thought that *conflicts* (strikes) were a better way to reach their goal.[47] They distrusted the proposed conflict settlement committees, because they feared the government would have much influence in the composition and operation of these and thought the government would be biased towards the employers.

Windmuller states: 'The leisurely pace of national debate, required by the need for obtaining a consensus among the dogma-bound views of society's constituent blocs, prevented the possibility of full-fledged PBO legislation before World War II.'[48] In some regards, *dogma-bound* may be too strong a statement: employers were open to bargaining but very pragmatically said that they did not want government officials without practical experience to rule the economy. Their willingness to negotiate, resulting from pillarized tradition as well as from a new view on capitalist order, prompted them to accept frequent consultation with the unions and the state. But in this consultative process, they blocked far-reaching top-down plans. The logic of influence resulted in bottom-up solutions rather than consenting with top-down designs. Their preference for bottom-up solutions stalled far-reaching social laws.

In 1937, a law was passed that allowed the government to either extend the bargaining agreement (collective labour agreement) to an entire industry or economic sector, including non-union members or else to nullify its provisions.[49] This was an example of the layering of labour institutions: small initiatives were succeeded by new rules that expanded the role of consultation. The first Act on Labour Contracts, issued in 1909, had included a careful exploration of the collective labour agreement. After World War I, the number of CAOs had risen sharply.[50] Now, in 1937, the minister of social affairs was given the power (on request of the social partners) to universalize collective labour agreements (regulating labour conditions and wage increases). Signed by the unions of a specific industrial sector, an agreement applied to all workers in that sector. This meant that labour unions did not need to have full coverage in a sector in order to represent all workers in that sector. Ironically, socialists in the parliament voted against this law (but were overruled), because it also contained the possibility that the minister would declare the provisions void in case the public interest demanded an opposite form of action.[51]

The effects of the 1937 law were larger than was expected at the time. It accepted unions as representatives disregarding union coverage. It was not allowed for employers to distinguish between union members and non-union members, which prevented underbidding by unorganized workers. Collective labour agreements on the basis of union bargaining were not uniquely Dutch. This institution has been applied in all Western European countries. In some countries, the conditions apply to non-union members on a voluntary basis (Denmark, Germany, Finland, Ireland, Italy, Sweden) and in others it is laid down in laws (Belgium, France, Austria, Portugal, Spain).[52]

What does this show us? Employers were willing to commit themselves to formal consultation because it drew the (hesitant) unions into this commitment as well, which they believed was good for harmonious labour relations. A major newspaper wrote in 1922 that employers found that these public laws restricted their freedom of movement, but also viewed some elements favourably. Harmonious relations between patrons and workers were stimulated, it built upon the insight that entrepreneurs were no longer 'monarchs', and individualism had finished flowering.[53]

2 The Sickness Act, 1920–1923

In 1913, a Sickness Act was introduced by the minister of agriculture, industry and trade, A.S. Talma. Remarkably, it only came into effect in 1930. It included compulsory insurance for sickness and medical care for salaried employees (independent entrepreneurs could join voluntarily). Both employers and employees would contribute equal payments to a fund, from which a sick employee could receive payment (six months, 70% of his wages).[54] The Councils of Labour, the regional concertation platforms, were originally meant to carry out the administration. This law from 1913 was accompanied by an Industrial Injury and Pension Act (Invaliditeits- en Oudersdomswet) that arranged entitlement for industrial injury, for old age for employees older than 70, and for widows. The entitlements were not indexed against inflation. This additional law came into force on 3 December 1919 in a slightly revised form.

In 1920, as part of the ongoing discussions, plans for an alternative Sickness Act were debated in the central consultation platform of the employer associations (the Centraal Overleg Werkgeversbonden).[55] By examining this agency, we can observe what employers talked about among each other, which concerns they raised in preparation of tripartite consultation, which would take place later on in the peak organization, the High Council of Labour.

This alternative proposal for the sickness and industrial injury insurance was drawn up by E.F. Posthuma, a director of the collective insurance firm Centraal Beheer who represented the employer association Maatschappij van Nijverheid (Society of Industry), and E. Kuypers of the peak union organization NVV (Nederlandsch Verbond van Vakverenigingen; Dutch Association of Trade Unions).[56] The chair of our employer's meeting, Mr J.J.M. Noback, announced on 27 October 1920 that the 'Posthuma-Kuper plan' was to be discussed.

During the discussion on this proposed sickness law, Posthuma said that he was afraid that the High Council of Labour would probably change the proposal in such a way that the employers would have to pay the entire provision, instead of sharing the cost with the unions. He stated that, in practice, this was already often the case, and conceded that actually it would be no problem to supply the full sickness pay even to a level of 80% (instead of 70%) of the wage, under the explicit condition that the *administration* of the law would be carried out by the employers themselves. This would still be cheaper because they would be much stricter in admission. He expected that the union NVV would agree that bureaucratic interference of the Chambers of Labour in this case would be undesirable.

But other employer representatives hesitated. They did not expect that the unions (who were not present in this preparatory meeting) would agree to the fact that employers took control into their own hands. The unions would probably demand some degree of codetermination. In reply to this concern, Posthuma emphasized that he thought that *cooperation* on the administration of the Sickness Act was possible without problem. Another objection expressed during the meeting was that if workers would not contribute financially, they would feel fewer incentives to keep down the number of sickness incidences. Others, by contrast, stated that the worker contribution could be part of their gross wage. If the workers would have to take care of 20% of the costs, there would remain a healthy incentive to reduce inflow. The discussion was concluded by most representatives remarking in a rather modest way that they merely expressed their *personal views*, not formally as representatives. Posthuma was given the assignment to continue to develop his proposal.

During the next meeting of the employer section of the High Council of Labour, on 28 January 1921, the proposal for full coverage by employers was accepted: all members, representing different employer associations, agreed to take this collective stand.[57] The Sickness Act would also be applicable to those who were not a member of a union (this is an early foreshadowing of the law of 1937 that made a Collective Wage Agreement binding for the entire sector). One member of an employer association remarked that he was sure that the association he represented would *not* agree with these changes in the original Sickness Act plan. He stated that he himself did not object but that it was his duty to draw attention to the fact that his association would not collaborate. This was a clear sign of a logic of membership, which is important for the functioning of an interest group involved in consultation, since it means that representatives take the lead in finding compromise.

When the issue came into the High Council of Labour, on 7 April 1921, it turned out that 'almost all organized employers and workers, except for the Christian unions', voted in favour of the new Posthuma–Kuper plan for the Sickness Act. Only the Christian-democratic unions and employer associations were not happy with the initiative. But despite such differences in opinion, the general feeling was that these social laws had to be accepted in one form or another. Employer representatives expressed fear of the unacceptable possibility that the unions would laugh since they would win either way (whether via the original Talma law or via the Posthuma–Kupers law). It was also stated that this was a matter of personal pride rather than a principal rejection![58]

In short, control was viewed as more important than financial cost. As Bruggeman and Camijn write, 'the employers were satisfied with the eventual result'.[59]

3 Unemployment Act

On 7 July 1921, the Unemployment Act was discussed by the employer section of the High Council of Labour.[60] This law had to replace the 1917 'Unemployment resolution' and the subsequent 'Unemployment Insurance Emergency Act' of 1919.[61] However, no new law was accepted until the war.[62] Employers were divided on the issue whether the employer should contribute to unemployment benefits for involuntary unemployed employees. At this point, the secretary pointed out that rejection meant an exit from consultation and that would mean that no influence could be exerted on outcomes. The employer representatives then preferred voice over exit. Nonetheless, they felt they still did not want to contribute directly to such 'generous' unemployment provisions. They had an interesting argument for this. They stated that in the early 1920s the economy was in a recession and that they needed all available capital to continue already-existing jobs rather than finance entitlements for the unemployed. But other employers, including the chair M. Triebels and the secretary, repeatedly argued in favor of contributing to unemployment provisions. On 11 August 1921, they decided that they could vote in favor of the 'Unemployment Act', on condition that it would *only* operate in times of 'normal' economic conditions and 'normal unemployment' and not during economic crisis![63]

On 15 September 1921 they stated again that they were willing to support unemployment benefits at a later moment in time (all further objections were ignored). It shows that they valued participation in the consultative process highly, in order to be there to influence results.[64] However, when the minister was advised by the advisory 'Unemployment Council' (Werkloosheidsraad) in October, in the final draft, the comments made by the employers were ignored entirely. This raised considerable irritation.[65] Fortunately for them, no law was passed.

On 15 February 1923, several representatives again expressed concern that the unemployment law would be disadvantageous for entrepreneurs during a recession. Several members stated that they should never have joined the consultative meeting with the government and the unions, because it showed that 'one commits oneself to something that is not desirable.' But a larger group expressed satisfaction that permanent consultation had prevented the minister of labour to introduce an Unemployment Act without consulting the employers at all![66] In 1928, the final advice to the government by the High Council of Labour stated that employers did not think it was fair to pay unemployment benefits to workers who had not earned the right to receive an income. They also objected to workers paying contributions for unemployment benefits through the unions, since, they said, the unions were essentially their opponents.[67] Thus, that particular law was postponed. We can conclude that control was higher on the agenda than cost, and in order to expand control, they expressly valued consultation.

Post-war hesitation and take-off

After the war, the introduction of broader welfare state laws could not be stopped by hesitant employer representatives. National unemployment insurance was introduced in 1952.[68] Universal pensions were introduced in 1947 and (formally) in 1956.[69] The Sickness Act was extended in 1939, following the German example of a general sickness law. In that year, Minister of Social Affairs C. Romme announced a new law, in which a 'Council for Sickness Funding' (Ziekenfondsraad) would survey the sickness funds that distributed healthcare remunerations to all workers below a certain wage threshold. This type of healthcare funding was introduced during the war so that in effect a national health service was realized by the German occupying regime. After the war, in 1949, it was continued. The system functioned until 1999, when it was replaced by the College voor Zorgverzekeringen (CVZ).[70]

By comparison, the German health insurance law of 1884 was almost fifty years ahead of its Dutch counterpart, the Sickness Act of 1930. Such laws had been introduced in the United Kingdom in 1911 and in Denmark in 1917. A universal public pensions law was introduced in Germany in 1889, in the United Kingdom in 1908 and in the Netherlands only in 1956 (1947), although it should be remembered that there had been company pensions since Stork introduced the first one in 1881. In the United Kingdom, an industrial injury law was introduced at about the same time as in the Netherlands: the 1897 Workman's Compensation Act.

The realization that the state could be held responsible for the distribution of welfare benefits gained way during World War II, particularly after publication in 1942 by Lord Beveridge of *Social Insurances and Allied Services* (1942), followed in 1944 by *Full Employment in a Free Society*. For the Netherlands, the Beveridge Report inspired the 'Commissie Van Rhijn' to write several reports in 1945–6, of which the first has been called the 'birth certificate of the Dutch welfare state'. But there was little political support for the idea of centralized social laws in Beveridgean style as advocated in the Van Rhijn Report – it met with strong resistance, despite extensive public attention.[71]

The upshot was that even then, the expansion of the welfare state did not immediately take off. Apart from the fact that Prime Minister Willem Drees was a prudent politician who was careful with the state's finances, there were other reasons for a slow expansion of social security. The pillars, through unions and employer organizations, still operated in the pre-war tradition. Within the new consultative PBO structure, a 'guided wage policy' was agreed on, which limited space for wage-related entitlements. Industrialization policy and wage restraint slowed down welfare state expansion. The unions did still not demand an expansion of welfare state provisions in the early 1950s: this would have gone against the agreement to keep wage costs down.[72] But the improved Sickness/Healthcare Act (1947), the temporary Pensions Act (1947) and the Unemployment Act (1952) were major improvements at the time.

When recovery and subsequent economic expansion was on the way, the social partners and the government coalitions agreed to introduce more generous and decommodified universal state laws. First, they installed old-age pensions, next disability and then unemployment benefits. The consultative bodies supported the guided wage policy which aimed to keep wage costs low (to stimulate investment and thus generate jobs). In the 1960s, with booming economic growth and full employment, wages could no longer be suppressed. At this time, additional social laws could be introduced because the costs of these were viewed as a social wage, and thus part of the wage bargaining process, where there was room for increase.

An impressive expansion of social laws brought the welfare state from a modest level to one of the most generous social systems, almost (but not quite) competing with Sweden as a yardstick for generosity. In quick succession, the Dutch government introduced the Widows and Orphans Act (1958), Child Allowance Act (1962), Unemployment Benefit Act (1964), Healthcare Act (1964), and the important Disability Act (1966).

Summarizing, we can state that the Dutch confessional parties by preferring 'subsidiarity' (decentralized provisions) slowed down the introduction of national, state-led provisions. There were no social democrats represented in the coalition governments before 1939 who could fight for the state-led solution. Liberal politicians did not see social transfers as a priority for state finances and favored subsidizing the agricultural sector (farmers had strong lobby groups), although there were social liberals who did put social security on the political agenda. Several laws were conceived before the war, but they were only realized after decades and were employer-oriented, not universal. Suspicious of central government intervention, the Dutch Catholic and Protestant parties were against social provisions by the state (exemplified by the Dutch-Reformed politician Abraham Kuyper, who was politically active between 1874 and 1920). Until 1939, ideological differences made it impossible for the confessional parties to cooperate with the socialists. In the Netherlands, the social democrats were not represented in coalition governments before the war, and the unions were not strong enough to demand state laws on social protection. In the meantime, the elites of the confessional and liberal blocs or pillars cooperated in the face of external threat and established a consultative mechanism in labour relations, which in the future would benefit welfare state expansion.

Conclusion

In the Netherlands, expansion of social laws took place in conjunction with the development of a coordinated market economy. These developments consolidated social peace while the unions and social democrats gained a stronger position in the political economy. In welfare state development we observe procrastination in the inter-war period and a relative generosity of the Dutch state welfare state laws that were introduced in the 1950s and 1960s. This development can be explained by the rise and acceptance of coordinating institutions. This implies that I do not emphasize labour union power, nor the role of organized business interest, but the development of institutionalized consultative platforms, supported by state law, as the main drivers of welfare state development. Naturally, once the platforms were in place, the social partners could voice their opinions or exert their power. It is remarkable that the discussions about increasing social protection and about giving more voice to stakeholders are strongly intertwined.

The perspective of employers on social laws changed once they were drawn into the bargaining and consultation system. Various examples show that employers bargained repeatedly for the best, or least objectionable, deal. As can be expected, objections were based on the past, such as unions not sticking to agreements. They did not foresee that the negotiated agreements would evolve into many comprehensive deals which unions would not be tempted to break at all, for example a strong, institutionalized bargaining position. Remarkably, in discussions about the Sickness Act, issues of control dominated over the financial costs of the provisions.

Actor preferences can be understood by applying historical institutionalism literature rather than rational choice literature. Representatives increasingly feel obliged to take a constructive stand, and they are not unwilling to consider certain initiatives as theoretical possibilities, while their rank and file would reject these outright. At a certain point someone would raise a substantial objection, which moved the outcome into the direction of an alternative solution – sometimes compromise, sometimes postponing the entire issue. As a result, the outcome of consultation with members of opposing interest groups was valued more than theoretical objections of the original rank and file.

This story illustrates the institutionalist view that deliberative processes generate new actor preferences. During the inter-war period, the coordinating institutions attempted to develop a shared approach to economic problems by uniting employer views and the views of representatives of the unions and the government. In particular, employers were a heterogeneous bloc. Various types of firms (small and large, liberal and Christian-Democrat) did not see eye to eye on social issues. Dutch welfare state expansion was put on hold while increased worker co-determination and information sharing were being discussed. The *increasing support view* provides a good perspective on the development of the coordinated welfare state. The post-war boom in welfare spending could only come about because a consultative platform was established in the inter-war period. Thus, ironically, the pre-war decades of disagreement resulted in far-reaching post-war social laws and a coordinated system that still exists today.

Consultation between employer and union representatives repeatedly displayed a willingness to accept compromise and moderated outcomes. The bargaining platform was also used as a vehicle for damage control: to prevent worse outcomes, both groups searched for the lesser evil. But we should keep in mind that the state had a very important role as the initiator of new initiatives and setting the agenda of the negotiations.

These observations show that the formative period of institutionalized consultation left a mark on the post-war coordinated market economy by developing *informal* institutions of conflict solving by speech. This was the foundation of the post-war consultative system. The viewpoints of firms were consolidated and expressed through inter-firm cooperation, which, in a comparative perspective, was strong in the Netherlands in the 1920s and 1930s. Coordination among firms was not centrally organized by the state, but instead the result of voluntary coordination and information exchange. Most prominent was the integration of employers in the national policy formation process through boards and commissions. These formed an institutional setting in which welfare state laws were discussed and accepted after the Second World War.

Institutionalized consultation had a basis in religious differences in a multiparty system: it aimed to deal with rising social-democratic pressure and was inspired by the developments outside the country, such as World War I. It should be kept in mind that in a coordinated economy, bargaining, conflict and distrust repeatedly came up. *Consensus democracy* is a much too rosy term for a system that only was established with gradually increasing support.

Notes

1 I am grateful to Bram Hulshoff for his assistance with the archival research.
2 Fioretos et al. (2016), 3–18.
3 Schmitter and Streeck (1991), 47–53.
4 De Rooy (2002), 30–31.
5 Van Zanden and Van Riel (2004), 108; Postma (2017).
6 Wielenga (2009), 41; De Rooy (2002), 155.
7 Prak and Van Zanden (2013), 201.
8 Hall and Soskice (2001), 1–68. On the Netherlands, see Touwen (2014a).
9 Lindert (2004), 186–188.
10 Katzenstein (1985).
11 Rainio-Niemi (2008). See also Mokyr (2006), 8–12.
12 Esping-Andersen (1990), 76.
13 Van Leeuwen (1998), specifically 277. See also De Swaan (1988), 50.
14 Kaufmann (2012), 340.
15 Touwen (2014a), 160. See also Touwen (2014b).
16 Wielenga (2009), 76–77; De Rooy (2002), 164–165.
17 See Van Zanden and Van Riel (2004).
18 Van Veen (2013), specifically 33.
19 Van Veen (2013); Gijsenbergh (2012); Couperus (2012).
20 Nijhof and Van den Berg (2012), 185.
21 I focus on what is often called neo-corporatism. By contrast, in totalitarian systems, the state *dictates* labour relations.
22 Hertogh (1998), 60–69; Nijhof and Van den Berg (2012), 47, 52. To administer the law, the *Rijksverzekeringsbank* was established in 1901. In 1956 it became the *Sociale Verzekeringsbank*, which supervised from 1987 on the former Councils of Labour as regional offices.
23 Lindert (2004), 46.
24 Touwen (2001), 4.
25 Nijhof and Van den Berg (2012), 48.
26 See for example Harmsen and Reinalda (1975); Hazenbosch (2009); Van der Velden (2004).
27 Sickness payments had to be organized by the Councils of Labour (Raden van Arbeid, 1919). These 39 regional Councils of Labour (Raden van Arbeid) were founded in 1919. The chairs of the councils were appointed by the minister of labour. The Councils of Labour were the successors of the Chambers of Labuor of 1897 that were stimulated by anti-revolutionary Christian-democrat politicians who hoped that they would avert the threat of revolution and were officially abolished in 1923.
28 Schuyt (1991), 3–4.
29 For a basic introduction to the Dutch welfare state see Noordam (1998). See also Van Gerwen and Van Leeuwen (2000); Roebroek and Hertogh (1998); Trommel et al. (2004).
30 Jackson (2010). See for a brief analysis of Dutch cartelization and competition policy in the twentieth century as a form of institutional change: Touwen (2018).
31 Martin and Swank (2012), 32.
32 Jackson (2010).

33 Lijphart (1968). See for the debates Blom and Talsma (2000) and De Rooy (1995). From a Marxist point of view, pillarization formed a strategy of elites to consolidate their powerbase in the class struggle. Wielenga (2009), 242.
34 Visser (2013).
35 In the late nineteenth and early twentieth centuries, a series of different social laws were passed, which were evidence of increasing state intervention without yet establishing a full-fledged welfare state.
36 The Algemene Werkgevers Vereniging (General Employers Association, established in 1919 as Zaanse Werkgevers Vereniging) planned to merge with VNO-NCW in 1997, in which year it became AWVN, but in 2008 the merger was cancelled. Bruggeman and Camijn (1999), 293.
37 Bruggeman and Camijn (1999), 61–75.
38 The two confessional peak associations combined their efforts in 1967 into the Federation of Christian Employers Confederations (Federatie van Christelijke Werkgevers Verbonden). The merger with the non-confessional peak organizations took place as late as 1995. Alongside the resulting VNO-NCW, the employers' organizations for small and medium-sized companies (MKB) and the agricultural peak organization (LTO) continued to exist.
39 Tros et al. (2004), 51–52.
40 Windmuller (1969), 231, 259.
41 Jonker (1991).
42 Gijsenbergh (2012).
43 International Institute of Social History, Amsterdam (IISH), Archief Florentinus Marinus Wibaut, inventory number 330, 1. Second meeting of the *Commissie voor de Bedrijfsorganisatie*, Monday 12 April 1920. Department of Labour, The Hague. It was also called 'Commissie voor de bedrijfsorganisatie en medezeggenschap'.
44 Tros et al. (2004), 55.
45 Hazenbosch (2009), 96.
46 Nijhof and Van den Berg (2012), 68–69.
47 IISH, Wibaut, inventory number 330 (1920), Sixth meeting of the *Commissie voor de Bedrijfsorganisatie*, 1–10.
48 Windmuller (1969), 288.
49 The 'Wet-AVV' (Wet op het algemeen verbindend en onverbindend verklaren van bepalingen van collectieve arbeidsovereenkomsten). This law from 1937 built on an earlier law from 1927, which, in turn, had been prepared by the High Council of Labour since 1919.
50 Harmsen and Reinalda (1975), 426–429.
51 Windmuller (1969), 73–78.
52 Tros et al. (2004), 103–104.
53 *Algemeen Handelsblad* 2 February 1923. See also IISH, Wibaut, inventory number 330.
54 Bruggeman and Camijn (1999), 109.
55 This platform, also called Centraal Overleg in Arbeidszaken voor Werkgeversbonden, was established by the Association of Dutch Employers (Vereniging der Nederlandsche Werkgevers, VNW) in 1920. After 1945 the departments dealing with social affairs of the VNW and the Centraal Overleg in Arbeidszaken voor Werkgeversbonden were merged into the Centraal Sociaal Werkgevers-Verbond. See Nationaal Archief, Den Haag [NL-HaNA], Centraal Overleg Werkgeversbonden, 1920–1945, nummer toegang 2.19.103.04, inventarisnummer 2, 1–2.
56 Bruggeman and Camijn (1999), 107–109. NVV is the peak union association that was established in 1915 by 15 unions. It merged in 1977 with FNV.
57 NL-HaNA, Centr. Overleg Werkgeversbonden, 2.19.103.04, inv.nr. 2, 2.
58 NL-HaNA, Centr. Overleg Werkgeversbonden, 1920–1945, nummer toegang 2.19.103.04, inventarisnummer 2, 1–2.

59 Bruggeman and Camijn (1999), 109.
60 NL-HaNA, Centr. Overleg Werkgeversbonden, 2.19.103.04, inv.nr. 2, 9, 2–4. General Meeting of the Centraal Overleg Werkgeversbonden (GM), 7 July 1921.
61 In Dutch: *Werkloosheidsbesluit* and *Werkloosheids-verzekeringsnoodwet.*
62 Hertogh (1998), 222–223.
63 NL-HaNA, Centr. Overleg Werkgeversbonden, 2.19.103.04, inv.nr. 2, 9, 1. GM, 11 August 1921, Scheepvaarthuis, Amsterdam.
64 NL-HaNA, Centr. Overleg Werkgeversbonden, 2.19.103.04, inv.nr. 2, 9, 1–3. GM, 15 September 1921, Scheepvaarthuis, Amsterdam.
65 NL-HaNA, Centr. Overleg Werkgeversbonden, 2.19.103.04, inv.nr. 2, 9, 2. GM, 27 October 1921, Industrieele Club, Amsterdam.
66 NL-HaNA, Centr. Overleg Werkgeversbonden, 2.19.103.04, inv.nr. 2, 9, 3. GM, 15 February 1923, Scheepvaarthuis, Amsterdam.
67 Hertogh (1998), 224.
68 The 1952 law was called 'Wachtgeld en Werkeloosheidsregeling', WW.
69 Between 1947 and 1956 there had been an interim law, the Noodwet Ouderdomsvoorziening.
70 Vonk (2012).
71 Schuyt (1991), 3.
72 The notion that wage restraint was achieved *in exchange* for welfare state provisions is not correct for the Netherlands. Van Kersbergen (1995), 130. Wage restraint resurfaced in the 1980s as a consensus solution. See Touwen (2008).

References

Blom, J. C. H., & Talsma, J. (eds.) (2000). *Verzuiling voorbij: Godsdienst, stand en natie in de lange negentiende eeuw.* Amsterdam: Het Spinhuis.

Bruggeman, J., & Camijn, A. (1999). *Ondernemers verbonden: 100 jaar centrale ondernemingsorganisatie in Nederland.* Wormer: Inmerc.

Couperus, S. (2012). Fixing Democracy? Political Representation and the Crisis of Democracy in Interwar Europe and the Netherlands. In J. Gijsenbergh, S. Hollander, T. Houwen, & W. de Jong (eds.), *Creative Crises of Democracy* (pp. 269–290). Brussels: Peter Lang.

Esping-Andersen, G. (1990). *The Three Worlds of Welfare Capitalism.* Princeton: Princeton University Press.

Fioretos, O., Falleti, T. G., & Sheingate, A. (2016). Historical Institutionalism in Political Science. In idem, *The Oxford Handbook of Historical Institutionalism* (pp. 3–18). Oxford: Oxford University Press.

Gerwen, J. van, & van Leeuwen, M. (2000). *Zoeken naar zekerheid: Risico's, preventie, verzekeringen en andere sociale zekerheidsregelingen in Nederland 1500–2000.* Amsterdam: Amsterdam University Press.

Gijsenbergh, J. (2012). Crisis of Democracy or Creative Reform? Dutch Debates on the Repression of Parliamentary Representatives and Political Parties, 1933–1940. In J. Gijsenbergh, S. Hollander, T. Houwen, & W. de Jong (eds.), *Creative Crises of Democracy* (pp. 237–267). Brussels: Peter Lang.

Hall, P. A., & Soskice, D. (eds.) (2001). *Varieties of Capitalism: The Institutional Foundations of Comparative Advantage.* Oxford: Oxford University Press.

Harmsen, G., & Reinalda, B. (1975). *Voor de bevrijding van de arbeid: Beknopte geschiedenis van de Nederlandse vakbeweging.* Nijmegen: SUN.

Hazenbosch, P. (2009). *Voor het volk om Christus' wil: een geschiedenis van het CNV.* Hilversum: Verloren.

Hertogh, M. (1998). *Geene wet, maar de Heer: de confessionele ordening van het Nederlandse sociale zekerheidsstelsel, 1870–1975*. The Hague: VUGA.

Jackson, B. (2010). At the Origins of Neoliberalism: The Free Economy and the Strong State, 1930–1947. *The Historical Journal, 53*(1), 129–151.

Jonker, J. (1991). Sinecures or Sinews of Power: Interlocking Directorships and Bank-industry Relations in the Netherlands, 1910–1940. *Economic and Social History in the Netherlands, 3*, 119–131.

Katzenstein, P. J. (1985). *Small States in World Markets: Industrial Policy in Europe*. London: Cornell University Press.

Kaufmann, F. X. (2012). *European Foundations of the Welfare State*. New York: Oxford University Press.

Kersbergen, K. van (1995). *Social Capitalism: A Study of Christian Democracy and the Welfare State*. London: Routledge.

Leeuwen, M. H. D. van (1998). Armenzorg 1800–1912: Erfenis van de republiek. In J. van Gerwen, & M. H. D. van Leeuwen (eds.), *Studies over Zekerheidsarrangementen: Risico's, risicobestrijding en verzekeringen in Nederland vanaf de Middeleeuwen* (pp. 276–316). Amsterdam: NEHA.

Lijphart, A. (1968). *The Politics of Accommodation: Pluralism and Democracy in the Netherlands*. Berkeley: University of California Press. (In Dutch: *Verzuiling, pacificatie en kentering in de Nederlandse politiek*. Amsterdam: De Bussy, 1968).

Lindert, P. H. (2004). *Growing Public: Social Spending and Economic Growth since the Eighteenth Century*. Two volumes. Cambridge: Cambridge University Press.

Martin, C. J., & Swank, D. (2012). *The Political Construction of Business Interests: Coordination, Growth, and Equality*. Cambridge: Cambridge University Press.

Mokyr, J. (2006). Preface: Successful Small Open Economies and the Importance of Good Institutions. In J. Ojala, J. Eloranta, & J. Jalava (eds.), *The Road to Prosperity: An Economic History of Finland* (pp. 8–12). Helsinki: SKS.

Nijhof, E., & van den Berg, A. (2012). *Het menselijk kapitaal: Sociaal ondernemersbeleid in Nederland. Bedrijfsleven in Nederland in de Twintigste Eeuw, vol. 4*. Amsterdam: Boom.

Noordam, F. (1998). Sociale zekerheid 1950–2000. In J. van Gerwen, & M. H. D. van Leeuwen (eds.), *Studies over zekerheidsarrangementen: Risico, risicobestrijding en verzekeringen in Nederland vanaf de middeleeuwen* (pp. 807–853). Amsterdam/Den Haag: NEHA/Verbond van Verzekeraars.

Postma, J. (2017). *Alexander Gogel (1765–1821): Grondlegger van de Nederlandse staat*. Hilversum: Verloren.

Prak, M., & van Zanden, J. L. (2013). *Nederland en het poldermodel: Sociaal-economische geschiedenis van Nederland 1000–2000*. Amsterdam: Bert Bakker.

Rainio-Niemi, J. (2008). *Small State Cultures of Consensus State Traditions and Consensus-Seeking in the Neo-Corporatist and Neutrality Policies in Post-1945 Austria and Finland*. PhD Dissertation. Helsinki: University of Helsinki.

Roebroek, J. M., & Hertogh, M. (1998). *De beschavende invloed des tijds: Twee eeuwen sociale politiek, verzorgingsstaat en sociale zekerheid in Nederland*. The Hague: VUGA.

Rooy, P. de (1995). Zes studies over verzuiling. *Bijdragen en Mededelingen betreffende de Geschiedenis der Nederlanden/Low Countries Historical Review, 110*, 380–392.

Rooy, P. de (2002). *Republiek van rivaliteiten: Nederland sinds 1913*. Amsterdam: Metz en Schild.

Schmitter, P. C., & Streeck, W. (1991). The Organization of Business Interests: Studying the Associative Action of Business in Advanced Industrial Societies. *MPIfG Discussion Paper 99/1*. Cologne: Max Planck Institüt für Gesellschaftforschung.

Schuyt, C. J. M. (1991). *Op zoek naar het hart van de verzorgingsstaat.* Leiden/Antwerpen: Stenfert Kroese.

Swaan, A. de (1988). *In Care of the State: Health Care, Education and Welfare in Europe and the USA in the Modern Era.* Cambridge: Polity.

Touwen, J. (2001). *Extremes in the Archipelago: Trade and Economic Development in the Outer Islands of Indonesia, 1900–1942.* Leiden: KITLV Press.

Touwen, J. (2008). How Does a Coordinated Market Economy Evolve? Effects of Policy Learning in the Netherlands in the 1980s. *Labor History, 49*(4), 439–464.

Touwen, J. (2014a). *Coordination in Transition: The Netherlands and the World Economy, 1950–2010.* Leiden: Brill.

Touwen, J. (2014b). The Hybrid Variety: Lessons in Non-Market Coordination from the Business System in the Netherlands, 1950–2010. *Enterprise and Society, 15*(4), 849–884.

Touwen, J. (2018). A Changing Landscape: Institutions and Institutional Change in the Dutch Economy. In P. Brandon, S. Go, & W. Verstegen (eds.), *Navigating History: Economy, Society, Knowledge and Nature. Essays in honor of Prof. Dr. C.A. Davids* (pp. 81–101). Leiden: Brill.

Trommel, W., van der Veen, R., & Schuyt, K. (eds.) (2004). *De herverdeelde samenleving: Ontwikkeling en herziening van de Nederlandse verzorgingsstaat.* Amsterdam: Amsterdam University Press.

Tros, F. H., Albeda, W., & Dercksen, W. J. (2004). *Arbeidsverhoudingen in Nederland.* Alphen aan de Rijn: Samsom.

Veen, A. van (2013). De Kamers van Arbeid: Experimenten met politieke vertegenwoordiging in Nederland rond 1900. *BMGN – Low Countries Historical Review, 128*(2), 31–61.

Velden, S. van der (2004). *Werknemers in Actie: Twee Eeuwen Stakingen, Bedrijfsbezettingen en andere acties In Nederland.* Amsterdam: Aksant.

Visser, J. (2013). Wage Bargaining Institutions: From Crisis to Crisis. *DG EcoFin Economic Papers No 488.* Brussels: European Commission.

Vonk, R. (2012). Een taak voor de staat? De Duitse bezetting en de invoering van de verplichte ziekenfondsverzekering in Nederland, 1939–1949. *Bijdragen en Mededelingen betreffende de Geschiedenis der Nederlanden/Low Countries Historical Review, 127*(3), 3–28.

Wielenga, F. (2009). *Nederland in de twintigste eeuw.* Amsterdam: Boom.

Windmuller, J. P. (1969). *Labor Relations in the Netherlands.* Ithaca, NY: Cornell University Press.

Zanden, J. L. van, & van Riel, A. (2004). *The Strictures of Inheritance: The Dutch Economy in the Nineteenth Century.* Princeton: Princeton University Press.

6 Social cohesion through policy coordination

The state, interests and institutions in Austria and Finland after 1945

Johanna Rainio-Niemi

The post-1945 period in the Western world stands out in scholarly literature as an era of growing societal stability, cohesion, and the welfare state. In the years when the post-1945 institutional and political model of governance was in the making across West European societies, contemporaries had memories and experiences of two types of a state. First were the still prevailing practices of a strong, controlled wartime state, and second, were the memories of states struggling with the pre-war decades' economic, political and social turbulence and societal fragmentation. How would a 'new normalcy' of the state, its practices and images, be after the wartime controls and exceptional authorities were lifted?

The wartime states had built much of their capacity upon the fact of being widely freed by the exceptional circumstances from many constitutional, democratic, political and economic constraints that limited their powers in peacetime society. When the wartime controls of public life were lifted, the claims for opening up of the, by now, heavily interventionist state to wider participation grew respectively. In analyses of the post-1945 era, the strength of the states often stand out, yet post-1945 was not an era of the state only. Quite the contrary, the key question was how to balance the increasingly active and, in many ways, mobilized non-state society with the empowered interventionist state – both being legacies of the 'total' nature of the wartime governance. The re-adjustment of the exercise of higher state power to the peacetime webs of checks and balances – distributing public power to different layers within the state, granting rights to individual citizens and associational autonomy to different groups and entities – did not happen without caution, even hesitance. The inability (or an outright refusal in some places) to find a functioning balance between the state's authority and societal democracy and participation had been a stumbling stone before the war. It had derailed democratic systems of governance and the peace in Europe, replacing them with aggressive authoritarianism, dictatorships and warfare. The forced cohesion of the war had put these battles on hold in democratic states, and in the authoritarian states, destroyed the socio-political frameworks almost entirely. Yet many of the most critical questions that had been acute in the 1920–1930s remained open

DOI: 10.4324/9780429503870-7

still, and in addition, the war had evoked a range of new questions concerning the shape of the new post-war 'normalcy'.

In this context, a more rational, productive and coordinated state agency arose to be a widely shared desire among the public policy administrators and political leaderships. Coordination appeared a key to productivity rises and more effective economic policy, and responded, more widely, to the dilemma of the balance between the interfering state and the participation-willing society. Building on institutional and ideational legacies from the wartime planning and control, the drive for more coordination also functioned as a preventive reaction to how socio-economic conditions and failed public policy coordination were perceived to have facilitated the disasters of the 1930s. Across European societies, the newly ambitious post-war bureaucracies had learned the lessons of the 1930s and of the wartime controls, and were eager now to implement programmes of social and economic 'modernization'. Limitations given, these policy aims were socio-economically more aware than had been the case before.

The belief in coordination was not a national affair only. There was no post-1945 "New Deal" in the United States, but in Europe, the US dominated aid and reconstruction schemes, such as the European Recovery Plan (ERP), came with strong strings attached concerning the ways of conducting more coordinated – and, simultaneously, more cooperative and consultative – public and economic policies. Reflecting the widespread belief in the causality among economic prosperity, social peace and a viable democracy, the search for stability was inherent to the search for economic growth and embedded with the post-war reconstruction schemes. As put by Milward and Sorensen,

> industrialization was thought of as the basis of an increase in output, industrial modernization as the basis of an improvement in overall productivity, increases in output and improvements in productivity as the basis of economic growth and, eventually, the concept of economic growth as the quickest way towards consensual politics within the stronger nation.[1]

However, in a peacetime society, the implementation of the more coordinated public and economic policies was politically and administratively a more complicated issue than it would have been under the wartime exceptional circumstances. The building of respective bureaucratic and administrative capacities in each local context, to quote Peter Evans, required much institutional innovation, being anything but a conservative strategy. The pooling, sharing and coordinating of the uses of public authority in society required a new type of institutional capacities from the state's public policy administrators. They needed capacities to be able to "engage and guide societal actors as well as to oppose and negotiate with them."[2] The finding a model that would be sustainable in the local context of constitutional procedures, political life, democracy and economics happened nowhere without contestation, trial and error. The pathways to modern, societally cohesive post-1945 welfare states were paved with twists, turns and failures to introduce a new type of coordination, consultation and cooperation instruments and platforms.

This chapter looks more closely at two examples of the post-1945 institution (re)building and their diverging historical and societal contexts. Both cases, Austria and Finland, are known in today's research literature as advanced post-1945 welfare states and, by deep contrast to these more contemporary images, as examples of deep societal fragmentation, polarization and conflict, and of the authoritarian currents of the 1920s and 1930s. This chapter discusses the state's integrative and institutional capacities first in broader and longer historical perspectives and focuses then on the critical decade and a half from the mid-1940s onwards. The chapter ends with an analysis of two failed early to mid-1950s attempts at the creation of the institutional matrices for more coordination in economic and socio-economic policy-making.

The two efforts, the government's Economic Directorate (Wirtschaftsdirektorium der Bundesregierung, hereafter ED) in Austria (1951–1954), and the series of the economic council type of institutions in Finland (1951–1956) have gained no thorough attention in the scrutiny on the rise of post-1945 neo-corporatism in the two countries. Both efforts were prestigious, directly linked to the government power and had all the most eminent actors in economic life participating. Arguing that these failures were critically important in the pushing of key actors in both societies towards more sustainable solutions, the chapter also open important insights into how the pathways were found to the different models of neo-corporatism and the post-1945 welfare states. How did Austria evolve into "one of the most corporatist post-war economies" and into the paragon of distinctively "societal" type of corporatism where "social partners" dominated and the state involvement was nominal?[3] On which grounds did Finland, in contrast, evolve into a case for "fair-weather" corporatism, standing out within the group of other Nordic welfare states as both most state-dependent and conflict-ridden?[4] Finally, Austria's case, in particular, also underscores the very constitutive ways in which the adaptation, response and even resistance to international and cross-nationally circulated economic policy impulses – stemming here especially from within the ERP, and the Organization for European Economic Cooperation (OEEC) – shaped the domestic search for more coordinated and consultative modes of economic policy-making.

Lessons learned from the 1930s: towards a neo-corporatist coordination state

A key component of the post-war model of "coordinated capitalism" – as it has been called by Barry Eichengreen – was the "set of norms and conventions, some informal, other embodied in law, to coordinate the actions of the social partners and solve a set of problems that decentralized markets could not."[5] A critical precondition for the "set" to come into being was a sufficiently centralized, autonomous and impartial state that had enough capacity to guide and negotiate with groups in society. Second, its introduction required that the "field" of interests was re-organized into institutionally symmetrical, internally hierarchical confederations, federations and associations that could be given principally equal roles in the coordination and negotiations with the state over the guidelines of public economic policy. This system became to be known since mid-1960s by the name neo-corporatism, the organizations and confederations representing business and employers, wage earners and trade unions, and, third, agricultural producers being given a key role.[6]

Professional-functional forms of organization and representation are an old phenomenon as such, both intertwining with and preceding the modern parliamentarian, electoral modes of democracy. It was in the 20th century only that the concept of corporatism – referring to the cooperation of the large, central-level interest organizations with one another and with state authorities – emerged. In the European context, a main historical distinction was the differentiation between the neo-corporatist and the authoritarian, mostly fascist corporatism of the 1930s. The latter, in many places, sought to "improve" the weaknesses of parliamentarian democracy or replace the multiparty democratic representation by formally unpolitical, one-party functional-corporate representation, the Austrian Christian corporate *Ständestaat* together with Mussolini's Italy being prime examples.[7] Severely discredited by these experiences, the concept of corporatism did go through a renaissance since the mid-1960s. At this point, political and economic scientists were able to observe the dramatic rise across capitalist, democratic societies of the arrangements whereby the public authorities worked systematically together with major interest groups, and these worked together to achieve productivity and maintain socio-economic and labour-market stability. The phenomenon seemed most advanced in those small state societies that, simultaneously, were developing ambitious welfare state policies in Europe (cf. Sweden, Switzerland, Austria).[8]

Tracing the concepts' scholarly uses, Molina and Rhodes notice the rapid shift of locus of corporatist literature from political scientific to political economy analyses by the 1970s. Having been, in Molina and Rhodes's words, almost "obsessed" with corporatism in the 1970s and 1980s, the political economists' interest, however, eroded with the rise of neo-liberalism towards the 1990s. In the 2000s, the increased macro-political concertation of interests, also within the European integration framework, opened new leeway to the political science and governance-orientated streams of analysis.[9] A similar trend from the dominance of political economy of the 1970s–1980s' towards more nuanced understandings of corporatism can be observed also in the field of historical studies analysis. Yet, the variety of ways in which public intellectuals – in the middle of the experienced crises of democracy during inter-war and wartime Europe – were rethinking corporatism, representation and governance, and elaborating aspects of "functional"[10] and "defensive" democracy, have gone widely unnoticed.

A rethinking of the lessons learned from the 1930s corporatism and fascism was at the heart of the so-called militant or defensive democracy debates arising on both sides of the Atlantic, especially among the emigres from German-speaking Europe, in the turn of the 1930s–1940s. Looking at how corporatism had functioned under fascism, the key question was how to harness corporatism for democracy's support. The main reference was not at all the wartime state but the pre-war political polarization, economic turbulence and societal fragmentation that were understood as root causes for the fall of pluralist, multiparty democracy, the rise of authoritarianism. In contemporary thinkers' minds, the extremism and authoritarianism of the 1930s sprang from the failure of pre-war leaders to manage socio-economic inequalities – due to the lack of political will and ability to share power, and due to the absence of respective institutional incentives. By overlooking the mobilizing appeal of emotionalism and the 'cult of irrationality' among the voters, and, second, by neglecting the need for effective institutional constraints to the uses of power by majorities, the pre-war pro-democratic leaders had lost the large working-class masses to fascism and national socialism.

The urgent task of the post-war generation, "our generation", as the US-based public intellectual Max Lerner wrote, was to keep power buried in majorities and collectivism from becoming "tyrannical". The second task related to the education of the power holders and, especially, the most powerful industrial, economic and administrative elites, to the respect of the "rules and virtues of pluralist democracy". As several authors concluded at the time, neither fascists or National Socialists had seized the power, had they not been supported, openly and tacitly, by a large enough segment of powerful elites at the top of economic, industrial, military and administrative life.[11] The key lesson, accordingly, was that the future of pluralist, tolerant democracy required the replacement of the "authoritarian monopoly capitalism", "manipulated by the interests of the few" with a system that guaranteed equal participation in the institutions of public socio-economic policy-making by all key interests groups that had significance to national income and production. In the creation of such a system, the public authorities and the state had to have a key role.[12] Indeed, whereas from the 1970s onwards, neo-corporatist arrangements were criticized as non-democratic, overtly technocratic and bureaucratic modes of policy-making, handing public decision-making power to powerful extra-parliamentary economic interests, in the post-1945 context, the promotion of new corporatism broke through to defend democracy with an eye to what had just happened in the 1930s.

The following sections examine the institutional pathways to more coordinated and, at the same time, neo-corporatist policy-making in Austria and Finland by looking, first, at the longer historical trajectories of the state's capacity and legitimacy in the two societies. The focus moves on to the societal context after 1945 within which the trends to coordination and corporatism were in the making through trial and error – more often so than is generally recognized in the main steam neo-corporatist literature. Regardless of major differences – Austria arising from the ashes of national socialism to the main symbol for societal corporatism and political hyper-stability, Finland being a case for state-depended corporatism that rested on the sound administrative state's capacities yet suffered from chronic instability of the political state – the basic underlying dilemmas to solve were largely similar. These dilemmas concerned (a) the balance of power between the administrative state and the political state, (b) the desired and possible role of the central state in society in general, and (c) the relations among the groups in society, their willingness to cooperate and/or abide the rules of cooperation and coordination set by the public authorities.

Legacies and capacities of the state: a historical overview

In the Habsburg Empire's predominantly German-speaking Austrian provinces, political organization and interest representation had taken place mainly through three "pillars", the pillars being catholic conservative, the socialist and the pan-German. The imperial rule had been mainly indirect and left therefore only weak and discredited legacies in terms of integrative and centralized powers. After 1918, the making of an autonomous, institutionally strong yet democratic state authority was paralyzed, neglected and de-legitimized in many ways.[13] Reflective of this, Austria's new constitution (1920) empowered parliament and, hence, the political parties with the largest mandates in parliament, that is, the socialists and the catholic conservatives. Post-1920 Austria was a full-fledged "party-state," depending, in practice, on the two main political "camps" ability to cooperate and compromise. In a society plagued by economic troubles, a lack of cohesion and deepening fragmentation and polarization, the ability to compromise proved weak, the two parties growing increasingly hostile to one another. By the mid-1920s, parliament – that is the state – was paralyzed by these hostilities and from 1927 onwards, the conflicts were already spreading to streets, the two blocs preparing paramilitary warfare against one another. To this constellation, the rising tide of national socialism, building on a pan-German political vision, added a third "corner" since the early 1930s. A fourth element intertwining in internal strife and paralysis was the exceptionally intense international involvement of the League of Nations' Economic and Financial Organisation and other actors of international banking and financial community during what has been called as the first, modern bail-out in history.[14]

In the summer of 1933, the ruling Catholic conservative government – in reference to political unrest and economic emergency – closed down Parliament and outlawed, first, all paramilitary and later all public political activities by the other political parties. The authoritarian one-party state, the Austro-Fascist Christian Corporate State (Ständestaat) was inaugurated on 1 May 1934. The National Socialist–led Anschluss to Germany liquidated this state in 1938, yet the Ständestaat created, in an embryonic form, a blueprint for a state in which a multiparty parliament based on electoral-territorial representation gave way to an institution based on a distinctively corporate-functional representation through economic chambers.[15]

Regarding the central state's institutional and integrative capacities, and traditions, Finland is almost an opposite to Austria. Administrative statehood had a long history, much longer than sovereign statehood (1917/1919). The Grand Duchy of Finland (1809–1917) was internally autonomous polity, structured in the model of governance Finland inherited from the centuries as an integral part of the Kingdom of Sweden. The autonomous administrative semi-state operated in accordance with a self-adopted constitutional order inherited from late 18th-century Sweden and adjusted to the context of Finland's autonomy within the Russian Empire. In a modernizing society, this semi-state grew into a notably capable, proactive agent in society.[16]

A distinctive feature of Finland's administrative state's history is that regardless of its institutional and integrative capacities, the sharing of supreme, sovereign political state power – once it became available – proved difficult. A key segment of the autonomous semi-states power became sharable already after the notably early introduction of general franchise and a unicameral parliament in 1906. With the first election (1907) ending with a social-democrat landslide victory and parliament majority, hesitance started growing on both the Russian and the domestic side. Parliament could not start its work, first, because of a new wave of imperial Russia's administrative integration programmes and then, because of the outbreak of World War I. When the full state sovereignty was achieved in December 1917, it took no longer than weeks after the country was in a civil war between the whites and the reds. The conflict concerned the constitution: the whites had their powerbase in the government; within the structures of the administrative state, the reds held the majority in Parliament; and both sides wished to draft the constitution accordingly.

The civil war ended with the white side's victory in May 1918. The winner's revenge on the reds was hard, the prison camp death rates exceeding the wartime losses many times over. The war effectively demolished the carefully cultivated (pre-independence) images of one unified nation and left the society of the new independent state bitterly divided.[17] The war also divided the political left into two halves: to the social democrats who rejected revolutionary means and to the more radical left whose emigrant party leadership resided in Moscow since 1918.

However, in a context where administrative cohesion and narrations of national unity had long been valued as the best asset of a small nation (against the Russian empire), the restoration of the lost societal and administrative cohesion soon re-emerged as a state political priority. The winning white side dominated this inter-war decades' reunification, but there were two strategies within: one more exclusionist, the other more integrationist, overlapping and competing with one another throughout the 1920s and 1930s. In the early 1930s, the exclusionist strategy gained in strength. Joining conservative-populist masses with conservative elites at the top of political, economic and military life in the interest of the uprooting of all types of socialism from Finland, the exclusionist forces managed to push through the so-called communist laws in Parliament in 1930. In consequence, all communist public activities were banned in reference to high treason. The ban formally covered far-right political extremism, too, but was applied more vigorously on the leftist side.[18] The legal ban of political extremism was to remain valid throughout the 1930s and the Second World war until the year 1944.

At the critical juncture of the early 1930s, Finland chose a different pathway compared to the other Nordic countries as well as compared to fascist systems of many other new small countries of Eastern Central Europe. While Austria, for instance, established a one-party authoritarian corporate state, the Nordic countries of the 1930s became famous for their explicitly democratic corporatist and political cross-class compromises and agreements in the early 1930s already. Finland's, by contrast to the other Nordic countries, leaned on legal bans, sanctions and exceptional state/government authorities for the controlling of those political and socio-economic elements that were considered most risky to the existing political and economic order. This strategy was visible also in the socio-economic field, being reflected in absence of any institutionalized labour-market negotiations in the Nordic style. There were no institutional incentives for collective agreements, wages were defined at the workplace level and the trade unions not recognized as legitimate collective representatives of the labour-side interests.[19]

The existing practices gained support from the legal sanctioning of all types of (actual and suspected) far-left public activities, including within the trade unions, but could be justified equally by the economic performance. Finland was one of the most rapidly growing economies in the inter-war era in Europe and was, in comparison to some other small, new states, hit relatively mildly by the 1930s' recession. Export syndicates and cartels, and, within the domestic sector, agricultural and domestic industries' could pursue effective cartelist and protectionist strategies to maintain export industries' price competitiveness and, on the other hand, shelter domestic production from competition – for instance through lowering of wages, layoffs and rationalization.[20] On the international arenas, the representatives of young Finland even were proud of their country's success through explicitly non-Keynesian policies.[21]

This general line of economic policy held more or less until the outbreak of World War II. The war against the Soviet Union, starting in late 1939, changed the scene entirely, however. The necessities of the wartime economy forced employers, businesses, agricultural producers and politicians close to them to take the labour force issues and interests seriously. For a small state's war performance, the issues of national cohesion grew tremendously in significance. Indeed, as an element of wartime governance, the employers' central organization was pushed to recognize the trade union confederation as the collective representative of the labour and as a reciprocal negotiation partner in January 1940.[22] However symbolic and provisional by intention – and brought into being by war, crisis and exception – the "January Engagement" did remove one of the main institutional obstacles on the way towards more encompassing corporatist cooperation between central organizations. The administrative state, in particular, proved resilient in holding on to the options for more systematically coordinated and controlled resource and policy planning that the "engagement" – now for the first time involving and engaging the labour side as well – promised. In addition, a key element, a backbone even of the wartime "enforced corporatism" was a solid body of exceptional legislation that enabled extra powers to the state and the all-party government (far left excluded) in society, politics and economic policy-making throughout the war. The legacies of wartime controlled or enforced state-led corporatism proved long-lasting also after the end of the war.

Institutionally enforced power sharing and hyper-stability in Austria versus return of the politics and chronic government instability in Finland

Whereas the Austria of 1918 to 1938 is a textbook example of a 'failed' 20th-century nation and state building in Europe, the Second Republic of 1945/1955 is equally famous for its rapid and successful power sharing and stability. After 1945, political elites not only cooperated but institutionalized their cooperation. The main differences were changes in the "quality of interest politics" and in the ways in which the "politics of interests" was connected to public policy-making.[23] Two aspects were of particular relevance here: first was the establishment and rigidly institutionalized power sharing within an encompassing system of three, self-governing socio-economic chambers – one for labour and wage-earners, second for business and employers and the third for agricultural producers. The second key element was the continuation of the, now institutionally reinforced, power sharing between the two main parties that re-established their operations after the wartime repression, the Social Democrats (SPÖ) and the Christian Democrats (ÖVP).

Austria's chamber system is unique in the context of post-1945 Europe. Membership in one of the chambers was now compulsory for citizens who were employees, employers or otherwise active in business or agricultural production. The chambers had wide delegated public powers in social and economic policy and labour-market issues and solid participation and veto rights in respective public policy-making. The novelty of the post-1945 system was the formally equal position of the Chamber of Labour (AK). The AK provided the main operational platform for the Austrian Trade Union Federation (*Österreichischer Gewerkschaftsbund*, hereafter ÖGB) that provided an umbrella organization for all trade unions and associations irrespective of their political party affiliations. Together with the Chamber of Business leadership, the ÖGB played a key part in the enactment of the law on the AK and, hence, the establishment of the chambers system. The "social partners" operating through the chambers grew into powerful para-statist actors in post-1945 Austria.[24]

The other cornerstone of the post-1945 power sharing were the continued practices of the early 1920s "Parteistaat". After 1945, the two main parties, re-established now as the Social Democratic Party of Austria (SPÖ) and the Austrian People's Party (ÖVP) shared the government power for over twenty years, until 1966. With a majority of about 90% of votes in Parliament, there was no functional opposition during this time in Austria. Furthermore, while the two-party coalition discontinued in 1966, the parties nevertheless continued to hold the approximately equal shares of the votes in Parliament (together 90% of the votes). This situation made the two parties dependent on mutual consent, compromises and the extraordinary practices of power sharing that continued to live on by proxy through the so-called Proporz.[25] This system of proportionality cut across layers of public administration and civil servant recruitment and guaranteed an equal share of the administrative posts and positions to each of the parties, establishing, in a longer run, a rather unique form of systematic, institutionalized patronage and clientelism.[26]

Compared to the regime collapse in post-war Austria, in Finland, the war reinforced the already solid images of a strong, centralized administrative state and its institutional preconditions to act as a coordinating agent in society and economy.[27] During the war, politics were mute, at least in public, all political parties – except the legally banned far left – taking part in governments and the joint war effort against the Soviet Union. After the war, reconstruction tasks were immense and war indemnities a great challenge – especially as Finland, by contrast to Austria, stayed away from the ERP and OEEC and, due to the wartime alliance with Germany, was initially not among the recipients of allied international wartime and immediate post-war aid schemes either (e.g. the United Nations Relief and Rehabilitation Administration). These circumstances justified regulation and exceptional state authorities in Finland for years to come. Simultaneously, the political discussion on the need for normalization and the principles of new upcoming 'normality' started right after the end of the wartime control of politics and public life.[28]

Concerning societal cohesion and consensus, one of the main changes concerned party politics and political life in general. The 'extremist' ends of the political party spectrum – the far left, most notably – had been legally banned since 1930, and the repercussions of the ban had naturally influenced the trade union movement as well. On virtue of the Interim Peace Treaty with the Soviet Union (autumn 1944), the ban on the extreme left was repelled and, simultaneously, a range of organizations at the heart of wartime public–private axis of governance – including the Civil Guard movement – were outlawed as 'fascists'.[29] In the spring 1945 elections, the far left gained 23.5% of the votes, compared to the social democrats' 25.8% and the Agrarian Union's 21,35%. These three big parties ruled Finland in a coalition until 1948. In 1948, the far-left alliance lost eleven of its seats and was not to participate in any government coalitions until 1966. Yet, with about 20% support (until the late 1980s), the question of the far left's participation in government was raised after every election and in connection with every government change.[30] The latter were to be many.

Compared to the hyper-stability of Austria's government coalitions between 1945 and 1966, post-1945 Finland is a case for chronic government instability. More than 20 governments ruled in Finland between 1945 and 1966, the average life span of a government being nine months.[31] In Austria, the coalition parties could lean on approximately 90% support in Parliament, whereas Finland's short-lived governments were mostly weak, short-lived minority governments or formally non-political, temporary caretaker governments composed of experts and civil servants. More often than not, these governments were ruling through temporary exceptional legislation and through a series of successive temporary economic enabling acts, in particular.

The return of the far left to politics and society resonated on the trade union movement as well. Already during the war, the trade union confederation – under an exclusively social democratic/non-communist leadership at that time – had grown into a recognized, powerful actor. Multiple institutional ties bound it to the core structures of wartime governance and economy, and this did not end with the end of the war, quite the contrary. One of the milestones was the law on wage control (June 1945) that obliged the trade union confederation and the employer organizations to define together the wages for each category of workers according to standardized wage and publicly available pay calculation principles. Besides the institutional framework, the wage control mechanisms created a new type of 'publicity' around jointly negotiated labour-market issues.[32] Characteristic of the basic pattern for years to come, however, the overall framework was both provided and sanctioned by the state and supported by the government's exceptional authorities. By 1947, an entire legal and institutional framework was in place for the central organizations to cooperate.

The influence gained through the new channels of participation was reflected on the SAK membership: from the circa 100 000 members at the end of 1944, the number doubled by the summer of 1945 and tripled by the end of the year.[33] Yet, the post-war confederation also was strained by heavy open and latent power struggles between the two main orientations within the political left. In addition, between 1958 and 1968, the confederation was disintegrated – not because of the social democrats versus communists divide but because of the Cold War – spirited ideological disputes within the social-democratic side concerning the 'right' attitude to communism.[34]

The extensive economic regulation, including wage, price and trade control were bound with temporary enabling acts that, on the other hand, required the government's constant involvement and, further, constant negotiations to achieve the necessary qualified majorities in Parliament. The governments grew into actively involved, main actors in the most heated labour-market and economic policy questions, whether desired or not. The most common reason for a government fall in 1945–1966 was, indeed, a conflict between some or all the main socio-economic interest parties. The struggles between the wage earners and the producers, between the employees and employers or all three on the wages versus prices, terms of export competitiveness versus wages and/or work conditions easily spilled over, derailing a cabinet after another and disturbing efforts to more broadly based 'Red–Green' majority governments between the social democrats and the Agrarian Union. Like in most post-1945 Western European societies, the interlinkages between the social democrats and the trade union movement, the agrarian political movement (Agrarian Union in Finland) and the agrarian producers' movement, the smaller conservative and bourgeois parties and the business and export interests were naturally close. In Finland, however, the social democratic party and the trade union confederation, SAK, also were often at odds with one another, both seeking an active role in the government and in parliament. The relationship between the Agrarian Producers' Confederation, MTK, and the Agrarian Union was strained as well, the political party being headed by Urho Kekkonen, who, before being elected as to the president of the republic in 1956 (until 1981), had nation-wide political ambitions instead of merely agrarian ones.[35]

In a context of three bigger political parties (social democrats, agrarians and the far left), each with about a 20% share of the votes, a range of smaller parties with strong veto rights and an active involvement of the labour market, agrarian producer and business interests in parliamentary politics, the shifts in alliances were frequently in order. The routine of enabling acts required qualified majorities, forcing weak and fragile minority governments into constant seek of allies, also outside of Parliament. The search for compromises ended often in a deadlock, other times to ad hoc solutions ('cow trading') that were politically, economically or administratively unsustainable in a longer run. Attempts at more sustainable Red–Green governments, with broader backing in Parliament, were particularly strained by the possibility that one of the parties (in practice, mostly the Agrarian Union) would seek tactical support at the expense of the coalition partner (the social democrats) from the far left or, directly, from the trade union confederation.

The tensions in the realm of the government, Parliament and interest-group politics, combined with, first, the notably low threshold of employing exceptional authority through enabling acts, and, second, the administrative state's solid capacity to provide an institutional matrix of platforms and procedures for policy coordination, cooperation and consultation, set the basic pattern in Finland for years to come. Without exceptional government authorities (enabling acts), many key decisions would simply have been politically impossible. Yet, once political decisions were there, the well-established administrative state could quickly set the scene through the variety of governance tools and platforms ready at hand for coordinated public policy drafting. This institutional readiness stands out in a comparative perspective to Austria, where the constitution limited central state-level action, agencies, and platforms. In Finland, on the other hand, the cooperation between the interest parties and political parties grew extraordinarily dependent from two elements: first, on the tireless, proactive work of the administrative state and, second, on the government's exceptional authorities that served to control the destabilizing influences from the highly conflictual field of party politics. The following case studies illuminate the differences in more detail.

Coordination state in the making: two failed institutions

The earliest efforts to the introduction of more coordination, cooperation and consultation to economic policies in post-war Austria and Finland related to the wage, price and inflation control. Since the early 1950s, the attempts to more centralized and coordinated, state-guided yet consultative economic policy-making intensified. The two efforts analyzed here, namely, the government's Economic Directorate (Wirtschaftsdirektorium der Bundesregierung, hereafter ED) from 1951 to 1954 in Austria and the institutional histories of the Economic Policy Planning Council/Economic Council (Talouspoliittinen suunnitteluneuvosto/Talousneuvosto) that was recommissioned several times in Finland between 1951 and 1956, both failed but were, nevertheless, important steps on the pathway to more coordinated and neo-corporatist policy-making.

In Austria, this most prestigious effort for the creation of an institutionally separate economic policy coordination platform at the central state level was directly related to the country's participation in the ERP and the OEEC. The idea of a new agency popped up to the government agenda in connection with the preparations for the OEEC's January 1951 meeting, where the organization was expected to present a plan for a transatlantic, Washington-led regulation of the production and distribution of raw materials because of the outbreak of the Korean War. The fulfilling of the "American requirements," it was assumed within the government, would require a new type of central state-level coordination regardless of the fact that Austria was divided into four occupation zones controlled by the Allied Powers. As Foreign Minister Karl Gruber was able to tell after returning from the meeting the American requirements were not binding yet political pressure for their implementation was heavy and connected with the option of receiving further US aid.[36]

Among the government, the 'American requirements' were the initial source for the ideas on new coordination agency. Once the idea of a new agency – without explicit indication of the 'American' origins of the idea – became public, it was soon embedded with wider domestic debates on the most desired ways of making economic policy. There was a variety of interpretations, aspirations, and concerns.

First and most acutely, the American requirements raised constitutional and administrative-technical questions within the government and administration: in a context in which power was shared among a range of strong semi-autonomous component units within the state (the chambers, provinces, exceptionally strong ministerial competencies), the options for a quick, centralized state-level action were inherently limited. These concerns were reflected on the government intern discussions on whether the ED should or could be an organ of the government "as a whole", whether it should locate under the Federal Chancellor's Office (BKA) or operate under the guidance of the most relevant ministry. The second set of questions concerned the issue of whether the new coordination agency should and could have competencies of its own or a more limited advisory mandate.[37] Third, how would the new agency relate to the existing commissions, especially to the Economic Commission and the Foreign Trade Commission within which the chambers' veto-rights were strong? This question led to the more fundamental discussion about the most desirable role of the chambers and the Trade Union Federation ÖGB in Austria's economic policy-making in general.

The government parties *could* have chosen to present the idea of a new coordination agency as a strictly limited and temporary set of measures related to the Korean War.[38] The idea, however, obviously evoked genuine broader interest within both coalition parties beyond the actual origins of it. The ÖVP's ministers, who coordinated their stances within the chamber of business and employers, welcomed the opportunity of revising the existing economic policy practices. The ED, in this perspective, was a promise of less complicated decision-making whereas the existing practices, in this perspective, involved too many commissions, too many 'external' participants and too many veto rights. The SPÖ was coordinating its stances with the AK and the ÖGB and initially welcomed the ED as a step to more effective, centralized 'economic planning'. On this side, no one, especially not the ÖGB, was ready to bargain about the chambers' legally guaranteed participation and veto rights. Without constant guarding of these rights, it was noted, Austria would soon be back to the 1930s-style authoritarian corporatism.[39]

Once the draft act on the ED arrived at Parliament to be discussed at the parliament's constitutional committee, the discussion intensified. According to the draft, the new agency was to coordinate work done in various ministries (inter-ministerial coordination at the central government level) and locate, administratively, under the Federal Chancellors Office (BKA) with the chancellor as the chair. The ED's task, further, was to provide the overall guidelines for economic policy-making and its mandate was to be provisional, for one year at a time. According to this first proposal, there were to be two types of members. The chancellor, the vice chancellor, and the relevant ministers (the minister of internal affairs, of social administration, of finance, of agriculture and forestry, of the nationalized industries, and of foreign affairs) would be voting members whereas the president of the Austrian National Bank and the presidents of the chambers and of the trade union federation ÖGB were members with "advisory votes" only.[40]

The parliament's constitutional committee removed the category of advisory votes altogether.[41] This move had already caused a heated debate in the National Assembly between the president of the ÖGB, who was a member of Parliament and one of the chairs of the National Assembly, and the president of the Chamber of Business, who equally was a member of Parliament. The former had accused the latter on attempts to centralize economic policy power, in practice, under the (ÖVP-led) Ministry of Trade, and the latter accused the former of the promotion of the "dictatorship of one single chamber" at the expense of wider national economic considerations.[42]

Before the issue officially landed the National Assembly's Plenary Session, it returned to the government due to the constitutional committee's amendments.

At this point, the European Cooperation Agency (ECA) Special Mission in Austria intervened. The ECA High Commissioner expressed the ECA's dissatisfaction with the Austrian government's passivity and repeated the criticism of the many institutional weaknesses of the prevailing economic policy-making system. In future, all further aid to Austria was to be explicitly conditional on the government's ability to introduce effective, more centralized coordination capacity.[43]

When the National Assembly Plenary Session discussed a new draft in early April 1951, the idea of "advisory votes" for the chambers and others were back in. The two tiny opposition parties were critical, but the proposal was nevertheless approved with the government parties' generous shares of votes. According to the SPÖ, the establishment of the ED was now in the vital interest of the "small, poor and occupied Austrian state." A key part of Austria's current economic problems boiled down, the SPÖ speaker noted, to the external manipulation of the coal prices (especially Polish coal prices) which further were an element in the broader attempts to disturb Austria's economic and societal stability. In the exceptionally difficult global political circumstances, the ED was a necessary tool for the defence of economic and societal stability and cohesion.[44]

The formal decision notwithstanding (May 1951), the search for less complicated procedures around the chambers' "excessive influence" went on intensely among the government officials. As the BKA legal advisors pointed out, the ambiguity of the new framework would in fact provide flexibility in implementation. Discussions also continued between the government officials, the European Cooperation Agency (ECA) Special Mission in Austria and the Austrian Central Bureau for European Recovery Programme Issues (ZERP). As Chancellor Figl (ÖVP) noted in the government-intern discussions, the international message was clear: the existing procedures of economic policy-making were too complicated, too slow and far too dependent on far too many "non-governmental outsiders". Simultaneously, it becomes equally clear from the materials that the government was not about to change the prevailing system in any more thorough or formal manner. This was politically not possible as the parliament dealings had shown, and second, under the continuing division of Austria into four occupation zones, including the Soviet presence in the Eastern parts of Austria, government was not willing to open any more profound discussions on the ground rules of Austria's economic or foreign trade policy-making. Stability was highly desirable under these circumstances. Also constitutional legal advisors suggested the use of case-specific, small and ad hoc ministerial committees that could consult chambers and other "outsiders" to the extent that was seen necessary or desirable in each specific case.[45] Without any other solution in sight, this turned into the routine, all sides simultaneously growing increasingly dissatisfied or disillusioned, however. The ÖVP and its partners lost interest, and the ÖGB grew critical of the way in which the involved parties were neglecting the ED's potentials to be developed into a new, effective policy-making platform.[46]

The ED's first mandate, approved in May 1951, was to expire in June 1952. Already in March 1952, came the news on the termination of the US aid for Europe around the very same time as the mandate would expire. The ERP programme was ending and the new aid and assistance schemes being retargeted to facilitate European national defence capabilities.[47] The foreseeable end of the ERP evoked an intense economic policy debate in Austria in the spring of 1952 and the discussion also covered the ED. In April 1952, the trade unions' ÖGB published a "ten point programme" which promoted full employment as the prerequisite for social and political stability in the country, the chambers' right to participate and the need for a strong-enough the state. Under the prevailing circumstances and to manage the transition caused by the end of the ERP, it would be wise to renew the ED's mandate for no less than two more years, saw the ÖGB.[48] In the Business Chamber's view, by contrast, time was ripe for the termination of all unnecessary administrative impediments to "normal" economic policy-making. This included the termination of the ED and the whole range of other commission-type of platforms.[49] Also the U.S. High Commissioner's Office participated in these discussions by publishing a listing of four main factors that, in the Office's view, set the scene for the future economic growth in Austria. The first two factors were the chambers' unique, legally grounded influence, and, altogether, the exceptionally 'well-organised' politics of interests, pursued most actively by the trade union movement. The other two were the deeply embedded cartel practices and the subjugation of exceptionally large sectors of economic life to big banking conglomerates or to direct state control (nationalised industries).[50] The reception of the 'American' views was twofold: the political left welcomed the US High Commissioner's criticism of cartels as hinders to free prices, the ÖVP side, on its part, welcomed the remarks on the chambers' potentially stagnating influence. However, illustrative of the ground on which the Austrian system was built, the Christian Social journal *Die Furche* (close to the ideological foundations of the ÖVP) chose to defend both cartels and the chambers. Cartels were seen as effective means to control the "dark sides" of unlimited competition, and the chambers as the main embodiment of democracy in economic life, a unique social innovation that combined economic autonomy with social responsibility and served to generate social cohesion and peace in society.[51]

In late March 1952, the ED faced a new challenge as the Provincial Government of Vorarlberg requested the Constitutional Court to scrutinize whether the ED's role above the ministries and as an inter-ministerial coordinator was a violation of the constitutionally anchored autonomy and competencies of individual ministers.[52] This investigation paralyzed the ED in many ways, yet, in May 1952, the government did propose an extension of the ED's mandate for two more years, until 1 July 1954, quite in line with the ÖGB's suggestion. The ÖVP approved but expressed the explicit wish that this "not so small committee of the government" would convene as seldom as possible, preferably not at all.[53]

Despite the extension, the ED's activities dried up in practice in 1952–1953. The few meetings were very short and marked by the repeated reminders by the chair that, in accordance with the Constitutional Court's recent decision, the ED was not entitled to discuss matters that were under ministerial competences.[54] After June 1953, the ED no more convened, the economic policy initiative clearly shifting to the ministries and, especially, to the new energetic minister of finance Reinhard Kamitz (ÖVP). The ED had become, as the daily paper *Die Presse* put it, a "completely useless institution," and in 1954, the termination of its mandate was no more discussed to any detail.[55]

Economic policy planning council in Finland

In Finland, the early 1950s were marked by attempts to form broad-based Red–Green coalitions between the two 'non-communist' big parties, the Agrarian Union and the social democrats. In economic policy, these years witnessed ambitious stabilization programmes, including a shift from the more narrowly understood price–wage controls towards more broadly coordinated, productivity-orientated policies.[56] Characteristic were also the attempts of linking the "agrarian income" to the overall system of price and wage determination. Just like in Austria, the early 1950s were years of intense economic policy debates and institutional (re)formulation in a situation marked by the gradual ending of the most urgent post-war reconstruction tasks and finding of the parameters of 'new normality.'

In spring 1951, the new Red–Green government was closely involved in the negotiation of "a truce" (*linnarauha*) on labour market which also included a commitment of the parties to the government's economic stabilization plan. The signatories of the truce were Prime Minister Kekkonen (Agrarian Union) together with the leaders of the employer's federation, STK; the Agrarian Producers' Central Union, MTK; the Swedish-speaking Agrarian Producers' Central Union, SLC; the Trade Unions' Confederation, SAK; and a range of other smaller employers' unions (Liiketyönantajain keskusliitto, LTK; Maataloustyönantajien keskusliitto), as well as the central union for white-collar wage earners (Henkisen työn keskusliitto). The institutional core of the truce was provided by the Economic Policy Planning Council (*talouspoliittinen suunnitteluneuvosto*), commissioned by the government as an arena, the administrative framework and the provider of necessary expert knowledge for the signatories' cooperation and the longer-term planning of national economic stabilization.[57] Besides of the administration, the council consisted of a chair and over 30 representatives from all involved interest associations, including the smaller ones, a range of key members of parliament and the Council of State (ministers). The locus was the executive committee with six members from the most relevant ministries and the main interest organizations (the employers' STK, the trade unions' SAK and the agricultural producers' MTK). Among the contemporary public, the executive committee came to be known as "the Prime Minister's shadow cabinet."[58]

In a comparative perspective to Austrian, the administrative and procedural ease with which the economic planning council of 1951 came into being is striking. The well-established administrative state provided ready-made blueprints for such agencies, the long histories of the so-called state committees institution providing the most natural matrix.[59] Because of the pre-existing institutional blueprint for cooperation between the state and sectors in society, there simply was no need to such constitutional-legal or administrative-procedural discussion that, in fact, remained unresolved throughout the ED's histories in Austria. In Finland, there was a ready-made, undisputable model for cooperation that could be launched immediately. According to the well-established praxis, big issues were divided into smaller ones, theme-specific subcommittees and working groups were nominated, and requests for consultation were sent out to an even wider circle of experts and stakeholders to be heard in the subcommittees and working groups during the policy preparation. In accordance with the guidelines for the committee-type of institutions, the council was to produce a series of public reports with concrete proposals to be brought by the government to parliament. Most often, this type of reports would contain ready-cut draft laws that had been so widely pre-discussed that they seldom were amended by Parliament. The committees were the absolute core engine of a consensus-seeking policy-making style in Finland and as an institution, the economic planning council of 1951 was nothing special as such.

Between 1945 and 1965, there were to be altogether twelve major economic policy advisory councils/committees at work in Finland, seven of them between the years 1945 and 1955.[60] This frequency is indicative of two aspects. It indicates first the ease with which the post-war governments, out of tradition, were able to turn to the well-established administrative tools provided by the administrative state. Second, the high number is indicative also of the fact that something quite did not work out as usual. Until the end of the war, the socio-economic issues had been mainly dealt with through the administrative state, the element of politics having been more or less filtered out, muted or suppressed in different ways. Under the post-1945 circumstances where politics entered the scene more openly, the finding of a sustainable balance between the chronic instability of the 'political' side of the state, embodied by the frequency of the government changes, and the stability of the administrative state proved difficult. The case of the early 1950s economic councils provides an illustration of the point.

The Red–Green coalition that had commissioned the economic planning council in the spring of 1951, collapsed in the autumn. The new government, also on a Red–Green basis, re-assigned the economic planning council and in April 1952, it was able to send its preliminary draft for a long-term national economic stabilization programme for comments. These comments still pending, the main truce parties concluded that there were no grounds for compromise, let alone agreements. One of the most open conflicts, at this point, was between the Social Democratic Party and the SAK. The SAK had been active in the initiation of the council and had high expectations concerning its capacity to steer the economic policy course toward Keynesians full employment.[61] The disappointment was respectively deep and reflected on the SAK's criticism of the social democrats' inability to stand up to their principles within the prevailing government coalition.[62]

More generally, the years 1952 and 1953 were to be marked by intense economic policy debating in Finland. Besides the SAK's promotion of full employment, the other main topics on the agenda were the system of "agricultural income", on one hand, and the industrial production costs and export price competitiveness on the other. According to the representatives of the export industries, in a small open economy, price competitiveness had to be a priority but the currently emerging linking of the agricultural prices with industrial wages risked creating automatism of wage increases that would eat away competitiveness

The break in the programme preparations in the spring of 1952 severely paralyzed the economic planning council during these debates. The trade unions' SAK, a foremost support of the council in the beginning, lost interest, and the same applied to the Agrarian Union's prime minister Kekkonen. The council was no more convened to full sessions but the officials and the experts of the council continued working, providing up-to-date administrative-technical and socio-economic knowledge especially to the prime minister and his office.[63]

In the summer of 1953, the conservative National Coalition Party – a party with close contacts to the business and employer associations – issued a parliamentary interpellation concerning the eroding export competitiveness. Kekkonen's Red–Green government did not survive this challenge and was followed by a new Agrarian Union minority government in the autumn of 1953. This government again fell before the end of the year, being replaced by a formally unpolitical caretaker government. This expert government had contacts with the employers' STK and the representatives of export industries and was, from day one, expected to push through economic deregulation and a currency devaluation to cut costs at home and to restore export competitiveness abroad.

Although the provisional expert government had an entirely different political basis than the earlier Red–Green government, it, too, recommissioned the economic council. The chairperson remained the same but the most drastic change – indicative of future conflicts – was the withdrawal of the agricultural producers MTK from the council following the new government's announcement that the issue of agricultural income no more was to be on the council's agenda.[64]

The provisional expert government withdraw from office already after the March 1954 elections, the key parties behind the expert government – especially the conservative National Coalition party – suffering a severe electoral loss. Among the winning social democrat MPs, the number of representatives who came directly from the trade unions' SAK grew. The social-democratic MPs now included the president and many other leaders of the SAK and were soon to be ministers in a yet another Red–Green coalition headed this time not by Agrarian Union's Urho Kekkonen but a prime minister from the small, centrist-liberal Swedish People's Party. The SAK's new foothold within parliament and, especially, government shifted the SAK's earlier focus from economic councils to, more directly, to the government, ministries, and parliament.[65] In a familiar manner, this new government, too, re-assigned an Economic Policy Planning Council. The chair remaining the same, the main task was to conclude the report that was left unfinished back in the spring of 1952.

The council's final report (*Talouspolitiikan perusohjelma*) was to be not much longer in pages than were the seven dissenting opinions that followed the report text. The most incompatible views originated from the Employers' Confederation STK and the Trade Unions' Confederation SAK. One opinion was shared by all: the Economic Policy Planning Council did not work as an instrument of governance, and the main reason was the council's provisional and unclear mandate. Because of these weaknesses, participants could not trust the council's capacities, this making them unable and unwilling to engage in any binding compromises or commitments originating in this arena. The conclusions from this incapacity varied, however. According to the employers' STK, the economic council, just like councils and committees in general, were unnecessary if not detrimental to the healthiness of free economic life. The trade unions' SAK equally, recognized the weaknesses of the council as an institution and, therefore, spoke for the founding of a new ministry, solely focused on economic planning. The administrative staff of the economic council, in turn, would have preferred a council with less contacts to party politics and interest group negotiations. Their suggestion was the establishment of a permanent Economic Policy Planning Office (*talouspoliittinen suunnitelutoimisto*) under the Council of State Office – a clear-cut experts' agency providing high-level research, knowledge, and prognoses on domestic and international economic trends.[66]

The outcome of the years' long economic policy negotiation is highly illustrative of how the well-established traditions of the administrative state and the preference for 'unpolitical', legal solutions worked out in the 1950s context. Illustrative was also the reaction of the government that chose to issue a new, stronger statute on the Economic Council (Talousneuvosto). The new council was to operate under the Council of State Office with two years' mandate at a time. The council was not – this was underscored – a *permanent* state organ, yet the idea was that in practice, such councils would be in operation all the time, a new council being mandated once the old mandate was running out.[67] In addition, the government issued a statute on a separate Economic Planning Office (Taloudellinen suunnittelutoimisto) to serve the production of impartial, unpolitical expert knowledge.

The new statutes of 1955 did not solve the problems that had strained the economic policy planning councils, quite the contrary. The lack of trust between the currently reigning Red–Green government and the administrative staff of the new, more solidly institutionalized Economic Council deepened. In course of 1955, the government – as a side effect of complex package of bargaining – finally completed the synchronization of agricultural income (*maataloustulo*) with the levels of income for industrial wage earners. The decision needed to be approved in Parliament, and the government, in fact, needed a whole series of economic enabling acts to push the bill through. At this point, the social democrats refused their support to one of the key enabling acts. The centrist-liberal and conservative political forces that opposed the routine of enabling acts generally, joined in. Consequently, the new enabling act did not get necessary support, and the government's decision on agricultural incomes bogged down in late 1955.

The relations between the government, especially Prime Minister Kekkonen and the economic council leadership broke down. The Prime Minister openly accused the council and the planning office leadership of politically imbalanced analyses that, in the guise of administrative and impartial knowledge, had supported especially the employers' and export industries' cause.[68] As a result, the government and its ministers (many of them from the SAK) kept all the main economic policy decisions inside the government, utilizing direct bilateral channels of the cabinet members to the leading heights of the SAK and the Agrarian side. In January 1956, just before the presidential elections, in which Prime Minister Kekkonen was a main candidate, the agricultural producers' MTK persuaded the government into approving increases in milk prices to compensate for the failure of the agricultural income decision. The trade unions' SAK responded by demanding wage increases to compensate for the price increases. The situation escalated into a general strike that started the same day as the newly elected president Kekkonen took office.[69]

At this point, the economic council was fully marginalized. Under the general strike, the council leadership a few times requested of whether the government would like to hear the council's opinion or use its services but was never replied. In October 1956, after the general strike and the start of the new president, the council's long-time chair Teuvo Aura announced his resignation.[70] After this point, there was to be a break to the use of the economic council type of institutions in Finland. In 1959, the agrarian minority government commissioned an inquiry concerning the economic councils as an institution. Yet, it was only in the 1960s that a further economic council – based on the revised statute of 1955 – was to be deployed again.

A key difference of between the councils of the 1950s and the 1960s was to be the latter's focus on international and European economic environment. Finland was an associate member of the European Free Trade Association (EFTA) since 1961 and the economic councils of the 1960s were to be particularly focused on the study of how to introduce incomes policies in the model of the OEEC recommendations in Finland too. In this planning, the economic councils were seen as the main platform for incomes policy formulation and even a new law on economic councils was introduced with this in mind in January 1966. This was just before the parliamentary elections after which the far left returned to the government coalition for the first time since 1948.[71]

Contrary to the mid-1960s plans, the economic councils had no role whatsoever in the process that eventually led to the first incomes policy agreement in 1968. Further, in the early 1970s, the incomes policy issues were explicitly removed from the statues that defined possible councils' possible agendas. The incomes policies were to be negotiated between the main interest organizations, however, with notable government involvement and support by the administrative state, the economic councils excluded. The government hence continued relying on the instrument of enabling acts to push through the various dimensions agreed in the negotiations, and the administrative state continued providing the platform of state committees for the related policy drafting. Economic councils in the style of the 1966 law were not to be involved.

Conclusion

In reference to Western Europe's extraordinary economic development between 1945 and 1973, Barry Eichengreen speaks of a distinctive model of "coordinated capitalism." A key element within was "the set of norms and conventions, some informal, others embodied in law that helped to coordinate the actions of the social partners and solve a set of problems that decentralized markets could not." As this chapter has shown, in post-war Austria and Finland, the architects of public socio-economic policy took efforts to establish more coordinated modes of policy-making. Underpinning these efforts, in the first post-war decade, in particular, was the wish for a more prosperous and cohesive future, arising centrally from the experiences of social, economic and political turbulence and polarization of the 1920s and 1930s and the catastrophes of World War II. On the other hand, the wish of more coordination and cohesion required new institutional capacities and new political will to cooperation and compromises.

Finland, historically, was a case for strong administrative capacities of the state and, simultaneously, a case for chronic government instability cause, also, by close entanglement between the socio-economic interest politics and government/parliamentary politics. The government routinely managed this instability through the means of exceptional authorities and government enabling acts.

Austria was a case for both formally and informally enforced power sharing within the realm of politics and, institutionally rather separately, of the realm of socio-economic interests (the chambers). On many occasions, Austria's distinctive power sharing practices run in deep contrast to the central-level coordination attempts. The central level state's institutional and administrative capacities were historically weak and burdened. In post-1945 Austria, however, the enforced power-sharing practices quickly and effectively managed to stabilize the previously centrifugal and scattered society. Within a few decades only, Austria's extraordinary system of power sharing transcended the layers of governance from parliament to government, from the top of the state to the local level, reaching out to cover the sectors of socio-economic and labour market policy. This praxis of power sharing generated 'hyper-stability' that calls for its like in post-1945 Europe. Yet, in a longer run, this power sharing evolved into an equally striking system of institutionalized patronage. In post-1945 Finland, on the other hand, the finding of a functioning balance between the well-established administrative state and the only now unrestricted democratic politics took time and effort. The end result was a system of 'fair-weather' neo-corporatism that remained extensively depended on the government's exceptional authorities (enabling acts) and on the administrative state's institutional capacities (the state committees). This system was and remained vulnerable to conflicts and politics and was fragile in many ways. Yet, it too established routines of its own, the role of enabling acts gradually diminishing towards the 1980s.

In neither of the analyzed cases did the economic council type of institutions prove to be the answer to the needs and desires for more coordinated, consultative and cooperative modes of policy-making. Regardless of the initial interest in and prestige of these attempts, the closer to the government power the attempted platforms of policy coordination and interest settlement came, the more fundamental the related conflicts of interest tended to grow. Above all, the analysis of the two 'failed' attempts reminds us that developments that may, in hindsight, appear as straightforward national pathways towards cohesive societies of the modern welfare states were, in reality, a historically contingent series of outcomes from the mixtures of intentions some succeeding, others failing and some coming out ahead as different from what was intended initially.

Notes

1 Milward and Sorensen (1993), 6–7. See also e.g. Milward (1984, 2000); a highly interesting account on the post-war productivity drive see Tweraser (1995).
2 Evans (2005), 26–47, 36.
3 Ebbinghaus and Visser (2000), 77; on Austria's model of neo-corporatism more thoroughly, see e.g. Katzenstein (1984). The differentiation between societal and state corporatism initially drawn by Schmitter in 1974 (reprinted 1981). Cf. also Schmitter (1985).
4 For Finland's model, see Pekkarinen (1992); Rehn (1996).
5 Eichengreen (2007), 4–5.
6 There were many variations among neo-corporatist systems. The research literature typically classifies variations nationally and, primarily, on the basis of the state's role and the extent to which public status was attributed to the main interest associations in society. In Offe's definition, the degree of corporatization increased with (1) the extent to which the resources of an interest association were supplied by the state, (2) the extent to which the range of representation was defined through public political decisions, (3) the regulation of internal relations between rank-and-file members and executive members of associations and, finally, (4) the extent to which interest associations were licensed and invited to assume, together with a specified set of other participants, a role in legislation, the judicial system, policy planning and implementation, or granted a right of *Selbstverwaltung* (self-administration). Offe (1981), 136–137, 140–141.
7 Costa Pinto (2017). For more see e.g., Harrison (1980).
8 For instance, Katzenstein (1985).
9 Molina and Rhodes (2002), 305–31, 305.
10 For an opening towards this type of historical analysis see, Couperus (2019); Capoccia (2005), 252–266, 252.
11 Lerner (1939/1943).
12 Karl Loewenstein's review on Lerner's pamphlet (1939).

13 The first Republic of Austria was, famously, a state that "nobody wanted." In the end of World War I, all major nationalities of the collapsed Austro-Hungarian Empire declared its full state sovereignty and the nine "leftover" provinces, including the imperial capital Vienna, formed a German Austria. A few weeks later, the provisional leaders of this leftover state unanimously declared their wish to join the German Reich. The Peace Treaty of St. Germain forbade this accession, e.g. Andics (1962).
14 Hanisch (1994); Kuprian (2002); Gerlich and Campbell (2002); Mattl (1984); Marcus (2018).
15 Talós and Neugebauer (1984); Binder (1997); Maderthaner (2002).
16 Jussila (1999); Polvinen (1996). Cf. also Huxley (1990); Rainio-Niemi (2019).
17 For more see e.g., Tepora and Roselius (2014); Haapala and Tikka (2012).
18 Capoccia (2005); Alapuro (1998); Hentilä (1999).
19 More on the Finnish version of 1930s' "historical compromise" e.g. Kettunen (2005); Karvonen and Lindström (1997).
20 Hjerppe and Jalava (2006); Hjerppe (1989); Heikkinen (2000). Export trade, especially, pulp, newsprint and plywood industries, kept good profit margins and the drop in sales profits could be compensated through relatively unrestricted rationalization measures and, indeed, through the lowering of wages and layoffs.
21 Kettunen (2002), 25–26.
22 Kettunen (2001); Paavonen (1987).
23 Talós (1993, 1985). Also e.g. Talós and Kittel (1996); Stourzh and Grandner (1986).
24 Talós and Kittel (1995); Talós (1997).
25 Rauchensteiner (1987); Enderle-Burcel (1995); Engelmann (2001); Sully (1989).
26 The "degeneration" of power-sharing and proporz and the labelling of it as corruption later became a majorasste for the rising right wing neo-nationalist populism in Austria. Rothstein (2011), 137. Cf. also Heinisch (2002).
27 Tiihonen (1985); Selovuori (1985).
28 For instance, Ojala et al. (2006); Paavonen (1998); Aunesluoma (2011).
29 After 1945, the far left formed an electoral alliance, the Democratic League of the Finnish People (Suomen Kansan Demokraattinen Liitto, henceforth SKDL). The Finnish Communist Party (Suomen Kommunistinen Puolue, SKP) whose leadership resided in Moscow was the biggest member in this electoral alliance.
30 Zilliacus (1995); Lavery (2006); Nevakivi (1999).
31 Hyvämäki (1977); Jääskeläinen (1980); see also Selovuori (1985).
32 Bergholm (2003). More generally on the formation of the policy model Kauppinen (1994); Bergholm (2015); Haataja (1993).
33 Hyvämäki (1977), 276.
34 In the late 1950s, a faction promoted less compromising policies vis-à-vis communists within the movement broke off from the SAK. The re-integration – which went on since 1963 – was one of the key requisites for the introduction of incomes policy pacts in Finland in 1968.
35 For instance, Bergholm (2005) offers detailed insight into the complex relationship between the SAK and the SDP at the time. For Agrarian perspectives, see Hokkanen (2002). On the business perspectives, Wuokko et al. (2019).
36 See e.g., ÖStA/AdR, BKA/Ministerratsprotokolle, Ministerrat 19.12.1950 (Nr. 230); 16.1.29151 (Nr. 232); BKA/ZERP, OEEC Paris 5.12. 1950, Ratsbecshluss betr. Rohstoff (Zl. 524.204-ERP/3/50); ÖStA/AdR/Bundesministerium für Handel und Wiederaufbau (hereafter BMfHuW), Wirtschaftsabteilung 1945–1954, Karton 41, "Stellungnahme zu Ratsbeschluss der OEEC bezüglich Rohstoff-Versorgung."
37 ÖeStA/AdR, BKA/ Ministerratsprotokolle, Ministerrat 23.1. 2951 (Nr. 233).
38 This type of a "narrow" interpretation concerning a clearly provisional, ad hoc, temporarily limited and US-related nature of the ED gained in weight in the coming years among the representatives of business, employers and the ÖVP.

39 ÖStA/AdR, BKA, Ministerratsprotokolle, Ministerrat 16.1. 1951: Wirtschaftsabteilung, Presseschaus 1949–1953, KARTON H/39: *Neues Österreich* 31.1. 1951; *Die Presse* 31.1. 1951; *Volkstimme* 31.1. 1951.

40 ÖstA/AdR, BKA/Ministerratsprotokolle, Ministerrat, 20.2.1951 Nr. 237, "Entwurf eines Bundesgesetzes über die Errichtung eines Wirtschaftsdirektoriums der Bundesregierung."

41 ÖstA/AdR, BKA/Ministerratsprotokolle, Die Sitzung des Ministerrates am 20.2.1951, "Entwurf eines Bundesgesetzes über die Errichtung eines Wirtschaftsdirektoriums der Bundesregierung"; Austrian Parliament Archives (hereafter APA), Nationalrat der Republik Österreich, (hereafter NR), Ausschüsse u. Unterausschüsse VI. G.P, Ausschuss für Verfassung und Verwaltungsreform. Protokoll über die Sitzung 27.2 1951.

42 ÖeStA/AdR, BKA/Ministerratsprotokolle, Ministerrat 6.3.1951; 49. Sitzung des Nationalrates der Republik Österreich, VI. G. P. 7.3. 1951, pp. 1843–1844; 1847–1948.

43 This intervention was followed by an intense exchange of letters between the Special Mission and its main discussion partner on the Austrian side, the Central Bureau for ERP Issues (BKA-Zentralbüro für ERP-Angelegenheiten, hereafter ZERP). ZERP was the main link between the domestic and international economic policy authorities from 1950 to 1953. "Paradoxically," as Hans Seidel has put it, the ZERP was one of the most active promoters of economic planning and coordination in Austria. See e.g., Seidel (2000), 264–265, 275.

44 Nr. 337 d.B. zu den sten.Protokollen des Nationalrates (VI.G.P., 29.3.1951) "Bericht und Antrag des Handelsausschusses betreffend den Entwurf eines Bundesgesetzes über die Regelung des Warenverkehrs mit dem Ausland (Aussenhandelsverkehrsgesetz 1951); Sitzung des Nationalrates der Republik Österreich 4.4.1951, 1887–1889; 1892–93; 1899–1903; Bundesgesetzblatt für die Republik Österreich Jg. 1951, BGBl. 104–108 Ausgegeben am 21. Mai 1951, 487–488; The ÖGB Yearbook 1951, 43.

45 ÖstA/AdR, BKA, Ministerratsprotokolle, Ministerrat 5.6. 1951; 12.6. 1951.

46 ÖstA/AdR, BKA, Inneres, 1. Sitzung des Wirtschaftsdirektoriums 27–30.6. 1951; (2. Forsetzung am 31.7. 1951); 2. Sitzung des WD 13.7. 1951; 10. Sitzung des WD's 2.10. 1951; On mediating activities oft he ZERP see e.g. ÖeStA/AdR, BKA/ZERP, Verfassungsdienst BKA (Zl. 63.327–2a/1951) to BKA-ZERP (Zl. 620201; Grundzahl 609.247-ERP/3/51) 3.10.1951; BKA/ZERP (Geschäftszahl, A.E. 621251–3/51) Taucher to the Minister for Trade and Reconstruction Dr. Kolb 19.10.1951; BKA/ZERP (Geschäftszahl, A.E. 624624; 623.324-ERP/3/51); BKA/ZERP A.E. 624624, Zl. 623.324-ERP/3/51; Stellungnahme zu dem Bericht und Antrag des BKA's-ZERP, (Zl. 623.324-ERP/3/51). The comments are dated 7.12. 1951 and can be found under BKA-ZERP Zl. 625.291–3/51 (Grundzahl 609.247-ERP/3/51); About ÖGB's discontent especially; ÖeStA/AdR, BKA, Inneres, Die 25. Sitzung des WDs 28.4.1952; cf. also the preceeding Sitzungs 20–24; on public discussion; ÖstA/AdR. BmfHuW, Wirtschaftsabteilung, Presseschau 1949–1953; *Wiener Zeitung* 19.4.1952.

47 ÖeStA/AdR, BKA, Inneres, WD, 24. Sitzung des WD's 31.3. 1952.

48 ÖstA/AdR. BmfHuW, Wirtschaftsabteilung, Presseschau 1949–1953, *Arbeit und Wirtschaft* 5(6), 1.1. 1952.

49 The ÖGB Yearbook 1952, 12–13, 33; Wien Bibliothek, Tagblatt-Archiv, ÖGB 1952, Mappe 331.881, "Ein Zehn-Punkte-Programm des Gewerkschaftsbundes. Für Stabilisierung aber gegen jede deflationistische Wirtschaftspolitik", *Arbeiter Zeitung* 5.4. 1952; ÖeStA/AdR, BMfHuW, Wirtschaftsabteilung, Karton 39/H, Presseschaus 1949–1953, *Wiener Zeitung* 19.4.1952. "Umstrittene Wirtschaftsgesetze", *Zukunft*, Heft 4, April 1952; "Konsumieren oder Investieren?" AZ 7.2. 1952, reprinted in Ausch 1963, 228–230; ÖeStA/AdR, BMfHuW, Wirtschaftsabteilung, Karton 39/H, Presseschaus 1949–1953, *Die Presse* 3.4.1952.

50 Johstone (1952); see also Seidel (2005), 566–568.

51 "Das Paradies der Kartelle" *AZ* 29.4. 1952 reprinted in Ausch 1963: 217–219.; "Marktfreiheit und Marktorganisation – im Licht amerikanischer Denkungsart." *Die Furche*, Nr. 19, 10.5. 1952, see also, "Antwort der Verantwortung. Eine Replik zum 'Johnstone'-Bericht", *Die Furche* Nr. 22, 30.5. 1952.

52 Sammlung der Erkenntnisse und wichtigsten Beschlüsse des Verfassungsgerichtshofes, 17 Heft, Jahr 1952, Nr. 2323 Erk. V. 17 Juni 1952, G 7/52; BGBl. Nr. 105/1951, 182–183, 187. ÖeStA/AdR, BKA, Ministerratsprotokolle, Ministerrat am 29.4. 1952.

53 ÖeStA/AdR, BKA, Ministerratsprotokolle, Ministerrat 6.5. 1952; 550 der Beilagen zu den Stenographischen Protokollen des Nationalrates (VI.GP), 7.5. 1952, "Regierungsvorlage" and "Erläuternde Bemerkungen"; 91. Sitzung des Nationalrates der Republik Österreich, (VI. GP.), 27.5.1952, Stenographisches Protokoll, 3497–3501 (citation on page 3501).

54 ÖeStA/AdR, BKA, Inneres, Wirtschaftsdirektorium, die Sitzungen 29–35 des WDs 14.7.1952–3.6. 1953.

55 ÖeStA/AdR, BKA, Ministerratsprotokolle, Ministerrat 9.2. 1954; ÖeStA/AdR, BMf-HuW, Wirtschaftsabteilung, Presseschaus 39/H, "Brauchen wir noch eine Bewirtschaftung?" *Artikeldienst, Bundeskammer der Gewerblichen Wirtschaft* 11.3. 1954; *Die Presse* 22.5. 1954.

56 E.g. Bergholm (2005), 339–340; Hyvämäki (1977); Paavonen (1987).

57 Vakauttamisohjelma. Talouspoliittisen suunnitteluneuvoston ehdotukset niihin liittyvine selvityksineen vakauttamistoimenpiteiksi linnarauhan 30.9 1951 päättyessä (Stabilisation Programme. Economic Policy Planning Council's Recommendations for Economic Stabilisation after the Expire of the Truce Agreement on 30.9 1951), hereafter Stabilisation Programme 1951, 7.

58 The discussion in this chapter is based on the material deposited in the National Archives / The Council of State Archives (Valtioneuvoston arkisto, hereafter VNA), komitea-arkistot (hereafter Committee archives), Talousneuvosto (talouspoliittinen suunnitteluneuvosto) (hereafter Economic Policy Planning Council), 1951–1954, VN 4266, IV-V, V-VII, folders 1,4, 20–24.

59 The state committees as an institution that originated from the Swedish era and had developed into the main arena of policy and law preparation in modernizing societies of both Finland and Sweden (with national variations, of course). For more, see Rainio-Niemi (2010).

60 Voipio (1991). It may be noted that even though the term *council* in many contexts evokes a connotation of a constitutionally anchored council, "a real state organ" and the term *committee* being reserved for more ad hoc, provisional organs, in Finland, none of the economic councils of the 1950s (or before) was 'real state organs' but provisional and based on the statute on the state committees (including various types of committees).

61 Bergholm (2005), 311–312, 339–341, 350–351, 369. According to Bergholm, the SAK was the initiator of both the truce of 1951 and the creation of the respective council.

62 On the other hand, within the framework of the Economic Policy Planning Council, the council staff and the prime minister really took efforts to facilitate compromises. Such facilitation, according to Bergholm, had not been seen before. Bergholm (2005), 351, 359–362.

63 NA/VNA, Committee archives, Economic Policy Planning Council, especially folders 1, 4, 20–24; Hokkanen (2002), 105–108; see also Suomi (1990), 200–210. At this stage, the relationship between the head of the council (Teuvo Aura) and the prime minister grew very close – just to break a few years later when the council leadership, in Kekkonen's view, had grown too confident of its independent capacity to steer the country's economic policy.

64 NA/VNA, Committee archives, Economic Policy Planning Council, folder 4. The significance of the withdrawal was retrospectively underscored by Teuvo Aura, the chair

of the economic council until 1956, in a lecture in April 1959. Deposited in NA/VNA, Committee archives, Talousohjelmakomitea 1956–1960, (hereafter Economic Programme Committee 1956–1960), folder 1, "PM. Talousneuvostojärjestelmä maassamme" by Teuvo Aura, 21.4 1959; Cf. also Hokkanen (2002), 94–154.

65 E.g. Bergholm (2005), 397, 399, 415.

66 Talouspolitiikan perusohjelma 1954, 74 (hereafter, the Programme for Economic Policy 1954), 73–73, 76, 83–83.

67 Asetus talousneuvostosta ja talouspoliittisesta suunnittelutoimistosta/ Förordning om det ekonomiska rådet och den ekonomisk-politiska planeringsbyrån 30.12. 1954. A 538/54). Suomen Asetuskokoelma 1954.

68 The tensions between the government and the council personified in the prime minister, presidential election candidate (and the president-to-be) Urho Kekkonen and the chair of the Economic Council Teuvo Aura. In the presidential campaign, Aura openly supported the candidacy of Sakari Tuomioja (centrist liberal National Progressive Party), who advocated less regulated economic policy line. The government was outspoken in its criticism against the council: the council was accused of having supported the attempt to vote down the Enabling Act in Parliament, to bring down the government and, furthermore, had almost succeeded. Regardless of the new statute-based status, the prime minister warned the council leadership of the exaggerated expectations concerning the council's role and position in relation to the country's government and the prime minister. See the letter by the government's Ministerial Committee for Economic Affairs to the Economic Council on 8 May 1956. VNA, Committee archives, Economic Programme Committee 1956–1960, folder 1; cf. Tiihonen (1990), 23.

69 Bergholm (2005). See also Suomi (1990); Polvinen (2003).

70 NA/VNA, Committee archives, Economic Programme Committee 1956–1960, folders 1–4; see especially the folders 3 and 4, including Talousohjelmakomitean osamietintö talousneuvostoista (report concerning the use of economic councils), 3.9.1959. This report scrutinising the practice of economic councils ended up with a recommendation that the current economic councils would be replaced by a more permanent yet also more narrowly mandated, strictly advisory Economic Policy Advisory Board. In addition, the report presented a draft law for a separate government Economic Research Institute. While the Economic Council was not abolished as suggested by the report, a new Economic Policy Planning Office was established in the Council of State's Office, yet this was no Economic Research Institute in the sense suggested by the draft law.

71 NA/VNA, Committee Archives, Economic Council, IV-VI, 1962–66, folders 6–7; Talousneuvoston mietintö lähivuosien kasvupolitiikasta. Helsinki, 1965, 53, 58, 75; Laki Talousneuvostosta / Lag om ekonom6iska rådet 2/1966 (14.1. 1966). Suomen Asetuskokoelma 1966.

References

Archives

Austrian State Archive, Vienna [AdR/ÖStA]

Bundeskanzleramt [BKA]
Ministerratsprotokolle 2. Republik
Zentral Büro für ERP Angelegenheiten [ZERP]
Wirtschaftsdirektorium [WD]
Wirtschaftliches-Ministerkomitee [WiMiKo]
Bundesministerium für Handel und Wiederaufbau [BMfHuW]
Wirtschaftsabteilung 1945–1954
Wirtschaftsabteilung/Presseschaus 1949–1953

The National Archives of Finland/ The Council of State Archives, Helsinki [NA/VNA]

Committee Archives
Economic Policy Planning Council 1951–1954
(*Talouspoliittinen suunnitteluneuvosto 1951–1954*)
Economic Programme Committee 1959–1960
(*Talousohjelmakomitea 1959–1960*)

Vienna City Library, Vienna

Tagblatt Archiv

Printed Source Collections

Parliament Proceedings

Stenographische Protokolle des Nationalrates der Republik Österreich
Beilagen zu den Stenographischen Protokollen des Nationalrates Republik Österreich [d.B.]

Bibliography

Alapuro, R. (ed.) (1998). *Raja railona: Näkökulmia suojeluskuntiin*. Helsinki: WSOY.

Andics, H. (1962). *Der Staat den Keiner wollte: Österreich 1918–1938*. Freiburg, Basel, Wien: Herder.

Aunesluoma, J. (2011). *Vapaakaupan tiellä: Suomen kauppa- ja integraatiopolitiikka maailmansodista EU-aikaan*. Helsinki: SKS.

Bergholm, T. (2003). *History of SAK*. Helsinki: SAK.

Bergholm, T. (2005). *Sopimusyhteiskunnan synty I: Työehtosopimusten läpimurrosta yleislakkoon: Suomen Ammattiyhdistysten Keskusliitto SAK, 1944–1956*. Helsinki: Otava.

Bergholm, T. (2015). *Kaksoissidoksen synty: Suomen työmarkkinasuhteiden toimintatavan muotoutuminen 1944–1969*. Tampere: Työväen historian ja perinteen tutkimuksen seura.

Binder, D. A. (1997). Der 'Christliche Ständestaat' Österreich 1934–1938. In R. Steininger, & M. Gehler (eds.), *Österreich im 20 Jahrhundert: Von der Monarchie bis zum Zweiten Weltkrieg* (pp. 203–256). Köln: Böhlau.

Capoccia, G. (2005). *Defending Democracy: Reactions to Extremism in Interwar Europe*. Baltimore, London: Johns Hopkins University Press.

Costa Pinto, A. (ed.) (2017). *Corporatism and Fascism: The Corporatist Wave in Europe*. London, New York: Routledge.

Couperus, S. (2019). Democracy Not Lost? Functional Democracy as a Panacea for Crisis in Interwar Europe. *Journal of European Studies*, *49*(3–4), 252–266.

Ebbinghaus, B., & Visser, J. (2000). *Trade Unions in Western Europe since 1945*. New York, London: Palgrave Macmillan.

Eichengreen, B. (2007). *The European Economy Since 1945: Coordinated Capitalism and Beyond*. Princeton: Princeton University Press.

Enderle-Burcel, G. (1995). Die österreichischen Parteien 1945 bis 1955. In R. Sieder, H. Steinert, & E. Talós (eds.), *Österreich 1945–1955: Gesellschaft, Politik, Kultur*. Wien: Verlag für Gesellschaftskritik.

Engelmann, F. C. (2001). *Government by Diplomacy: The Austrian Coalition 1945–1966*. Wien: Braumüller.

Evans, P. (2005). Harnessing the State: Rebalancing Strategies for Monitoring and Motivation. In M. Lange, & D. Rueschemeyer (eds.), *States and Development: Historical Antecedents of Stagnation and Advance* (pp. 26–47). New York: Palgrave Macmillan.

Gerlich, P. & Campbell, D. F. J. (2002). Austria: From Compromise to Authoritarianism. In R. Steininger, G. Bischof, & M. Gehler (eds.), *Austria in the Twentieth Century*. New Brunswick, NJ: Transaction Publishers.

Haapala, P., & Tikka, M. (2012). Revolution, Civil War and Terror in Finland in 1918. In R. Gerwarth, & J. Horne (eds.), *War in Peace: Paramilitary Violence in Europe after the Great War* (pp. 72–84). Oxford: Oxford University Press.

Haataja, L. (1993). *Suomen malli 1940–1956: Työmarkkinajärjestelmän ja poliittisen järjestelmän vuorovaikutussuhde neuvottelujen vakiintumisesta keskityksen purkautumiseen*. Helsinki: Työministeriö.

Hanisch, E. (1994). *Der Lange Schatten des Staates: Österreichische Gesellschaftsgeschichte im 20. Jahrhundert*. Wien: Ueberreuter.

Harrison, R. J. (1980). *Pluralism and Corporatism: The Political Evolution of Modern Democracies*. Sydney, Melbourne: Allen & Unwin.

Heikkinen, S. (2000). *Paper for the World: The Finnish Paper Mills' Association Finnpap 1918–1996*. Helsinki: Otava.

Heinisch, R. (2002). *Populism, Proporz, Parian: Austria turns to the Right*. New York: Nova Scotia.

Hentilä, S. (1999). Independence between East and West: How did Finland Survive as a Democracy? In T. S. Lehtonen (ed.), *Europe's Northern Frontier: Perspectives on Finland's Western Identity*. Jyväskylä: PS-Kustannus.

Hjerppe, R. (1989). *The Finnish Economy 1860–1985: Growth and Structural Change*. Helsinki: Bank of Finland.

Hjerppe, R., & Jalava, J. (2006). Economic Growth and Structural Change: A Century and a Half of Catching-up. In J. Ojala, J. Eloranta, & J. Jalava (eds.), *The Road to Prosperity. An Economic History of Finland*. Helsinki: SKS.

Hokkanen, K. (2002). *Kekkosen maalaisliitto: Maalaisliitto-Keskustan historia 4*. Helsinki: Otava.

Huxley, S. D. (1990). *Constitutionalist Insurgency in Finland: Finnish Passive Resistance as a case of Nonmilitary Struggle in the European Resistance Tradition*. Helsinki: SHS.

Hyvämäki, L. (1977). *Valtioneuvoston historia 1917–1966, II: Ministeristöjen historia 1939–1966*. Helsinki: Valtion painatuskeskus.

Jääskeläinen, M. (1980). Sodanjälkeinen eduskunta (valtiopäivät 1945–1963). In *Suomen Kansanedustuslaitoksen Historia, 8*. Helsinki: Valtion painatuskeskus.

Johnstone, H. W. (1952). *The Restraint of Competition in the Austrian Economy*. Vienna: The Office of the U.S. High Commissioner.

Judt, T. (2005). *Postwar: A History of Europe Since 1945*. New York: Penguin Books.

Jussila, O. (1999). Finland as a Grand Duchy, 1809–1917. In O. Jussila, S. Hentilä, & J. Nevakivi (eds.), *From Grand Duchy to a Modern State: A Political History of Finland since 1809*. Bloomsbury, London: Hurst & Company.

Karvonen, L., & Lindström, U. (1997). Red-Green Crisis Agreements: The Great Depression in Scandinavia in Comparative Perspective. In V. Helander, & S. Sandberg (eds.), *Festskrift till Krister Ståhlberg*. Åbo: Åbo Akademi University Press.

Katzenstein, P. J. (1984). *Corporatism and Change: Austria, Switzerland and the Politics of Industry*. Ithaca, NY: Cornell University Press.

Katzenstein, P. J. (1985). *Small States in World Markets: Industrial Policy in Europe*. Ithaca and London: Cornell University Press.

Kauppinen T. (1994). *The Transformation of Finnish Labour Relations*. Labour Policy Studies 81. Helsinki: Ministry of Labour.

Kettunen, P. (2001). The Nordic Welfare State in Finland. *Scandinavian Journal of History, 26*(3), 225–247.

Kettunen, P. (2002). Suunnitelmataloudesta kansalliseen innovaatiojärjestelmään. In H. Blomberg, M. Hannikainen, & P. Kettunen (eds.), *Lama-kirja: Näkökulmia 1990-luvun talouskriisiin ja sen historiallisiin konteksteihin* (pp. 15–45). Turku: Kirja-Aurora.

Kettunen, P. (2005). The Power of International Comparison: A Perspective on the Making and Challenging of the Nordic Welfare State. In N. F. Christiansen et al. (eds.), *The Nordic Model of Welfare: A Historical Reappraisal*. Copenhagen: Museum Tusculanum Press.

Klausen, J. (1998). *War and Welfare: Europe and the United States, 1945 to the Present*. New York, London: Palgrave Macmillan.

Kuprian, H. J. W. (2002). On the Threshold of Twentieth Century: State and society in Austria before World War I. In R. Steininger, G. Bischof, & M. Gehler (eds.), *Austria in the Twentieth Century*. New Brunswick, NJ: Transaction Publishers.

Lavery, J. (2006). *The History of Finland*. Santa Barbara, California: Greenwood Press.

Lerner, M. (1939/1943). *It is Later than You Think: The Need for a Militant Democracy*. New York: The Viking Press.

Loewenstein, K. (1939). Book Review (Lerner 1939). *American Political Science Review, 33*(3), 519–521.

Maderthaner, W. (2002). 12 February 1934: Social Democracy and Civil War. In R. Steininger, G. Bischof, & M. Gehler (eds.), *Austria in the Twentieth Century*. New Brunswick, NJ: Transaction Publishers.

Maier, C. S. (1975). *Recasting Bourgeois Europe: Stabilization in France, Germany and Italy in the decade after WWI*. Princeton: Princeton University Press.

Marcus, N. (2018). *Austrian Reconstruction and the Collapse of Global Finance, 1921–31*. Cambridge, Massachusetts: Harvard University Press.

Mattl, S. (1984). Die Finanzdiktatur: Wirtschaftspolitik in Österreich 1933–1938. In E. Talós, & W. Neugebauer (eds.), *Austrofaschismus: Beiträge über Politik, Ökonomie und Kultur 1934–1938* (pp. 133–159). Vienna: Literaturverlag.

Milward, A., & Sorensen, V. (1993). Interdependence or Integration? A National Choice. In A. Milward et al. (eds.), *The Frontier of National Sovereignty: History and Theory 1945–1992*. London, New York: Routledge.

Milward, A. S. (1984). *The Reconstruction of Western Europe 1945–51*. London: Methuen & Co. Ltd.

Milward, A. S. (2000). *The European Rescue of the Nation State* (2nd ed.). London, New York: Routledge.

Molina, O., & Rhodes, M. (2002). Corporatism: The Past, Present and Future of a Concept. *Annual Review of Political Science, 5*, 305–331.

Nevakivi, J. (1999). From the Continuation War to the Present, 1944–1999. In O. Jussila, S. Hentilä, & J. Nevakivi (eds.), *From Grand Duchy to a Modern State: A Political History of Finland since 1809*. Bloomsbury, London: Hurst & Company.

Offe, C. (1981). The Attribution of Public Status to Interest Groups: Observations on the West German Case. In S. Berger (ed.), *Organizing Interests in Western Europe: Pluralism, Corporatism, and the Transformation of Politics*. Cambridge: Cambridge University Press.

Ojala, J., Eloranta, J., & Jalava, J. (eds.) (2006). *The Road to Prosperity: An Economic History of Finland*. Helsinki: SKS.

Paavonen, T. (1987). *Talouspolitiikka ja työmarkkinakehitys Suomessa toisen maailmansodan jälkeisellä jälleenrakennuskaudella vuosina 1944–1950*. Turku: Turun yliopisto.

Paavonen, T. (1998). *Suomalaisen protektionismin viimeinen vaihe: Suomen ulkomaankauppa- ja integraatiopolitiikka 1945–1961*. Helsinki: SHS.

Pekkarinen, J. (1992). Corporatism and Economic Performance in Sweden, Norway and Finland. In J. Pekkarinen, M. Pohjola, & B. Rowthorn (eds.), *Social Corporatism: The Superior Economic Model?* Oxford: Clarendon Press.

Polvinen, T. (1996). *Imperial Borderland*. Durham, NC: Duke University Press.

Rainio-Niemi, J. (2010). State Committees in Finland in Historical Comparative Perspective. In R. Alapuro, & H. Stenius (eds.), *Nordic Associations in a European Perspective* (pp. 241–267). Baden-Baden: Nomos.

Rainio-Niemi, J. (2019). Managing Fragile Democracy: Constitutionalist Ethos and Constrained Democracy in Finland. In M. Conway, & J. Rainio-Niemi (eds.), Special Issue on Fragile Democracy and the Nordic Countries, *Journal of Modern European History*, *17*(4), 519–538.

Rauchensteiner, M. (1987). *Die Zwei: Die grosse Koalition in Österreich 1945–1966*. Wien: ÖBV.

Rehn, O. (1996). *Corporatism and Industrial Competitiveness in Small European States: Austria, Finland and Sweden 1945–1995*. PhD Thesis. Oxford.

Rothstein, B. (2011). *The Quality of Government: Corruption Social Trust and Inequality in International Perspective*. Chicago: The University of Chicago Press.

Schmitter, P. C. (1981). Still the Century of Corporatism? In P. C. Schmitter, & G. Lehmbruch (eds.), *Trends Toward Corporatist Intermediation* (2nd ed.) New York: Sage Publications.

Schmitter, P. C. (1985). Neo-Corporatism and the State. In G. Wyn (ed.), *The Political Economy of Corporatism*. New York, London: Macmillan.

Seidel, H. (2005). *Österreichs Wirtschaft und Wirtschaftspolitik nach dem Zweiten Weltkrieg*. Wien: Manz-Verlag.

Selovuori, J. (ed.) (1985). *Power and Bureaucracy in Finland 1809–1998*. Helsinki: Edita.

Stourzh, G., & Grandner, M. (eds.) (1986). *Historische Wurzeln der Sozialpartnerschaft*. Wien: Verlag für Geschichte und Politik.

Sully, M. (1989). The Austrian Way? In A. Pelinka, & G. Plasser (eds.), *The Austrian Party System*. Boulder, CO: Westview.

Suomen asetuskokoelma (1954). Asetus talousneuvostosta ja talouspoliittisesta suunnittelutoimistosta/Förordning om det ekonomiska rådet och den ekonomisk-politiska planeringsbyrån 30.12.1954. A 538/54). Helsinki: Valtioneuvoston kirjapaino.

Suomen asetuskokoelma (1966). Laki Talousneuvostosta/Lag om ekonomiska rådet 2/1966 (14.1.1966). Helsinki: Valtioneuvoston kirjapaino.

Suomi, J. (1990). *Kuningastie: Urho Kekkonen 1950–1956*. Helsinki: Otava.

Talós, E. (1985). Sozialpartnerschaft: Zur Entwicklung und Entwicklungsdynamic kooperativ-konzertierter Politik in Österreich. In P. Gerlich, E. Grande, & W. C. Müller (eds.), *Sozialpartnerschaft in der Krise: Leistungen und Grenzen des Neokorporatismus in Österreich*. Köln: Böhlau.

Talós, E. (1993). Entwicklung, Kontinuität und Wandel der Sozialpartnerschaft. In E. Talós (ed.), *Sozialpartnerschaft: Kontinuität und Wandel eines Modells*. Wien: Verlag für Gesellschaftskritik.

Talós, E. (1997). Sozialpartnerschaft: Kooperation – Konzentierung – politische Regulierung. In H. Dachs et al. (eds.), *Handbuch des politischen Systems Österreich: Die zweite Republik*. Wien: Manz-Verlag.

Talós, E. & Kittel, B. (1995). Sozialpartnerschaft: zur Konstituierung einer Grundsäule der Zweiten Republik. In R. Sieder, H. Steinert, & E. Talós (eds.), *Österreich 1945–1955: Gesellschaft, Politik, Kultur*. Wien: Verlag für Gesellschaftskritik.

Talós, E. & Kittel, B. (1996). Roots of Austro-Corporatism: Institutional Preconditions and Cooperation Before and After 1945. In G. Bischof, & A. Pelinka (eds.), *Austro-Corporatism: Past, Present, Future*. Contemporary Austrian Studies vol. 4. New Brunswick, NJ: Transaction Publisher.

Talós, E. & Neugebauer, W. (eds.) (1984). *Austrofaschismus: Beiträge über Politik, Ökonomie und Kultur 1934–1938*. Wien: Verlag für Gesellschaftskritik.

Talousohjelmakomitea. Talousohjelmakomitean osamietintö talousneuvostoista (1959). Kom. 1959:47 (mon.), Helsinki. [The State Committee Report on the Economic Councils].

Talousohjelmakomitea. Talouspolitiikan perusohjelma (1954). Helsinki. [Programme for Economic Policy].

Talouspoliittinen suunnitteluneuvosto. Vakauttamisohjelma (1951). Talouspoliittisen suunnitteluneuvoston ehdotukset niihin liittyvine selvityksineen vakauttamistoimenpiteiksi linnarauhan 30.9 1951 päättyessä. Kom. 1951:13, Helsinki. [Stabilisation Programme 1951].

Tepora, T., & Roselius, A. (eds.) (2014). *The Finnish Civil War 1918: History, Memory, Legacy*. Leiden: Brill.

Tiihonen, S. (1985). *Valtioneuvosto koordinoijana: Teoria ja käytäntö vuosina 1939–1956*. Helsinki: Valtionvarainministeriö.

Tweraser, K. (1995). The Politics of Productivity and Corporatism: The Late Marshall Plan in Austria, 1950–1954. In G. Bischof (ed.), *Austria in the Nineteen Fifties*. New Brunswick, NJ: Transaction Publishers.

Voipio, I. B. (1991). *Talousneuvostot 1920 – sekä vastaavat eräissä Euroopan maissa*. VATT Discussion Papers. Helsinki: Government Institute for Economic Research.

Wuokko, M. et al. (2019). *Loputtomat kihlajaiset: Yritykset ja kolmikantakorporatismi Suomessa 1940–2020*. Helsinki: Siltala.

Zilliacus, K. O. K. (1995). *Finländsk kommunism i ljuset av väljarstod 1945–1991*. Helsingfors: Finska Vetenskaps-Societeten.

7 The German welfare state between path dependency, federalism, and political shocks, 19th and 20th centuries

Marcel Boldorf

Introduction

Germany is often cited as the world's first national state that provided a state-guaranteed system of social security. Indeed, the three pillars of social insurance, the health, the accident and the pensions' insurances were introduced as early as the 1880s to respond to problems of social fragmentation and class conflicts at the onset of Germany's industrialization. Germany's case is frequently mentioned as the prototype of a top-down model, resulting from industrial backwardness. The first aim of this chapter is to investigate the origins of the German welfare state and its implementation in the last decades of the 19th century. After that, the development of social security is explored in the long run. Although German politics were shaken by a series of shocks, such as the Nazi dictatorship, the welfare state had remarkable continuity. The reasons for that will be analyzed as an interplay between democratic or authoritarian regimes and the economy. From the beginnings of the welfare state, the redistribution of resources can be seen as its genuine duty. In the course of the 20th century and especially after World War II, the German welfare state turned to other perspectives: Under the influence of Keynesianism, social policy was regarded as a means for social planning in order to form the society. However, path dependency was a main characteristic of the German welfare state, and social policy was a preservative element which guaranteed social stability.

The development of Germany's social security system was embedded in a period of economic growth that began in the second half of the 19th century. The best indicator to measure increasing prosperity is the real wages which started to rise in the 1880s.

Within the long-lasting period of real wages growth, a significant period of stagnation can be identified. In the first half of the 20th century, the level of real wages remained on the same level, as the comparison of the 1913 and 1950 data shows. In the inter-war period, the level of pre-war real wages could only be reached in 1927, showing a tendency to a further rise, which was abruptly stopped by the Great Depression. In the Nazi era, real wages did not rise again despite a boom, which was exclusively based on the state demand for armament goods.

DOI: 10.4324/9780429503870-8

Table 7.1 Germany – real wages index (1913 = 100), 1820–1990

1820	64
1840	57
1860	60
1870	65
1880	58
1900	87
1913	**100**
1927/28	100
1929	112
1938	110
1950	116
1960	190
1970	330
1990	450

Source: Rainer Gömmel, Realeinkommen in Deutschland. Ein internationaler Vergleich (1810–1914), Nuremberg: Self-publishing, 1979 [also published in: Cologne: GESIS Datenarchiv, 2003, ZA 8167, www.gesis.org/histat/]; Christoph Buchheim: Einführung in die Wirtschaftsgeschichte, Munich: Beck, 1997, pp. 124–125 (real weekly wages). For the period after 1945, the data for the Federal Republic of Germany are shown.

The stagnation of growth ended after World War II, leading to three decades of growing prosperity which had never been experienced before. Considered as an economic miracle by contemporary witnesses, it was rather a period of reconstruction based on a spillover of human capital.[1] The accumulated know-how led to an outstanding growth of productivity and over-averaged growth rates until the long-term trend of secular growth was reached in the 1970s. Thus, two phases of real wages development can be distinguished: from 1950 to 1970, West German real wages almost tripled, whereas in the next 20 years they only rose by one third. This corresponded to the normalization of growth rates. The contemporary German politicians, however, sought for a long time to return to the outstanding growth rates of the post-war decades.

Looking back to the period before World War I, a period of continuous growth of real wages can be identified from the 1880s onwards. The decades before were characterized by stagnation, and between 1870 and 1880 even by a sharp decline of real wages. The onset of German industrialization was followed by an economic depression, which was regarded with scepticism by the bourgeois classes. They feared the consequences of migration, urbanization, the growing of an industrial proletariat and their political organizations. Germany's first steps of building up a social welfare state, however, were rather settled in the following period which held out in prospect a rise of wealth and prosperity.

The chapter is structured as follows: After explaining social fragmentation at the onset of Germany's Industrial Revolution, the three pillars of social security (health, accident and pension insurance), the core of the welfare state, are analyzed in the long run. After that, the importance of political and economic breaks in the era of the World Wars will be discussed. However, path dependency was the most significant characteristic of the German welfare state in the 20th century. Due to the German partition, the two German states were in a social policy competition. To conclude, the socio-political paradigms of the German unification and the transition to the 21st century are described.

Social fragmentation at the onset of German industrialization

In the European context, Germany was a latecomer in the process of industrialization. Alexander Gerschenkron developed the idea that Germany's relative backwardness made a jump necessary to catch up to the United Kingdom.[2] The introduction of a system of social security might be interpreted as an indispensable prerequisite for a rapid industrial transformation. When more closely examined, we can get aware that Germany's welfare traditions were reaching far back to the early modern period and the Middle Ages. However, the social reform of the 1880s coincided with a distinctive turn to conservatism, driven by Reich Chancellor Bismarck, one decade after the foundation of the German nation state.

Among the retarding factors of Germany's economic development in the first half of the 19th century, the territorial-political fragmentation has to be evoked. The German Confederation, created in 1815, still consisted of 40 single states, each having customs boundaries and its own fiscal and coinage system. The industrial gap between the western and eastern parts of the German territories was important. Germany lacked in fast communication means, and the transportation services were undeveloped. As external factors, the high competition on international markets must be evoked as well as the technological advance of the British industry. Therefore, Germany's growth was primarily extensive, just like England's at the first stage of its Industrial Revolution. In the 1840s, the income per capita was rather low compared to Britain. However, the obstacles to industrialization lost in importance because of improvements such as the German customs union, railway construction and knowledge enhancements through scientific research.

The social reality was characterized by a deep fragmentation and a rather unequal income distribution. In the period preceding the 1848 March Revolution, more than half of the inhabitants of German towns lived beyond the threshold of poverty. In Cologne, one third of the population was listed in the poor register, further 40 per cent lived in an emergency situation. In Mannheim, 45 per cent of the 22,500 inhabitants were in need, among them the majority of factory workers. The tax payment rates also give hints on poverty: In Berlin, 75 to 80 per cent of the craftsmen were free of tax in the 1840s because of their low incomes. In Hamburg, too, two thirds of the workers were tax-exempted because their income was below the local minimum wages.[3] In the countryside the situation was even worse: It is estimated that one a fifth of the population disposed of sufficient revenues to make their living.[4] Their situation even deteriorated when the commons were privatized in the course of the Prussian agrarian reforms.

According to the General Law Code for the Prussian States (Allgemeines Landrecht für die preußischen Staaten) of 1794, the hometown residency (Heimatprinzip) was the basis for the organization of poor relief.[5] It delegated the task of poor relief to local municipalities and cities. Only people who had acquired local citizenship were entitled to receive assistance. In the period of early industrialization, the hometown relief residence system frequently failed because of the increase of inner-German migration. When people left their homes seeking job opportunities and fell into poverty far from home, they had to return to their birthplace to claim poor relief. On their arrival, the claims were often rejected because of their long absence. The new industrial cities were keen on maintaining the hometown residency system because it gave the opportunity to deny the poor's claims of relief.

In Prussia, the law on the right of residence of 1842 abolished the home relief residency.[6] Instead, it defined rules for the integration of arriving migrants. Persons older than 24 years old had to stay more than two years in a municipality in order to acquire the right of residence. When a person in need possessed the residential right of relief, the town authorities could not refuse assistance to him. The law reform was primarily pushed by the agrarian lobby in the east which wanted to avoid the assistance of the people who had moved westward to the industrial centres.[7] The Prussian state reacted to the new requirements of the industrial society where mobility had risen. However, the financial problem was translocated to the places of arrival: Since the 1840s, and even more severe in the 1850s, the rising industrial towns lacked in financial means to provide relief for the residents who claimed public assistance. The problem was particularly serious for the so-called labouring poor – domestic servants, journeymen, day labourers or even factory workers. These workers were not able to earn a living, although they were working. Their wages were so low that they could hardly save any money for the strokes of fate. In the case of sickness or accident, they fell into complete distress because they were lacking financial means for medical care or personal aid.[8]

In that period, Prussia and other German states suffered from the effects of the last Malthusian crisis in the middle of the 1840s. It was due to constant population growth and a shortage of available food and employment opportunities. There was an ongoing shift of employment towards the industrial sector, and the importance of wage labour increased. The tension between population growth and labour supply had two consequences: First, open unemployment grew without being measurable because of the lack of adequate statistical sources. Second, hidden unemployment existed by downgrading workplaces, wage reductions, an extension of the work time and the substitution of male workers by female and child labour. Unemployment as a severe social problem could gradually be remedied with industrial expansion and the increase of labour supply.[9]

In view of the uncertain income conditions, all the members of a worker's household had to earn money to provide the basis of existence. If one wage earner became ill or disabled – especially the main breadwinner – the financial means turned to be insufficient to beware the family from falling into poverty. Even under normal conditions, workers were incapable to save money for their retirement and thus, poverty in old age was quite common. The early industrialization changed little in this regard, and in the middle of the 19th century, the traditional main reasons for pauperization such as illness, disability and old age were still prevailing.[10]

Summing up, the following new risks can be noticed in 19th-century society with its growing number of wage workers: (1) The workers' only means of subsistence was to sell their labour power for a wage; this being a fundamental difference to the former agrarian society, (2) new risks arose through the spread of industrial work, for instance the necessity of insurance against accidents at work, (3) family ties lost in importance, sharpening the traditional problem of old-age poverty. Thus, personal retirement arrangements were required, (4) the income situation did not allow to make savings for future needs.

The intellectual discourse of the German historical school of economics attacked the tyranny of Manchester Liberalism. The economist Adolph Wagner held in 1871 a public speech on social reforms which draw nationwide attention.[11] As other reformers, he claimed an active role of the state in a more and more fragmented society during a period of heavy industrialization. These ideas were not far from those of Reich Chancellor Bismarck. The latter one propagated the concept of a moderate and rational state socialism. However, this thinking did not correspond at all with progressive socialism but meant a conservative political turn. The reform-oriented conservatives enlarged the conception of property rights to public and state ownership. In the liberals' eyes, this was a form of state interventionism which diverged from freedom and progress. Conservatives such as Bismarck, however, had a patriarchal vision of the redistribution of resources: a concrete example for this were his plans to use the revenues from the state's monopoly on tobacco taxes to build up a pension scheme under the supervision of his government.[12]

Bismarck capitalized in 1878 two failed assassination attempts on the German emperor to persecute social democrats. While the Anti-Socialist Laws were debated in Parliament, the Prussian State's Ministry (Staatsministerium) was elaborating plans for the introduction of a social security system. They included measures for the integration of the working classes into the national state, thus overcoming the traditional poor legislation. Bismarck wanted to make the workers small state pensioners, even without claiming their co-financing by paying contributions. His concept of social security was part of an overall strategy: Internal nation building was linked to the idea of an authoritarian state which guaranteed security by social solidarity. Beyond that, the conservative turn consisted in extending the bureaucracy with reliable civil servants in order to regulate economic and social issues. By revitalizing the tradition of the strong state, the reforms of the 1848 revolution should be weakened and the political authority be consolidated.[13]

The three pillars of social security in the long run

When opening the fifth German Reichstag in the Berlin City Palace on 17 November 1881, Chancellor Bismarck read out a proclamation of Emperor William I, which reacted to the rejection of the first proposal of accident insurance by the Reichstag. This imperial message requested the parliament to deal again with the matter of social legislation. The government expressed its conviction that "the remedy of social ills cannot be exclusively achieved through the repression of Social Democratic excesses but must at the same time envisage constructive measures for the improvement of the workers' welfare".[14] With reference to workers' life risks, the Imperial Message developed a program to create insurance against accidents, illness and the risks of ageing for the working population, especially for industrial workers. The aim was the pacification of social conflicts, "to leave Our Fatherland new and permanent guarantees for its internal peace and to those in need that greater security and more generous assistance to which they are entitled". These prospective social reforms presented a mixture of authoritarian and autonomous structures. On the one hand, there was statutory insurance regulated by public law that exercised "caring compulsion". On the other hand, self-administration was at the base of organization, as it had been the case in the ancient social systems of the guilds. Some points were actually new: The social insurance introduced the right to receive benefits without testing indigence. Thus, the state recognized the existence of social causes for misery without blaming the deserving poor of being responsible for it. Thus, the promotion of individual welfare became a task of society.[15]

The social legislation introduced in the 1880s took account of the major life risks of workers and their families, which were divided into the four categories illness, accident, invalidity and old age, unemployment; they became the classical pillars of the German social policy. The subsequently installed compulsory state-run insurance system addressed three of the previously mentioned collective life risks: the health insurance of 1883, the accident insurance of 1884 and the invalidity and old-age insurance of 1889. Only in 1927 were the Unemployment Insurance Act and in 1994 the Long-term Care Insurance Act added. The following subsections give a longitudinal overview of the long-term development of the three fundamental pillars of the German social insurance from the end of the 19th to the beginning of the 21st century.

1 Health insurance

The Health Insurance Act (Gesetz über die Krankenversicherung der gewerblichen Arbeiter) of 15 June 1883 established a compulsory insurance regulated by imperial law and granted free medical treatment and medicaments for wage workers. Its organization took up the system of the traditional provident funds, especially those of craftspeople and guilds. Although the Act of 1883 stipulated the installation of local health insurance funds, they were only gradually established.[16] Two thirds of the insurance were financed by the workers, one third by the employer. Until the turn of the century, about 10 million of compulsorily insured persons were registered, the vast majority of them being male (see Table 7.2). From the third day of illness, the insured received sick payments up to a maximum of 13 weeks, as well as the expenses for medical and pharmaceutical treatments, after having consulted a contracted practitioner.[17] In 1913, by far the largest part of expenditures of the national health insurance (41 per cent) were spent to cover the loss of earnings due to illness. Twenty-four per cent of the rest of the expenditures were paid for medical treatments; more than 15 per cent, respectively, for medicaments and residential health facilities; and 4 per cent for pregnant women, women in child-bed and death assistance.[18] In the course of the century, along with an enormous increase of expenditures, these shares were subject to change: In 2003, that is, 90 years later, only about 5 per cent of the total expenditures were used for sick pay, whereas the largest parts were spent on residential health facilities (31 per cent), pharmaceutical (26 per cent) and medical treatments (21.5 per cent).[19] Meanwhile, the health insurance funds had to spend 6 per cent of the expenditures on administration. During the 20th century, the expenditures of the statutory health insurance increased, expressed as a share of the corresponding gross domestic product (GDP), from 0.5 per cent (1900) to 6.2 per cent (2000). This structural shift from sick pay to medicaments and residential health facilities corresponded to the growing cost-intensive provision of high-technology medicine.

Until 1925, the statistics only included the local, regional, company and craftspeople health insurances, and in 1927, the insurances for miners and in 1928, the maritime health insurance were added. During the Great Depression, the number of members decreased, and until 1931, it had fallen to 21.1 million,

Table 7.2 Membership in the German health insurance, 1890–2000

	Members (in millions)	*Male*	*Female*	*Members, as % of the population*
1890	6.6	5.3	1.3	13
1910	13.1	9.4	3.7	20
1925	18.2	11.3	7	29
1935	19.5	13	6.5	29
1955	18.3	11.9	6.4	37
1980	35.4	19.5	15.9	57
2000	51	25.8	25.2	62

Source: Marcel Boldorf, Sozialpolitik, in: Thomas Rahlf (ed.), Deutschland in Daten. Zeitreihen zur Historischen Statistik. Bonn: Bundeszentrale für politische Bildung, 2015, p. 90.

that is one third of the total population. The absolute and relative decline in membership until 1935 was a result of the Nazi's expulsion of certain independent professions from the compulsory insurance. Even more important was the refusal of benefit entitlements to stigmatized social groups.

After some disparate evolutions during the period of occupation, the first chancellor of the Federal Republic of Germany, Konrad Adenauer, pushed to maintain the multiple-payer health insurance or to re-establish it. His government also restored the self-administration by employees and employers which had been abolished by the Nazi regime.[20] One of the first legislative measures in the early 1950s, was to extend the insurance coverage to refugees and expellees for the former German territories in the east, to returning German soldiers and German Democratic Republic (GDR) refugees. The largest rise in members was caused in 1957 by the Pension Reform that included all old-age pensioners in the statutory health insurance. The social-liberal government extended the insurance coverage to prevention and long-time care, and in 1972 the peasants and in 1975 the university students were included in the national health insurance.[21] By the end of the century, the statutory compulsory health insurance had expanded to larger parts of the population, including more and more women. In 2000, for the first time ever, fewer than half of the members were male and women were the majority.

2 Accident insurance

In the 1880s, the political debate centred on the question of whether the accident insurance should be state-independent and financed by premiums or if it should be funded by Reich subsidies.[22] Bismarck opted for a statutory insurance which would let the workers without any premium payment. At the end, the installed system was financed only through employers' contributions and without state subsidies. Its carriers became the Employers' Liability Insurance Associations (Berufsgenossenschaften), regulated by public law and including the employers of the insured companies. All blue- and white-collar workers who earned up to 2000 marks per year were insured compulsorily. The Imperial Liability Act (Reichshaftpflichtgesetz) of 1871 had maintained the principle that workers were only entitled to receive benefits when the employer could be made responsible for the damage. In case of accidents caused by force majeure or by the carelessness of the worker, the casualty would not receive any benefit. The new accident insurance replaced these regulations by the right to receive benefits, thus socializing the risks.[23]

At the beginning, the accident insurance had only been conceived for the manufacturing sector. Successively, more occupational groups were included, for example in 1884/85 the national mail and the telegraph administration, the railways, the navy and the army; in 1886 the agriculture and forestry sectors; and in 1887 the construction industry and the maritime transport sector.[24] The number of insured persons continued to increase because the accidents insurance associations of other sectors joint it, and other groups such as soldiers and prisoners were included. By the turn of the century, the accident insurance had almost 20 million members and until World War I about 30 million. The organization was quite scattered: In 1913, there were 58 industrial and 49 agricultural Employers' Liability Insurance Associations, plus 561 on the local level.[25]

In the inter-war period, the coverage was extended to commercial and administration employees and to individual professions. The risks now included the registration of occupational diseases and accidents on the way to and from work. The benefits covered medical treatments to restore the capacity for work. During the Nazi era, the statistically relevant changes were related to the approval of more occupational diseases and the inclusion of accidents in vocational training. Altogether, the realignment of the organizational structure was less significant than in the health insurance.[26] In the Federal Republic, the accident insurance was reorganizing according to the traditional structures and only slightly modified by the Accident Insurance Act (Unfallversicherungsgesetz) of 1952. One of the social-liberal coalition's modifications was the extension of the coverage to schoolchildren and day-care centres.[27] In this sector of social security, a continuous expansion of the group of entitled persons can be observed, too.

3 Pension insurance

The Invalidity and Old-Age Insurance Act (Gesetz über die Invaliditäts- und Altersversicherung), published on 22 June 1889, applied to all workers and employees over 16 years with an annual income below 2000 marks. However, by the end of the century, pensions were mainly paid in cases of invalidity and only granted to secure the livelihood for people who had reached the age of 70. The contribution rate for pensions was only 1.7 per cent of the work income, and it was paid in equal shares by both workers and employers. Accordingly, the benefits were low, and in case of death, they were not meant to maintain the survivors (widows and orphans).[28]

The old-age and invalidity pension had two components: first, the Reich subsidy (Reichszuschuss), a uniform pay of 50 marks per year which reflected Bismarck's paternalistic motives; second, the insurance-based pension which, in case of invalidity, consisted of a basic amount of 60 marks and an increment which depended on the contribution period and the paid-in deposit. The old-age pension only consisted of the variable amount. In this case, the basic amount was regarded as dispensable, since the old-age pensioners were supposed to receive higher pensions because of their longer insurance period. For many years, the old-age pension was just seen as a pension for invalidity caused by the decreasing ability to work. For political reasons, however, the conditions for entitlement were extended, and the benefits were funded by current contributions; that is there was a pay-as-you-go financing plus a state subsidy. At the same time, funds were built up in order to convert the insurance, in the long term, into a capital-based system. Given the low benefits, the pension insurance built up a considerable capital stock until 1913 which was, however, annihilated by the war inflation.[29] Benefits for orphans and widows were only introduced by the Reich Insurance Act (Reichsversicherungsordnung) of July 1911. Coverage was however only given in the case of invalidity. The employee insurance (Angestelltenversicherung), established for white-collar workers in the same year, worked without Reich subsidies until 1945. Gradually, the retirement age was lowered to 65 years. Despite the state subsidies during the inflation of 1922/23, the pensions sank into insignificance. The new beginning was based again on the pay-as-you-go principle. Up until the Nazi dictatorship, financial recovery was of top priority. After achieving full employment in 1937, there was a greater scope for extension, which was carried out according to the selection criteria of the Nazi regime.[30]

An example for such an extension was the Wehrmacht Welfare and Maintenance Act (Wehrmachtfürsorge und -versorgungsgesetz) of 1938, symbolizing the remilitarization of the war victims' care.[31] The act considered the military service as a service of honour and replaced the war victims' pension with a disability allowance (Versehrtengeld) what, in a certain way, linked up with the military regulations of the German Empire. A differentiated system of allowances led to the fact that the basic pension lost relevance and that military aspects like rank became more important to determine the amount of benefits. Compared to the victims of World War I, the soldiers of the new Wehrmacht received a more differentiated and higher pension. Furthermore, the care for several groups of disabled civilians was regulated on a military basis. Among them there were the members of the Reich Labour Service, the participants of the "national uprising" (Volkssturm), the SS and the police. After the war, the Allied abolished immediately these kinds of military elements added by the Nazi administration.

After World War II, the dual organization of the pension insurance for employees and the workers' insurance funds was maintained. In the currency reform of 1948, pensions were exchanged at a ratio of RM 1: DM 1, while the rate for the remainder was RM 10: DM 1. The Social Insurance Adjustment Act (Sozialversicherungs-Anpassungsgesetz) of 17 June 1949 introduced a minimum pension to the old-age and invalidity insurance which was higher than the standard rates of poor relief.[32] The benefits for blue- and white-collar workers were partially aligned: The workers' widows were now entitled to pensions. Regarding the requirement to receive invalidity pensions, the degree of reduced work ability was lowered from two thirds to 50 per cent. In 1953, the right of getting benefits was extended to the German refugees and expellees from the former eastern Reich territories.

A milestone in the development of social policy was the Pensions Reform that concluded Konrad Adenauer's second chancellorship. In January 1957, a majority in the Bundestag, including the social democrats but not the liberal Free Democratic Party (FDP), voted for the reform act. Pensions were no longer meant to be a supplement for elderly citizens but a wage replacement;

pensioners thus benefitted from economic growth. The average pension level increased immediately by 60 per cent, and since 1959 the pensions were annually adjusted to the real wage development. The new system was based on the idea of an intergenerational contract; for example the working population paid for the pensions of the retired generation. In this pay-as-you-go system, the collected contributions were directly spent to finance the pensions and supplemented by increasing Federal subsidies.[33]

In 1957 the coverage of the statutory pension insurance was extended to peasants and in 1960 to self-employed craftspeople. The Pension Reform Act (Rentenreformgesetz) of 1972 introduced, for the first time, a flexibilization of the pension age which allowed an earlier retirement. Under Chancellor Willy Brandt, the statutory insurance was opened to freelancers and housewives; they were given the opportunity to build up pension rights by paying voluntary contributions.[34]

During the 1980s, the effective retirement age declined, according to collective agreements on the level of companies. In 1989, almost every second male pensioner retired early. After the unification of the two German states, about 4 million pensioners from the former GDR were integrated into the West German pension system. With effect from 1 January 1992, the Pensions Transition Act (Rentenüberleitungsgesetz) applied the system of wage-related pensions to the territory of the new federal states. Until 2001, the age threshold was gradually raised, and the number of early retirements declined. In November 2002, the Commission for Sustainable Financing of the Social Insurance System, later known as Rürup Commission, started a discussion about raising the retirement age up to 67.[35] The successive reduction of incentives for early retirement led to the result that, in 2013, among the 60- to 65-year-olds, there were once again more people at work than retired.[36]

Political breaks: the Weimar Republic and national socialism

Beyond the continuities in the core German of social security, there were significant breaks in the history of German social policy. One important caesura was the military defeat of 1918. The demission of the emperor Wilhelm II entailed a shift of the political forces to the left. The trade unions succeeded in consolidating the power that they had gained during the war. They had sent representatives into the state bureaucracy and managed to be recognized as equal tariff partners. In order to improve the economic and social situation and regulate the demobilization, they formed a common body with the employers, the Central Working Community (Zentralarbeitsgemeinschaft).[37] In an agreement of November 1918, the trade unions could achieve some long-pursued goals: the introduction of the eight-hour workday without reducing weekly loans, which meant a strong rise in wages; the confirmation of the workers councils installed in 1916 with the Auxiliary Service Law (Hilfsdienstgesetz); the creation of a binding arbitration system guaranteed, if necessary, by the state. These social milestones were enforced step by step during the following years, for instance in the Works Council Act (Betriebsrätegesetz) of 1920.[38]

While wartime inflation continued, the government used its influence to adapt the wages to the constantly growing prices. There was a so-called inflation consensus: The ongoing wage–price spiral allowed the working population to keep its living standard. Under these circumstances, the Weimar governments realized a certain ideology of egalitarianism which helped maintain social peace.[39] Actually, the number of strike actions had fallen. However, the fragile arrangement came to an end in the hyperinflation of 1923. This break led to an eruption of unemployment, the number exceeding the mark of 2 million in February 1926 whereas the real wages still remained under the pre-war level.[40] The economic instability and the lack of economic growth resulted in "an increasingly fragmented and polarized society".[41] In the Reichstag elections, the parties of the extreme left and right gained more and more voters. The Central Working Community proved to be inoperable, and the labour-market players were confronting each other without any will to seek compromises. This culminated in the Great Ruhr lockout of 1928, during which the Ruhr industrialists banned 230,000 steelworkers from the factories. The Weimar democracy failed because it was unable to unify an increasingly fragmented society by social policy means.[42]

Thus, social policy measures were mostly gap fillers in a period of a continuing crisis. As shown, some amendments were made to the social insurance system. The main improvements in the welfare systems could be noticed in the relief for the victims of war and inflation. Special relief systems were introduced for these groups which were regarded as "patriote victims". Despite the innovation of the unemployment insurance, most of the unemployed dropped out of the system. After 26 weeks, people reached the end of their eligibility to receive unemployment insurance benefits.[43] They had to rely on public relief, and the state had to finance an Emergency Aid (Krisenfürsorge) in order to release the municipalities from social welfare payments. However, the lack of social cohesion pushed the takeover of power by the national socialist regime.

When Hitler came to power, he did not seize vigorous measures to fight the causes of mass unemployment, although he pretended to do so.[44] Instead, he pursued the aim of making the country ready for war once again. Tax reductions and economic incentives were oriented on the armament industries. The slight improvement of the economic situation benefited from a tailwind. On the labour market, the regime was seeking possibilities for the provision of work. Social policy measures were compatible with the Nazis' aims in demographic and family policies. An excellent example for that are the marriage loans (Ehestandsdarlehen). For every married couple, an interest-free loan was granted for home furnishing. However, the newlyweds had to give proof of their Aryan origin and political loyalty. The loan was reduced by a quarter with every newborn child, thus being paid in full at the fourth birth. However, the success was moderate as only 17 per cent of 2 million couples received a marriage loan until 1943. Other Nazi family policy measures were maintained after the war, among them the laws on maternity regulation and on child allowances. The Maternity Protection Act (Mutterschutzgesetz) of 17 May 1942, based on a 1927 law, introduced dismissal protection and an employment ban for employed women becoming mothers. These elements were readopted later in the Federal law of 1952. Child allowances were introduced for the first time in September 1935 as one-time payments; then in April 1936, it was extended to monthly payments. This regulation framework was taken up in the Child Allowance Act (Kindergeldgesetz) of 1954.[45]

The racist national socialist policy was applied to Jews and other minorities resulting in their exclusion from the welfare system. The self-administration of social insurances was abolished and superseded by an authoritarian governance. Despite such negative actions, Götz Aly pretends that millions of simple Germans enjoyed an improvement of the living standard in the Nazi era.[46] He construes them as beneficiaries from the German plundering of occupied countries in Europe. This was completely wrong as the first supply shortages in food could be noticed as early as in 1934. Social transfers were shortened, for instance the relief payments of social welfare. People in need did not benefit from the Nazi regime and the rest of the population paid the bill of Hitler's war when they lost their cash savings in the currency reform of 1948. Although authoritarian, the Nazi regime did not succeed in reinforcing social cohesion within German society.

Path dependency as the main characteristic of the German welfare state in the 20th century

The inter-war period was an era with few changes in the basic institutional structure of the German welfare state. This is why the term *path dependency* is used to describe the persistence of welfare policy despite the fundamental caesuras in German history, above all the Nazi dictatorship. When it is used, it does not include the idea of a determined historical process. Basically, the outcome of situations such as the hyper-inflation of 1922/23 or the Great Depression of 1929 was open. Despite such ruptures, the Bismarck social insurance system survived, and its three main pillars were maintained. Radical changes were unknown, and the system was rather characterized by gradual amendments.

The scholarly debate on path dependency focuses on the caesura of 1945. It is common sense that this year was a deep rupture. That the Allies took care about a redemocratization of Germany and abolished racist and exclusionary elements in social legislation. Thus, the after-war period was characterized by a reorientation in many terms. In this context, it has been stated that the German social security system was "on the verge of a break in continuity and of a new beginning."[47] The Manpower Division of the Allied Council worked out a draft for a compulsory social insurance which deviated considerably from the traditional German principles. It was oriented on the British Beverdige plan aiming at introducing a model that would encompass the entire nation, thus breaking with the traditionally German organization according to specific groups and classes of the population. It would have meant to change the old-age pension into a uniform basic state pension and the health insurance into a kind of National Health Service which was largely tax-financed. The reform project mobilized a strong German opposition. The remaining civil servants of the Reich Ministry of Labour and a large number of interested parties – up to the trade unions – stood together to defend the traditional German system. They voted for preserving path dependency instead of opening up to internationally discussed concepts. Thus, there were hardly any fundamental changes to the basic framework of social insurance in the early years of the Federal Republic of Germany.

Such a kind of path dependency was typical for the evolution of the German social system. The astonishing phenomenon continued until the end of the 20th century, facing challenges, such as de-nationalization, European integration and globalization. But how can this path dependency be explained? It was not deterministic but resulted from the setting of a network of actors, often called corporatism. The German system can be described as a specific governance characterized by a symbiotic relationship of lobby groups in the political or economic sphere. Beyond their respective tasks, these groups fulfilled common tasks that brought them closer together. In the era of Konrad Adenauer's chancellorship (1949–1963), the phenomenon was particularly pronounced: Every week, representatives of pressure groups and lobbies had auditions with the chancellor in the Bonn Federal Chancellery in order to influence the government's policy. In social policy, the most powerful associations were the Federation of German Trade Unions (Deutscher Gewerkschaftsbund), the Confederation of German Employers' Associations (Bundesvereinigung der Deutschen Arbeitgeberverbände) and the main Christian associations such as Caritas and Diakonie. In 1957, a total number of 578 bureaus existed in Bonn which all tried to achieve their lobbyist goals.[48] They had a considerable impact because of their connections and networks with the government, although the German constitutional laws reserved the forming of political conscience exclusively to the political parties.[49] Because of this lobbying, the Christian Democratic Union (CDU)-led governments were permanently seeking for compromises among the interests of industrialists, the trade unions, the peasants, medium-sized businesses and the representatives of civil services.[50]

In general terms, the German way of organizing the welfare state was characterized by strong networks of political interests, monopolies of representatives, complex hierarchies and a low level of competition between those groups. This was a typical element of West German democracy, differing in this point from other Western political systems. There were a lot of veto players and co-regents which participated in the state's governance. These participation opportunities were rather hindering reforms from the inside than promoting institutional changes.[51]

How did the pressure of corporatist lobby groups influence on social policy? Even when the federal government changed, only a part of the authority was altered. A large number of civil servants remained in place, and thus, eras of reforms did not result in fundamental changes of the political, economic and social structures. The evolution of the German welfare state can be better described as an ongoing introduction of amendments. This can be observed for core areas of social policy from the foundation of the Federal Republic in 1949 to the mid-seventies. Continuous lines appeared more clearly than breaks, ruptures or junctions. The political scientist Manfred G. Schmidt has worked out this specificity of West German state governance and called it as a steady policy of the intermediate way ("Politik des mittleren Weges").[52]

One of the consequences of path dependency was that decisions which created new institutions or normative patterns of administrative behaviour could only be modified at a great expense.[53] When alternatives were not supposed to be more cost-effective, the administrations tended to maintain the traditional arrangements. Moreover, path dependency sent a signal to the policymakers that their room of manoeuvre was narrow. As the framework of political governance was fixed, there were very few possibilities to alter the strategic orientation and the content alignment of social policy. Thus, political changes took place in clear-cut and limited boundaries, and a radical solution had little chance of being realized.

The stability of bureaucracy was surely one of the main reasons for this kind of continuity: The welfare state was highly administrated by civil servants. These officials often had begun their career in the Weimar Republic and served throughout the Third Reich until the foundation of the Federal Republic of Germany.[54] Until the middle of the 1960s, especially the medium-ranking civil servants such as the heads of departments, sub-departments or important divisions remained in place. The average employee looked back on a long administration career, being a specialist who ensured a smooth operation and administration of the same kind of tasks. After 1945, a large number of social democrats who had been dismissed during the Nazi era re-entered the federal administration guaranteeing a continuity to the period prior to the dictatorship. The specific West German arrangement of corporatism and lobbying was suitable for overcoming fragmentation. Social consensus was at least maintained over the period of accelerated growth which ended in the mid-70ies. After that, the increase in unemployment was generating a sense of crisis.

Impacts of the competition between the two German states

If a noteworthy rupture of path dependency happened during the second half of the 20th century, this was the West German pension insurance reform of 1957. It meant a deep structural change which deviated from the traditions of the Bismarck insurance system.[55] Its implementation was not only a sign of increasing prosperity but also a result of the fact that social policy played a crucial role in the competition between the West and the East.

In East Germany, the post–World War social insurance was conceived as a unitary system which set an end to the diversity of organization. Issues of social welfare were more centralized, and the main attention was paid to work integration measures. Thus, social policy was systematically neglected. This corresponded with the Marxist theory that it was of minor importance, being a relic of the capitalist system. Lacking in original concepts, the Socialist Unity Party (SED) maintained large parts of the traditional institutional framework, thus retaining a high degree of path dependency in the GDR. The new central trade union, the Free German Trade Union Federation (Freier Deutscher Gewerkschaftsbund, FDGB), became responsible for the administration of the social insurance. Some welfare branches, such as the unemployment insurance and municipal social relief, were marginalized. Expenditures on social welfare were several times subject to severe financial cuts. As social policy was regarded as a tool for shaping society, the official documents avoided the use of the term until the 1960s.[56]

In terms of economics, the competition of the two German states was at its height in 1957. In West Germany, this year marked a milestone because a remarkable level of prosperity could be reached.[57] The established expectations of the 1950s had been transformed into a prosperity experience, and West Germany left behind the obligation of being modest. In this context, the Bundestag voted for the earlier described pension insurance reform, introducing inflation-adapted pensions which should supersede wage payments. This kind of pension set up the starting point of a redistribution of resources between the generations. However, the reform also had unintended effects: Rent payments became a financial burden for the public treasury because in the following decades, the share of retired people was growing and the number of contributors sinking.

By the end of the 1950s, the pensions reform became a challenge in the inner-German competition. On one hand, it had a crucial importance for the consolidation of the Federal Republic of Germany as a means of keeping social peace. On the other hand, it sent a strong signal eastwards: West Germany kept its importance as a migration alternative for the population of the GDR. The SED got immediately aware of the attraction effect of the new pensions system in the West. This initiated a discussion about an own socialist reform. The debate rapidly turned to another main thrust as the SED reflected on the possibility of adapting to the recently introduced Soviet reform project. Such a turn would have meant to transfer the paying of benefits to the companies.[58]

However, this plan was abandoned because it would have levered out the GDR pensions system. Certainly, it would have transferred a further financial burden to the remaining private-owned companies what corresponded to the regime's aims. But the contributions for the majority of the workers, which were employed in the state sector, would have been paid by the national treasury. As this would have led to a considerable rise in government spendings, the adoption project was quickly abandoned. The GDR government had no concepts to reply to the West German reform. The high level of pensions reached in the West could not be granted in the East. The SED responded to the ambitious Western project by stopping the hazardous race in welfare policy.

This decision was a sign of the approaching economic crisis which finally led to the erection of the Berlin Wall in 1961.

As the economic experiment of the new economic system failed at the end of the 1960s, the active role of the state in welfare policy was pushed on the agenda. The new political leader, Erich Honecker, created the slogan of the "unity of economic and social politics".[59] By doing so, he announced a consumption-oriented program which should provide a rise of the living standard of the working classes. Its socio-political core was an ambitious housing program which started in 1973 and could not fully be realized because of a lack of funding.

According to the interpretation of the SED, state socialism had to take care of the satisfaction of basic needs at low prices for the entire population. This conviction led to a fatal subvention policy. Most prices of everyday goods such as basic foodstuffs, children's clothes, public transport, services and rents were kept by regulations, although the costs were rising. This explained the state's high expenses for subventions in the respective economic sectors. At the time of Honecker's takeover of power, the subvention ration was already laid at 10 per cent of the National budget. Until the end of the 1980s, it rose to 25 per cent.[60] As government expenses for the financing of basic needs were constantly growing, these financial means were missing for other purposes, especially the financing of investments. That is why the subventions were a clear sign of the financial crisis which marked the end of the GDR. They were an indicator of the loss of purchase power among the East German population. They were less and less a contribution to general welfare, and thus, the welfare competition of the two German states was clearly lost by the eastern side.

Socio-political paradigms in the transition to the 21st century

Over the 20th century, the German welfare state experienced a shift in social welfare paradigms. Since the Bismarck era, the integration of the working classes by financial transfers was the main concern. After the turn of the century, the aspect of a fairer distribution of resources rose in importance, and the belief of social equity was derived from this. During the Weimar Republic, the number of political players increased by the growing power of the workers' movement and the government participation of pro-welfare parties, such as the social democrats and the Catholic Zentrum Party. Welfare policy experienced a further boost because the democratic parties used it as a tool to enlarge the numbers of followers and their political appreciation.[61]

The idea of averting the danger of subversive movements by social policy lost importance. First of all, this was an effect of growing incomes among broad sections of the population. At the same time, social budgets expanded, and fresh thinking about social policy arose. It took over the role of preserving social standards and of national self-assurance. Thus, the welfare state is today considered by historians as a German memory space (*lieu de mémoire*), due to its persistence and national peculiarity.[62]

The belief in the predictability of social development was enforced by the transition to a Keynesian economic policy in the 1960s. By applying new methods in politics and administration, social policy was supposed to play an active role by influencing social evolution. The idea of prevention gained in weight, and the goals of humanizing working life and reforming the society in touch with the citizens. Traditional elements, such as securing the subsistence level and protection from the vicissitudes of life, were superseded by the quest for greater equality through the reduction of income disparities.[63] In quantitative terms, this process was linked to the expansion of the ratio of social expenditures which can be observed in the second half of the 20th century.

The ratio of social expenditure reached its first height in 1975. This year, immediately after the first oil crisis, marked a turning point. The so-called stagflation of the 1970s (low growth combined with high inflation) set an end to the expansion of the welfare system. The financial circumstances got more and more unfavourable although the socio-liberal government was still willing to develop the welfare state. In the 1980s, too, the growth rates remained low compared to the post-war decades. Although the socio-economic framework changed, the most popular device in the German public was to continue in the same way as in the past. Vested rights in the core areas of social security were defended with courage and determination. There was a broad consensus in the struggle of maintaining the high social standards regarding the level of wages, unemployment benefits and job security. These themes became popular in public debates, inciting politicians to declarations that they were willing to satisfy these wishes. The reform of the welfare state was not considered as a necessary response to the change of the economic framework but as an indicator of a new misguided ideology referred to as neoliberalism.[64]

When becoming chancellor in 1982, Helmut Kohl stated his will to find ways to reduce expenditures for welfare purposes. Contrary to his announcements, his government only initiated slight changes in the existing scheme of social welfare. Of course, some social achievements were modified, but there were no fundamental structural reforms. Thus, his ambiguous governance was symptomatic of the lack of commitment to reform.

On the contrary, there was a consolidation of social expenditures on the level achieved in the 1970s (see Table 7.3). In the course of German unification, the expenditures even rose slightly again. The way West Germany coped with the changing framework differed remarkably from the policy of other Western industrialized nations, namely the United States and Great Britain. Margret Thatcher and Ronald Reagan decided for a turn to neo-liberalism and monetarism, and thus, in these countries, the 1980s were characterized by severe cuts in the system of social security.

Chancellor Helmut Kohl's policy also turned towards monetarism. At the same time, his government tried to lower the level of unemployment, considering this aim as task number one.[65] However, these ambitious aims could not be reached. In contrast, the number of unemployed increased from 1.8 million

Table 7.3 Social expenditure ratio in the Federal Republic of Germany, 1960–2008

Social expenditure ratio		*Shares of expenditures for*			
	Total	*Age*	*Health and invalidity*	*Family support*	*Unemployment*
1960	19.9	9.1	6.1	3.7	0.4
1970	22.5	9.5	7.3	4.6	0.5
1975	27.7	11	9.5	5.1	1.4
1980	27.3	10.9	9.9	4.7	1
1990	25	10.2	9.3	3.5	1.5
2000	28.3	11.8	10.8	3.2	2.1
2008	26.8	11.3	10.4	2.9	1.4

Source: Sensch, Jürgen: histat-data compilation. Germany's social expenditure, 1960–2010, Cologne: GESIS Datenarchiv, 2014 (ZA 8593), www.gesis.org/histat/.

by the end of 1982 to 2.3 million by the end of 1983. The German government reacted with the classical social policy tools: the shortening of working-life time by the Pre-Retirement Act (Vorruhestandsgesetz) of April 1984.[66] Despite that, the unemployment figure only fell slightly, remaining on the same level until the end of the German division.

Yet, the German welfare state was not facing ideological challenges. Regarding the change of the social and economic framework, its future could only be safeguarded by stimulating the efficiency of services and by assigning resources to future-oriented tasks. Above all, mass unemployment had to be fought, because it led to a constantly increasing need for financing. Although successive German governments declared the reduction of unemployment as their social priority, the reforms on the labour market were not carried out over decades. Over the unification of the German states, the unemployment figure grew to more than 5 million. Thus, there were no resources left for other challenges such as the ageing of the population or deficits in the education sector.

The criticism of expanding costs of the welfare state, which had long been put forward by economists, did not penetrate public consciousness until 1990. In a re-organized Europe, which was characterized by the expansion of the European Union to the east, the competition of location factors acquired new significance. High social costs were more and more interpreted as a disadvantage in international competitiveness. At the same time, the economic failure of the German unification led to large compensation expenses, which were also reflected in a rise of social expenditures (see Table 7.3). The Kohl government's persistent unwillingness to introduce reforms persisted until the social democrats and the Green Party took over the government in 1998. Chancellor Gerhard Schröder turned to a labour-centred social policy. In July 1999, a law introduced integration grants for the old-aged unemployed. Thus, social legislation definitively turned away from Kohl's policy of shortening working-life time. Job-creating schemes should be opened to larger groups of the society by applying structural reforms, initially conceived for the East German states, to the whole country.

The Schröder–Blair paper, published in 1999 under the title "The way ahead for Europe's Social Democrats", opted for an active labour-market policy. The two social democrat heads of government considered that a welfare state system which hinders the ability to find work urgently needs to be reformed. The subsequent reform policy of Chancellor Schröder was harshly criticized, evoking a one-sided orientation on the new middle classes formed by white-collar workers, skilled trades- and craftspeople, civil servants and young managers. Indeed, some of the social reforms were inspired by such a leitmotiv. Best known in that context were the 2003- to 2005-introduced "Laws for Modern Services in the Labour Market". In German, they are commonly called Hartz reforms, named after a 15-member committee chaired by Peter Hartz, who was then Volkswagen's personnel director. The most discussed was the fourth reform (Hartz IV) of January 2005 that brought together the former unemployment benefits for long-term unemployed (*Arbeitslosenhilfe*) and the social assistance (*Sozialhilfe*), leaving them both at the lower level of the former social assistance.[67]

Further problems of social policy at the beginning of the 21st century were the continuing weakness of growth and the low natural population growth. That promoted the search for new ways of financing the welfare state, with a particular focus on the old-age security and reforms in the health sector. In many respects, the debate on the social insurance was linked to former discussions on the welfare state, referring for instance to the failed health reform project of 1959 which intended to introduce additional payments to doctor's visits or to the ongoing discussion on lowering of the pension's level that started in 1975. The achievement of a growth-oriented, "activating" social policy, emphasizing the promotion of work, was based on the so-called productive social policy of the late 1960s. One can draw an important conclusion of the history of German social policy in the second half of the 20th century: An outstanding economic growth seems to be the precondition for the expansion of the welfare state.

Notes

1 Buchheim (1997), 95, referring to Jánossy (1969).
2 Gerschenkron (1962). See Lloyd's chapter in this book.
3 Wehler (1987), 280.
4 Sachße and Tennstedt (1983), 162.
5 Steinmetz (1993), 112.
6 Steinmetz (1993), 113–114.
7 Tennstedt (1983), 86–89.
8 Nipperday (1996), 191, 198.
9 Pierenkemper and Tilly (2005), 50–53, 80.
10 Fischer (1982), 83.
11 Grimmer-Solem (2003), 172.
12 Stolleis (2013), 52.

13 Steinmetz (1993), 142–143; Kocka (2016), 401–403.
14 Leichter (1979), 116. See also for the following citations.
15 Kocka (2016), 400.
16 Hoffman (2001), 48.
17 Stolleis (2013), 70; Frerich and Frey (1993), 97, 113.
18 Statistisches Jahrbuch [Statistical Yearbook] für das Deutsche Reich (1916), 372.
19 Statistisches Jahrbuch der Bundesrepublik Deutschland (2005), 199.
20 Stolleis (2003), 287. See also for the pension insurance: Mierzejewski (2016), 177.
21 Zöllner (1989), 380 sq.
22 Stolleis (2013), 65, 72.
23 Stolleis (2013), 56.
24 Stolleis (2013), 72–73.
25 Statistische Jahrbuch [Statistical Yearbook] für das Deutsche Reich (1915), 376–379.
26 Frerich and Frey (1993), 295; Stolleis (2003), 157, 200.
27 Zöllner (1989), 380 sq.; Frerich and Frey (1993), 64, 283.
28 Mierzejewski (2016), 18.
29 Hardach (2006), 167–173.
30 Hardach (2006), 230–233; Frerich and Frey (1993), 213, 300–303.
31 Stolleis (2013), 96.
32 Mierzejewski (2016), 165.
33 Mierzejewski (2016), 217–220.
34 Mierzejewski (2016), 208 sq; Frerich and Frey (1993), 49–57; Zöllner (1989), 376 sq.
35 Krause (2012), 175–178.
36 See the article "Mehr Ü-60-Erwerbstätige als Ruheständler", in: *Frankfurter Allgemeine Zeitung* (15th August 2013).
37 Feldman (1977), 82.
38 Stolleis (2013), 90, 126–127.
39 Feldman (1977), 137.
40 Bresciani-Turroni (2007), 406 (1st edition in Italian in 1931).
41 Young-Sun (1998), 16.
42 Kolb (2005), 180.
43 Stachura (1986), 11.
44 Buchheim (2008), 381–414.
45 Ruhl (1994), 317–330, 161–176.
46 Aly (2006), 310 sq. (chapter 13 "Nazi Socialism").
47 Hockerts (1981), 315–321.
48 Rudzio (1982), 33.
49 Bührer (1989), 147.
50 Schwarz (1995), 460.
51 Abelshauser (2016), 4; Werner (2006), 495–498.
52 Schmidt (1987), 139–177.
53 Conrad (1998), 104.
54 Löffler (2016), 181.
55 Conrad (1998), 113.
56 Schmidt (2013), 40–45; Boldorf (1998), 38–46, 253.
57 Hockerts (1990), 37.
58 Hoffmann (2005), 110.
59 Schmidt (2013), 68–69.
60 Steiner (2005), 34 sq.
61 Schmidt and Ostheim (2007), 215.
62 Kott (2001), 486.
63 Kaufmann (2001), 94.
64 Plumpe (2016), 274.

65 Leaman (2013), 86–87.
66 Weiss (1987), 80.
67 Leaman (2013), 159, 176.

References

Abelshauser, W. (ed.) (2016). *Das Bundeswirtschaftsministerium in der Ära der Sozialen Marktwirtschaft: Der deutsche Weg in der Wirtschaftspolitik* (Wirtschaftspolitik in Deutschland 1917–1990, vol. 4). Berlin: De Gruyter.

Aly, G. (2006). *Hitler's Beneficiaries: Plunder, Racial War, and the Nazi Welfare State.* New York: Metropolitan.

Boldorf, M. (1998). *Sozialfürsorge in der SBZ/DDR: Ursachen, Ausmaß und Bewältigung der Nachkriegsarmut.* Stuttgart: Steiner.

Bresciani-Turroni, C. (2007). *The Economics of Inflation: A Study of Currency Depreciation* in Post War Germany. Auburn: Ludwig von Mises Institute (1st edition in Italian in 1931).

Buchheim, C. (1997). *Einführung in die Wirtschaftsgeschichte.* Munich: Beck.

Buchheim, C. (2008). Das NS-Regime und die Überwindung der Weltwirtschaftskrise in Deutschland. *Vierteljahrshefte für Zeitgeschichte, 56*, 381–414.

Bührer, W. (1989). Unternehmerverbände. In W. Benz (ed.), *Geschichte der Bundesrepublik Deutschland, vol. 2: Wirtschaft* (pp. 140–168). Frankfurt am Main: Fischer.

Conrad, C. (1998). Alterssicherung. In H. G. Hockerts (ed.), *Drei Wege deutscher Sozialstaatlichkeit: NS-Diktatur, Bundesrepublik und DDR im Vergleich* (pp. 101–116). Munich: Oldenbourg.

Feldman, G. D. (1977). *Iron and Steel in the German Inflation, 1916–1923.* Princeton: Princeton University Press.

Fischer, W. (1982). Armut in der Geschichte: Erscheinungsformen und Lösungsversuche der "Sozialen Frage". In *Europa seit dem Mittelalter.* Göttingen: Vandenhoeck & Ruprecht.

Frankfurter Allgemeine Zeitung (2013). "Mehr Ü-60-Erwerbstätige als Ruheständler" (15th August 2013).

Frerich, J., & Frey, M. (1993). *Handbuch der Geschichte der Sozialpolitik in Deutschland, vol. 1: Von der vorindustriellen Zeit bis zum Ende des Dritten Reichs, vol. 3: Sozialpolitik in der Bundesrepublik Deutschland bis zur Herstellung der Deutschen Einheit.* Munich: Oldenbourg.

Gerschenkron, A. (1962). *Economic Backwardness in Historical Perspective: A Book of Essays.* Cambridge, MA: Harvard University Press.

Gömmel, R. (1979). *Realeinkommen in Deutschland: Ein internationaler Vergleich (1810–1914).* Nuremberg: Self-publishing.

Grimmer-Solem, E. (2003). *The Rise of Historical Economics and Social Reform in Germany, 1864–1894.* Oxford: Clarendon.

Hardach, G. (2006). *Der Generationenvertrag: Lebenslauf und Lebenseinkommen in Deutschland in zwei Jahrhunderten.* Berlin: Duncker & Humblot.

Hockerts, H. G. (1981). German post-war Social Policies against the Background of the Beverdige-Plan: Some Observations Preparatory to a Comparative Analysis. In W. Mommsen (ed.), *The Emergence of the Welfare State in Great Britain and Germany 1850–1950* (pp. 315–339). London: Croom Helm.

Hockerts, H. G. (1990). Metamorphosen des Wohlfahrtsstaates. In M. Broszat (ed.), *Zäsuren nach 1945: Essays zur Periodisierung der deutschen Nachkriegsgeschichte* (pp. 35–45). Munich: Oldenbourg.

Hoffman, B. (2001). *Wages of Sickness: The Politics of Health Insurance in Progressive America.* Chapel Hill: University of North Carolina Press.

Hoffmann, D. (2005). Leistungsprinzip und Versorgungsprinzip: Widersprüche in der DDR-Arbeitsgesellschaft. In D. Hoffmann, & M. Schwartz (eds.), *Sozialstaatlichkeit in der DDR: Sozialpolitische Entwicklungen im Spannungsfeld von Diktatur und Gesellschaft 1945/49–1989* (pp. 89–113). Munich: Oldenbourg.

Jánossy, F. (1969). *Das Ende des Wirtschaftswunders: Erscheinung und Wesen der wirtschaftlichen Entwicklung.* Frankfurt: Neue Kritik. (Engl.: *The End of the Economic Miracle: Appearance and Reality in Economic Development.* White Plains, 1971).

Kaufmann, F. X. (2001). Der Begriff Sozialpolitik und seine wissenschaftliche Deutung. In Bundesministerium für Arbeit und Sozialordnung/Bundesarchiv (eds.), *Geschichte der Sozialpolitik in Deutschland seit 1945, vol. 1: Grundlagen der Sozialpolitik* (pp. 3–101). Baden Baden: Nomos.

Kocka, J. (2016). Bismarck und die Entstehung des deutschen Sozialstaates. *Francia, 43*, 397–408.

Kolb, E. (2005). *The Weimar Republic*, 2nd edition. London/New York: Routledge.

Kott, S. (2001). Sozialstaat. In E. François, & H. Schulze (eds.), *Deutsche Erinnerungsorte, vol. 2* (pp. 485–501). Munich: Beck.

Krause, B. (2012). *Demografischer Wandel und verbandliche Interessenvermittlung*: "Rente mit 67" "und" "Wet VLP" im Vergleich. Münster: Waxmann.

Leaman, J. (2013). *The Political Economy of Germany under Chancellors Kohl and Schröder: Decline of the German model?* New York/Oxford: Berghahn Books.

Leichter, H. M. (1979). *A Comparative Approach to Policy Analysis: Health Care Policy in Four Nations.* Cambridge: Cambridge University Press.

Löffler, B. (2016). Personelle und institutionelle Strukturen des Bundeswirtschaftsministeriums. In Abelshauser (ed.), *Das Bundeswirtschaftsministerium in der Ära der Sozialen Marktwirtschaft: Der deutsche Weg in der Wirtschaftspolitik* (Wirtschaftspolitik in Deutschland 1917–1990, vol. 4) (pp. 95–191). Berlin: De Gruyter.

Mierzejewski, A. C. (2016). *A History of the German Public Pension System: Continuity and Change.* Lanham: Lexington Books.

Nipperday, T. (1996). *Germany from Napoleon to Bismarck, 1800–1866.* Princeton: Princeton University Press.

Pierenkemper, T., & Tilly, R. (2005). *The German Economy during the Nineteenth Century.* New York, Oxford: Berghahn.

Plumpe, W. (2016). *German Economic and Business History in the 19th and 20th Centuries.* London: Palgrave Macmillan.

Rudzio, W. (1982). *Die organisierte Demokratie: Parteien und Verbände in der Bundesrepublik*, 2nd ed. Stuttgart: Metzler.

Ruhl, K.-J. (1994). *Verordnete Unterordnung: Berufstätige Frauen zwischen Wirtschaftswachstum und konservativer Ideologie der Nachkriegszeit (1945–1963).* Munich: Oldenbourg.

Sachße, C., & Tennstedt, F. (1983). *Bettler, Gauner und Proleten: Armut und Armenfürsorge in der deutschen Geschichte.* Reinbek: Rowohlt.

Schmidt, M. G. (1987). West Germany: The Policy of the Middle Way. *Journal of Public Policy* 7, 139–177.

Schmidt, M. G. (2013). Social Policy in the German Democratic Republic. In M. G. Schmidt, & G. A. Ritter (eds.), *The Rise and Fall of a Socialist Welfare State: The German Democratic Republic (1949–1990) and German Unification (1990–1994)* (pp. 23–166). Berlin/Heidelberg: Springer.

Schmidt, M. G., & Ostheim, T. (2007). Sozialstaatlichkeit in Deutschland: Ein Fazit aus der Sicht der Theorien der vergleichenden Wohlfahrtsstaatsforschung. In M. G. Schmidt et al. (eds.), *Der Wohlfahrtsstaat: Eine Einführung in den historischen und internationalen Vergleich* (pp. 210–220). Wiesbaden: Verlag für Sozialwissenschaften.

Schwarz, H.-P. (1995). *Konrad Adenauer: A German Politician and Statesman in a Period of War, Revolution and Reconstruction, vol. 1: From the German Empire to the Federal Republic, 1876–1952.* Providence/Oxford: Berghahn Books.

Stachura, P. D. (ed.) (1986). *Unemployment and the Great Depression in Weimar Germany.* Houndmills: Palgrave Macmillan.

Stachura, P. D. (1986). Introduction. In P. D. Stachura, (ed.), *Unemployment and the Great Depression in Weimar Germany.* Houndmills: Palgrave Macmillan.

Statistisches Jahrbuch [Statistical Yearbook] für das Deutsche Reich 1915/1916 (1916/1917). Berlin: Kaiserliches Statistisches Amt.

Statistisches Jahrbuch der Bundesrepublik Deutschland (2005). Wiesbaden: Statistisches Bundesamt.

Steiner, A. (2005). Leistungen und Kosten: Das Verhältnis von wirtschaftlicher Leistungsfähigkeit und Sozialpolitik in der DDR. In Hoffmann, & Schwartz (eds.), *Sozialstaatlichkeit in der DDR* (pp. 31–45).

Steinmetz, G. (1993). *Regulating the Social: The Welfare State and Local Politics in Imperial Germany.* Princeton: Princeton University Press.

Stolleis, M. (2003). *Geschichte des Sozialrechts in Deutschland.* Stuttgart: UTB.

Stolleis, M. (2013). *Origins of the German Welfare State: Social Policy in Germany to 1945.* Heidelberg: Springer.

Tennstedt, F. (1983). *Vom Proleten zum Industriearbeiter: Arbeiterbewegung und Sozialpolitik in Deutschland 1800 bis 1914.* Cologne: Bund.

Wehler, H. U. (1987). *Deutsche Gesellschaftsgeschichte, vol. 2: Von der Reformära bis zur industriellen und politischen "Deutschen Doppelrevolution" 1815–1845/49.* Munich: Beck.

Weiss, M. (1987). *Labour Law and Industrial Relations in the Federal Republic of Germany.* Deventer: Kluwer Law and Taxation Publishers.

Werner, W. (2006). Vom Modell zum Auslaufmodell: Der Sozialstaat Bundesrepublik Deutschland verliert seine Vorbildfunktion in Europa. *Vierteljahrschrift für Sozial- und Wirtschaftsgeschichte, 93*, 495–498.

Young-Sun H. (1998). *Welfare, Modernity and the Weimar State, 1919–1933.* Princeton: Princeton University Press.

Zöllner, D. (1989). Sozialpolitik. In W. Benz (ed.), *Die Geschichte der Bundesrepublik Deutschland. Vol. 2: Wirtschaft* (pp. 362–392). Frankfurt am Main: Fischer.

8 Transition paths out of social fragmentation

The South African state, social welfare and nation building, 1950–2015

Grietjie Verhoef

Introduction

State formation in South Africa since colonial domination in the nineteenth century occurred as a process of social fragmentation under colonial allegiance and economic domination. State power to colonial capital was entrenched after decolonisation by awarding political power to the white society through the constitution of the Union of South Africa. Social fragmentation occurred on two levels: between white and indigenous African and other peoples of colour on one level, and between English-speaking European settlers and the emerging local Afrikaner society in South Africa. The dominant white society engineered socio-political modernisation for economic development, using entrepreneurial self-empowerment and State Owned Enterprises in a mixed economy. Social fragmentation was perpetuated on the grounds of ethnic and cultural diversity. Fragmented democracy existed. As Beveridge-style social welfare programmes were implemented across the Commonwealth, the South African state led by introducing the first universal pension provision, albeit racially differentiated. As the Western world used state welfare programmes to address social fragmentation post-1945, welfare programmes were fragmented on the basis of race. A model of peaceful racial coexistence in separate ethnically differentiated states was enforced. In the post-1945 simple majority rule state, this political model was internationally criticised as 'undemocratic'. Increasing opposition to social and political fragmentation resulted in the abdication of the white-controlled state to a single-majority rule in 1990. Since the beginning of the twenty-first century, state power, in effect, reinforced social fragmentation despite policies to overcome it. State power was central to capitalist economic modernisation in a racially segregated state up to the late 1980s. Global liberalisation swept across Africa, but a modified political economy of state power after 1990 re-instituted racial discrimination for so-called restitution of historical disadvantages. These policies enhanced state power and undermined liberal market performance. Delivery on social development goals failed because of a failed state, corruption and black economic empowerment policies favouring

DOI: 10.4324/9780429503870-9

an elite, rather than the broad, population. Political corruption and no growth perpetuate social fragmentation, now on both racial and class grounds.

Social fragmentation is generated by endogenous and exogenous impulses. In South Africa, major social fragmentation originated from the period of contact between southward-migrating African indigenous peoples and northward-penetrating European settlers since the seventeenth century. Social institutions of poor relief in Britain, the so-called friendly societies,[1] were voluntary associations preceding official poor relief measures of the British government. Such voluntary social institutions were also active in the societies that converged into the Union of South Africa in 1910. The complexity of social needs in South Africa is grounded in the historical unfolding of diversity of culture, ethnicity and race, and the organisation of state power. At the beginning of the twentieth century, four British colonies existed in southern Africa, of which two were recently subjected independent Afrikaner Republics. In all British colonies, the African population, the Coloured and the Indian population groups were excluded from central political decision-making. The historical unfolding of social fragmentation in South Africa therefore has two dimensions: the social dimension of poverty and the racial dimension of colour, which determined the choice of the nature and extent of social welfare provision. Despite these complexities, the South African state had introduced a relatively comprehensive set of social welfare provisions by the end of the 1940s. In the United Kingdom general social security only followed the Beveridge Report of 1942. Welfare provision in South Africa occurred against the context of the developments in the United Kingdom but was exceptional in scope. This could not satisfy the escalating social want. This chapter explores the development of diversified social security in South Africa and the progress towards transcending social fragmentation. Social fragmentation in South Africa also has a distinct racial dimension, moulded by the existential concerns for self-determination by the Afrikaner society that had developed in South Africa.

Taking care of those in need was observed to be a social responsibility, not a state function. Under the company rule of the Dutch East India Company between 1652 and 1795, there was not a 'state' in the Cape settlement taking responsibility for its 'subjects'. As free burghers left the service of the company, the responsibility for life was a private affair. Khoi and San communities engaged with the settlers but remained autonomous and self-reliant for subsistence and social want. Once British colonial control was established and expanded after 1806, the colonial society was divided between colonial officials, settlers and the indigenous population, either Khoi, San or African. The origin of social fragmentation between people of European descent and indigenous peoples on the African continent in southern Africa therefore has its origin in the seventeenth century. Racial fragmentation became a significant component of social fragmentation across Africa, and South Africa was no exception. The unique dimension in South Africa is the role performed by a new European indigenous entity, Afrikaners, after 1910 who collaborated with English-speaking British subjects, in entrenching political power. White people secured political power, in a similar way as did the liberation movements in Ghana, Nigeria, Kenya, Uganda, Zambia and other British colonies – through constitutional means from Britain. This was the formation of the South African Union in 1910. The British monarch was the head of the South African state, leaving people of colour outside the political system until 1994. The deep roots of social fragmentation acquired a distinct racial dimension but were by no means exclusively racial, as the explanation of Afrikaner social and economic marginalisation will highlight.

Transcending social fragmentation based on enshrined racial segregation failed to deliver a unitary egalitarian society in South Africa, because the state failed its developmental responsibilities. As this chapter shows, economic development during the twentieth century went a long way in bridging the welfare gap, both in white and black societies. In the post-1994 era, two factors exacerbated the fragile society divisions: population growth or immigration of 'refugees' and economic meltdown. With the reintroduction of statutory racial discrimination, social want has again acquired a racially defined character. In the following sections, the chapter explains ethnic-specific social self-empowerment actions, the white-controlled state welfare policies and the post-democratic 'precarious welfare state'[2] failure to address social transformation. In conclusion, the chapter considers the potential to bridge persistent social fragmentation in South Africa.

Social welfare and self-help empowerment

In the nineteenth century, as Afrikaners settled in the northern parts of the territory after the Great Trek commencing in the late 1830s, the emigrant white population was dependent on themselves. They engaged in subsistence agriculture and livestock farming. Fortunes were determined by climatic catastrophes of the nineteenth century, especially droughts, as well as the lack of economic diversification of the economy, and repeated confrontation with indigenous societies, which resulted by the late 1880s in a distinct manifestation of poverty.[3] The community took full responsibility for social want. The Afrikaners' church, the Dutch Reformed Church (DRC) in the Cape Colony was aware of the growing need amongst a portion of their members. In 1898, the Kakamas Settlement was established by the DRC on the farms Soetap and Kakamas on the banks of the Orange River to resettle poor white Afrikaners who had been left devastated by severe repeated droughts in 1895 and 1896 followed by the rinderpest epidemic, which wiped out large cattle stocks.[4] The DRC also established a trade school for young white men and a dedicated branch of the church to seek employment for unemployed men. The South African War of 1899–1902 exacerbated poverty deeply. Completely destroyed agricultural lands left both white and black people impoverished. The DRC took full responsibility for their poor (*onze armen*) and regarded action as its 'moral obligation'. In successive synods (annual church meetings), strategies were devised to address the growing urbanisation of Afrikaners and improved education to facilitate adaption to urban circumstances. The majority of the white rural population was familiar only with extensive agriculture and had no capital to intensify operations.

A 'bywoner' class (poor people living on the land of a wealthy landowner) developed and exploded after the war. The DRC concerned themselves in successive congresses constituted specifically to address the issue of white poverty in 1916, 1922 and 1923[5] and finally solicited the financial support of the US Carnegie Commission to conduct a comprehensive investigation into the phenomenon of white poverty. The Carnegie Commission reported in 1932 that more than 300 000 white people, primarily Afrikaners, were living in abject poverty. Afrikaner leaders across the spectrum of cultural, business and church leadership pulled together to seek avenues out of the dilemma facing their own people. The Ekonomiese Volkskongres (EVK) was called in 1939 as a collective effort of all Afrikaner stakeholders. The clarion call of the congress was 'A people saves itself! (*'n Volk red homself*). This approach to the resolution of the Afrikaner poverty phenomenon resulted in the strategic planning of concrete long-term solutions. The underlying principle was self-help and a stern warning against reliance on state welfare. Afrikaners internalised the responsibility for the problem of their poor. The Afrikaner leaders at the EVK reiterated that the roots of the problem lay in capacity and not welfare. Empowerment was a function of Afrikaners' capabilities. Those empowerment strategies included the establishment of an industrial finance house to provide funding to emerging Afrikaner entrepreneurs in order to facilitate meaningful access to business. Afrikaners contributed in £2 shares to the capital of Federale Volksbeleggings (FVB) in 1942 to set up their own industrial finance house. Furthermore, the EVK established a mutual assistance welfare organisation, the Reddingsdaadbondl (RDB) to collect subscriptions from members and to distribute the proceeds towards education bursaries for members, welfare support and skills training of young people. Afrikaner businessmen organised themselves into the Afrikaanse Handelsinstituut (AHI, Afrikaans Chamber of Commerce) to render mutual support to emerging Afrikaner entrepreneurs. In essence, the root cause of Afrikaner social displacement was the transition from full reliance on agriculture to growing landlessness and urbanisation. Newly urbanised Afrikaners did not have the skills profile to succeed in the mining, industrial or urban administration sectors.

Traditionally, the African communities cared for their poor in the communal homestead of the African chief. Land was communally owned and cultivated under the auspices of the traditional leader, who distributed food according to need. As droughts, the South African War and the cattle disease also affected African subsistence, and as the mineral discoveries opened opportunities for wage labour in mines and subsequently small industries, Africans also urbanised since the late nineteenth century. By 1911, 12.64 % of the African population (508 000) was urbanised, and by 1946, this had risen to 1 794 212.[6] Africans in the urban areas lived in slum conditions, experienced social displacement and suffered from exposure to disease. In these areas, voluntary organisations similar to the English friendly societies soon developed to supplement irregular income. These organisations are loosely known by the collective name of *stokvels* (originating from the word *stock fairs*) and functioned as rotating savings and credit associations. The *stokvels* collected savings on a rotating basis from trusted members for distribution at a later stage, for purposes of funeral needs, payment of debt, payment of education fees or simply to acquire luxury goods. These voluntary associations represented an urban self-help institution amongst Africans but was not institutionalised or strategically linked to a comprehensive survival or empowerment strategy of the African community.[7] Friendly societies were prevalent in the Cape Colony and later spread to other colonies under British administration, such as the Transvaal Colony. In the Cape Colony, friendly societies were organised by persons not serving in the colonial administration, since they were excluded from social services available to colonial officials, such as free medical services at state-funded hospitals – as had been the case in other British colonies in Africa (PRO: CO/5424/25; PRO: Co/5251:44207). The need for extensive welfare supplementation among English-speaking settlers was limited, but the self-help social organisation seemed to have penetrated the urbanised African societies fairly widely.[8] In 1905, the Civil Servants' Medical Benefit Society was established in Johannesburg as a friendly society to provide medical benefits to civil servants in an environment of escalating medical costs.[9]

Conditions of public distress manifested in the urban areas where white and African labour contested access to employment. Growing numbers of impoverished whites flocked to the cities where they competed with equally unskilled African labour, but the latter at a lower cost. The skilled white labour force, often English-speaking workers from the United States or the United Kingdom who were employed in the mining industry, organised themselves to protect employment opportunities against African competition. The state was slow in enacting legislation to protect its white constituency, but the assumption was, as expressed by John X Merriman, prime minister of the Cape Colony in 1895, that

> the European race in this country . . . held the country in the interest of civilisation, and in the interest of good government. . . . The white population was in a minority in this country, but they must be a dominant minority if they were to live there at all.[10]

As the Labour Party succeeded in an election agreement with the National Party in 1924 to take control of the South African government, the state gradually introduced statutory social security measures to secure employment protection to white workers. The Mines and Works Act, No 12 of 1911 reserved the issue of blasting certificates only to white workers (in the interest of safety) and later specified the number of African workers a white supervisor may oversee. As costs escalated in deep-level mining, mine owners sought to reduce the number of white employees in favour of more African employees, which in 1922 led to the most violent strike in the gold mining industry. The state suppressed the strike by military force. An agreement between the mine workers and the Chamber of Mines provided for the employment of racial quotas. In 1924 when the Pakt government of Hertzog took office, a series of statutes were passed to protect white workers – the Industrial Conciliation Act, No 11 of 1924, the Wage Act, no 27 of 1925 and the Mines and Works Amendment Act, no 25 of 1926. The Industrial Conciliation Act provided dispute resolution procedures to organised 'workers' – by definition, only white workers. The Wage Act provided for wage negotiations, agreements and minimum wages with 'workers'. The definition of *workers* excluded the majority of African workers. The Mines and Works Amendment Act sanctioned racial discrimination in certain employment categories in the mining industry. The Apprenticeship Act, No 26 of 1922 (amended 1944) made no distinction on the basis of race, but conditions for apprenticeships were formulated in such a way effectively excluding many Africans. The Native Urban Areas Act, No 21 of 1923 (amended 1945) enforced urban residential segregation and granted municipal authorities the right to issue permits, identify residential locations and control the influx of Africans to urban areas.[11] These measures served to enhance white worker protection and indirectly also social security by offering employment security to poor whites and by securing the exclusivity of skilled employment categories to the predominantly English skilled labour force. It can be argued that these statutes laid the foundation for the South African welfare state,[12] although the National Party government was less inclined towards the extension of welfare to everybody in need. The state preferred the principle of employment policies to put the unemployed in work rather than turning them into the recipients of grants.[13] The Carnegie Commission and the EVK reiterated that position.

In practice, the social conditions of many impoverished people in urban areas deteriorated in the aftermath of the Great War and the international depression. English liberal protagonists called for the extension of universal social welfare, especially those adversely affected by weakening economic conditions caused by the post-war depression and the Great Depression of the 1930s. English liberals representing the Africans in Parliament and on the Native Representative Council supported the calls for social security.[14] The appeal for relief of the plight of the elderly poor after the Spanish Flu epidemic of 1918 led to the passing of the Old Age Pensions Act, 1920. This introduced for the first time a means-tested non-contributory old-age pension for whites and coloured people, differentiated in scale on the basis of race.[15] A subsequent Commission of Inquiry into Old Age Pensions (the so-called Pienaar Commission) proposed in 1927 the introduction of a system of 'National Insurance' that would provide for risks of sickness, accident, premature death, invalidity, old age, unemployment and maternity.[16]

These proposals suited a developed economy and society, but in the case of South Africa, failed to take into account the capacity of the domestic economy. The National Party state was positively inclined towards the proposals of the Pienaar Commission, but full implementation was unaffordable. Old age pensions were extended to the adult dependents of pensioners and a child maintenance grant was introduced for poor children. In 1935, a dedicated section for social welfare was organised in the Department of Housing, but in 1937, a separate Department of Social Welfare was established.[17] The government was encouraged by the rising number of voluntary private organisations engaged in social welfare. One such initiative was the successive DRC congresses and the establishment of its committee on the poor. The EVK and subsequent actions to empower the unemployed and poor, were well received by the state. These initiatives aligned with the Government's position favouring economic growth and job creation to welfare transfer payments. The rejection by the Carnegie Commission in 1932 of state agency in taking responsibility for the resolution of the poor white problem, was interpreted by Seekings as anti-state welfarism,[18] as a renewed emphasis was placed on the agency of the community and of the church to address social want.

In fact, international developments had a profound impact on the unfolding of social welfare developments in South Africa after the publication of the Carnegie Report. The New Zealand Social Security Act of 1935 introduced state-funded social welfare[19] and in preparation for the termination of World War II, Western nations signed the Atlantic Charter in 1941. The latter committed the signatories to a world free of want, and Smuts pledged to follow article 5 of the charter committing signatories to the objective of securing improved labour standards, economic advancement and social security.[20] Smuts made it clear in Parliament that after the war steps would be taken to include also the native population, urban and rural, under measures of enhanced well-being (Hansard, 12/1/42: Col 5–6;6/3/42: Col 3316–3321). Smuts appointed the Social and Economic Planning Council (SEPC) in 1942 as a semi-official advisory body to report to the prime minister on social and economic policy matters. The SEPC committed itself to social security as one of its guiding principles. A Social Security Committee was appointed in 1943. In its first report, it proposed a full programme of pensions and health and employment insurance.[21] At the time of the release of the Beveridge Report in Britain, the Smuts government had been preparing the introduction of universal social security. In 1944, the Pensions Law Amendment Act was passed, introducing universal pensions for the first time in the British Commonwealth. This meant that all citizens were eligible to receive a pension. The government refrained from describing pensions as a 'right' on the grounds that many thousands of persons did not need such aid. The introduction of a compulsory contributing scheme was envisaged to deliver serious complications regarding existing state and private pension and provident funds. Apart from those considerations, it was apparent that such pension payments would increase state expenditure considerably (an estimate of £4 million per annum). In the government white paper outlining the policy considerations of the state, the state endorsed the principles of the proposals but explained the practical implementation to which the government would commit. The most important development was that Africans and Indians were included.[22] As the state could not afford the all-inclusive social security scheme, the new act introduced a non-contributory pension scheme, fully financed from existing sources and additional taxes for all the race groups in South Africa. Invalidity grants and blind pensions were improved. Child grants under the Children's Act were improved, and family allowances were extended in respect of the third child in a family of limited means. Unemployment benefits were expanded, and additional subsidies were offered to the provinces in respect of health services. These additional social security measures added an additional £16.3 million to the state's expenditure in 1947.[23] By 1946, the state paid out pensions to 140 000 Africans.[24]

In 1946 the Unemployment Insurance Act, of 1946 introduced unemployment insurance. The entire social welfare net by the end of United Party rule in 1948, was extensive. In 1941 pensions were introduced to war veterans through the War Pensions Act, No 45 of 1941 and No 44 of 1942. This paid pensions to war veterans, irrespective of race, who were not disabled but have fallen into circumstances of need. A variety of disability grants were paid to invalids, semi-fit persons and other dependent persons, such as blind and deaf people, certified epileptics and lepers. The state also provided housing for the totally unfit, such as settlements for the aged and unfit Europeans were settled in Hereford, Coloured persons at De Novo and Africans at Elandsdoorn.[25]

Social welfare in South Africa was comprehensive but racially differentiated. In other settler societies in Africa such as Southern Rhodesia, pensions were paid irrespective of race but with higher qualification criteria. No unemployment insurance was offered and disability grants were limited.[26] The exceptionalism of social security in South Africa was its universalism, a characteristic not applied internationally by the 1940s. Under the Hertzog Pakt government welfare was approached from a perspective of providing relief, while the conservative Afrikaner leadership approached welfare from the perspective of support aimed at restoring capacity to take care of oneself. Havenga, the minister of finance under Hertzog, placed more emphasis on policies to create employment than relief to the downward spiral of the depression, than increased fiscal expenditure.[27] The ethos of Afrikaner empowerment strategies threatened to derail the extension of the social security net. When Smuts was prime minister, he was more directly influenced by international developments in social security. Practical realism remained an important check on the implementation of the full scope of SEPC recommendation in 1943. The constraint of affordability constituted the barrier to universal race-blind implementation. In all the debates in Parliament the Smuts government subscribed to the principles of the SEPC proposals but fell short of implementation on the grounds of cost to the economy.[28]

The period between: separate development and economic growth

The National Party moved into office in 1948 on a clear mandate: preserve the future of the white people in South Africa. The disillusionment with Smuts after the war, coupled with the rising African militancy opposing colonial control in Africa, strengthened white anxiety about future self-determination in Africa. The National Party election victory paved the way for the extension of policies of racial segregation into a more systematic programme of separate development of the different races. The implication of this development for social welfare policies was that racial differentiation was entrenched. At no stage during National Party rule was any person who had become eligible for old-age pensions excluded from such benefits. No African worker was ever formally excluded from unemployment benefits, but the qualifications for eligibility excluded the majority of African workers technically. In the course of the next 25 years, social security provisions remained virtually unchanged from the extensive range of social welfare provisions of the late 1940s. The benefits paid remained racially differentiated and did not escalate in similar proportions for all beneficiaries.

This chapter does not address two important aspects of the comprehensive social security net, namely health and education provision. Suffice it to mention that proposals in 1944 by Dr Gluckmann for a national health scheme were rejected as too expensive and unaffordable to the small country.[29] Smuts stated in Parliament that "a national health scheme would necessitate far-reaching changes for which the country is not ready".[30] On education, there was no system of education for African children until Bantu Education was introduced in 1952 by the Malan government. Despite unwavering criticism against differentiated education provision, substantial growth in school attendance, performance and pass rates were achieved by the early 1970s.[31] Social welfare provision was therefore aligned with the policy of separate development after 1948.

The National Party was convinced that the peaceful coexistence of the different races in South Africa was only possible through political separation. Furthermore, the differences of culture, modernisation and aspirations between whites and the African population suggested rationality in separation. While Smuts had created expectations of an improved life for all after the war, the Malan government sought first to secure Afrikaner self-determination. Afrikaners were making significant progress with self-driven economic empowerment initiatives (the Second Volkskongres in 1952 declared white poverty something of the past – FAK, 1952) and Afrikaners had secured political power. The reality of Africa and South Africa was that an ambitious new African elite was rising, demanding the termination of colonial control, pan-Africanist solidarity and full citizenship rights in their own independent states.[32] In South Africa, the African Nationalist Congress (ANC) Youth League under Oliver Tambo, Nelson Mandela and Govan Mbeki wrestled power from the moderate ANC leadership and, as young radical leaders, embarked on a course of militant opposition to the National Party government. They mobilised the membership to mass protest and civil disobedience to realise their non-negotiable demands. In the context of militant African protests led by people such as Nnamdi Azikiwe, Kwame Nkrumah and Blaise Diagne, elsewhere in Africa, demands were made for full citizenship rights and equality in social security provision. The Freedom Charter of 1955 drafted by the ANC and its allies called for the recognition of the right to work, full unemployment benefits, equal pay for equal work, a minimum wage, paid leave, free and compulsory universal education, the right to housing, free medical treatment and hospitalisation for all based on a health scheme run by the state.[33] These demands dovetailed well with the SEPC proposals but were not received positively, since that would result in the end of white political power.

The reality in South Africa was that the population in 1911 consisted of 5.9 million people, of which 21.3% was white, 67.2% African, 8.7% Coloured and 2.5% Indian. By the end of the first decade in the twenty-first century, the total population exceeded 51 million people, of which the African section made up 79% and the white population 8.9% (see Table 8.1). The growth rate of the African section of the population consistently exceeded 2% to 2.6% per annum by 1960–1970, while the Coloured population grew by more than 3% per annum between 1950 and 1970. The population growth of whites fluctuated between 1.6% (1950–1960) and 2.14% (1960–1970).[34] At the beginning of the twentieth century, Afrikaners had made up around 55% of the white population, affording them a strong electorate influence.

Pan-Africanism was overtly opposed towards white self-determination aspirations. Economic power was firmly under the control of white businessmen and Afrikaners implemented dedicated strategies towards extending their stake

Table 8.1 Population of South Africa, 1911–2011**

	Africans	*Coloured*	*Indian*	*White*	*Total*
1911	4 019 000	525 000	152 000	1 276 319	5 972 757
1951	8 560 000	1 103 00	367 000	2 642 000	12 671 452
1960	10 928 000	1 509 000	477 000	3 088 000	16 002 797
1970	15 340 000	2 051 000	630 000	3 773 000	21 794 000
1980*	13 112 000	2 458 000	748 000	4 220 000	28 978 510
1996	31 127 631	3 600 446	1 045 596	4 434 697	40 583 574
2001	35 416 166	3994 505	1 115 467	4 293 640	44 819 778
2011	41 000 938	4 615 401	1 286 930	4 586 838	51 770 560
2015*** (mid-2015 est)	44 228 000	4 832 900	1 362 000	4 534 000	54 956 900
% growth	920.17%	779.1%	746.6%	259.3%	766.7%

Source: Statistics South Africa www.statssa.gov.za.

* Figures exclude Transkei, Boputhatswana, Ciskei and Venda as independent states.

** Selection of years to coincide with census years.

*** Statssa mid-2015 population estimates.

in the mainstream economy. By 1914, individual taxpayers constituted only 0.9% of the total population, and by 1951, this number had risen to 3.49%. The disparity between the generators of wealth and contributors to national income and those demanding state-sponsored social welfare was obvious. Strong growth in manufacturing during the post-war era, as well as strong performance in international resource prices supported strong GDP growth. Between 1950 and 1993, real GDP rose from R119 857 million to R514 887 million, growing at 4.2% between 1946 and 1950, 4.5% during the 1950s, 5.7% during the 1960s and then slumped to 3.4% growth between 1971 and 1980.[35] During this period of strong growth, which followed the performance of the Western world and South Africa's main trading partners in Britain and Europe, taxation remained the core source of government finance – 79% during the 1950s, 72% during the 1960s and 74% during the 1970s.[36] Tax rates increased significantly since the 1960s to fund state expenditure. In 1978 a 4% General Sales Tax (GST) was introduced, which had risen to 13% by the late 1980s. The significance of these macro-economic indicators is that a relatively small taxpayer base oiled the wheels of economic growth and diversification at a time when population growth placed a significant burden on economic resources.

The strong economic performance was soon halted as the decade of rising gold and oil prices marked the transition from rapid to moderate growth. Between 1961 and 1988 real per capita GDP growth slumped from 3.4% between 1961 and 1970, to 0.2% between 1979 and 1988.[37] The concerning factor was rising Government expenditure as a proportion of GDP, which indicated growth stimulated by Government spending and not productive expansion. Government expenditure rose from 12.72% of GDP in 1960 to 25.6% in the latter half of the 1980s.[38] During the period of contraction, state expenditure on social services displayed a distinct downward trend. As reflected in Table 8.2, government expenditure on social services (excluding health and education) declined as a portion of real government expenditure from 34% in

Table 8.2 Expenditure on social services/welfare, 1960–1993

	R'm nominal	*R'm real*	*% G expenditure nominal*	*% G expenditure Real*	*% GDP nominal*	*% GDP Real*
1960	201.3	28.8	34.0	34.0	4.0	3.0
1965	260.8	33.4	26.0	26.0	3.4	3.0
1970	286.6	31.2	12.2	12.2	2.3	2.0
1975	621.0	43.1	10.6	11.0	2.3	2.2
1980	1277.2	50.1	10.4	10.4	2.1	2.1
1985	3422.2	70.0	12.0	12.0	3.0	3.0
1990	40472.1	404.7	41.3	41.3	15.0	15.0
1993	57938.0	402.1	43.5	43.5	15.1	15.0
% growth	28681%	1296%				

Source: Central Statistical Services, 1960–1993.

1960 to 10.4% in 1975, which represented 3% of real GDP in 1960 and 2% of real GDP in 1975.

State expenditure on social services was reduced from the second-largest expenditure item of government expenditure in the 1960s to fourth position by the end of the 1980s. Why this shift occurred, is partly also illustrated by the policy implementation by the National Party after the 1950s. When the National Party assumed office, the minister of finance expressed a desire to limit the number of pensions and transfer payments to be made to Africans in urban areas. The new government preferred to put people in work or to provide social services more in accordance with 'Native customs and traditions'. In recognising the authority of traditional African authorities, the government wanted to 'reinstate the natural obligations of the Bantu authorities' with respect to their aged and children by transferring social transfers to them to administer.[39] The annual increase in pensions paid to Africans did not rise in equal proportions to those of the other population groups. Additional amounts were transferred to the African Welfare Trust Fund for distribution by the traditional authorities in their respective areas. The state transferred funds into the Trust Fund and authorised expenditures by traditional authorities as a measure of transferring responsibility to those authorities and facilitating the transfer of government skills to those authorities.[40] These measures constitute the escalating costs of duplicating administrative systems for the different ethnic African communities in accordance with the policy of separate development.[41]

The relative decline in expenditure on social services occurred on the back of increased expenditure on general administration and defence. As reflected in Table 8.2, state expenditure on social services/welfare rose in nominal terms from R201.3 million in 1960 to R57 938 million in 1993 (or R28.8 million in real terms to R402.1 million in 1993). As a proportion of total state expenditure, social expenditure dropped from 34% to12% in 1985 and then spiked to 43.5% in 1993. This constituted 15% of GDP in 1993. Government expenditure on general administration rose from 46.4% in 1960 as a proportion of total government expenditure to 67.9% in 1989. Defence expenditure rose in the same period from 10.4% of total government expenditure to almost 16% by the early 1980s.[42] The period between 1960 and 1980 was the period of systematic implementation of the Bantu Homeland policy, whereby ethnic African states were established and one, the Republic of Transkei, was granted independence in 1963. These added to state expenditure and only declined as the state started preparing for the transition to black majority rule since the mid-11980s. After the banning of political parties such as the ANC and the PAC (Pan Africanist Congress) and the Communist Party of South Africa in 1960, South Africa left the British Commonwealth, and domestic unrest was suppressed by force, and state expenditure on defence escalated. Between 1960 and 1980, the size of the public sector expanded significantly, with expenditure on the public sector rising from 22.3 % of GDP in 1946 to 26.3% in 1975 and expenditure on public corporations (e.g. ESCOM, ISCOR, SASOL, IDC) rose from 1.2% in 1946 to 6.8% in 1979.[43]

A fragmented society became a Humpty-Dumpty cracked society. While the master plan of political separation for peaceful coexistence was systematically undermined after the assassination of Dr H F Verwoerd in 1966, the state became increasingly repressive, opposition shifted to terrorism at home and from across the borders and the economy slumped under growing international sanctions, the global recession of the 1980s and a slowdown in domestic growth. These conditions increased, what Lindert calls, 'marginal deadweight costs which will choke off either the ability or the willingness to continue raising taxes and transfers'.[44] During the period of National Party rule between 1948 and the early 1980s, universal social welfare benefits were distributed to all citizens, but the racial differentiation coupled with strategies of redirecting benefit allocation through traditional authorities, in practice, opened the door to extensive administrative complexities and corruption. In reality, great discrepancies developed between the race groups' benefits. As Davenport and Saunders (2000) explain:

> [a]t bottom, the discrepancies resulted from hard business calculation and much as racial prejudice, and has to be seen as a reflection of the state's ability to pay a reasonable amount across the board, given the numerical discrepancies between the races and the relative lack of earning power of Africans.[45]

Between the early 1980s and 1990, the gap between social welfare transfers to the different race groups, was narrowed substantially. This gap in social expenditure per recipient was closed entirely by 1992.[46] It became increasingly apparent that social fragmentation was not simply a function of inequality in social welfare distribution but also social fragmentation based on racial, cultural and historical legacies. Transcending such fragmentation required non-racialism and a strong economy.

Developmental social welfare: a widening stream

The transition to a black majority government in South Africa occurred relatively peacefully. The ANC published a proposed plan for the restructuring of the economy and for development to eradicate poverty. Immediately after the ANC took office, the Reconstruction and Development Plan (RDP) was submitted as the government policy document.[47] The RDP set out five broad goals. The first was to meet basic needs through a massive programme of housing construction, land reform, basic service delivery, transport improvement, environmental protection, health services and nutrition and the transformation of the welfare system. The second goal was to improve human resource development through education. The third was economic development to address unemployment and industrial and business development. The fourth goal was democratisation, accountability and transparency of state institutions supported by a strengthened civil society. Finally, the RDP planned to decentralise the implementation of the ambitious plan. This 'promise to the people' at the first universal election soon proved to have created highly unrealistic expectations, which the government was forced to disavow.[48] As experienced by the Smuts government of the 1940s, the country's economic and fiscal constraints impeded the implementation of the RDP ambitions. Theoretically, such a comprehensive social security programme had the potential to overcome massive social and economic fragmentation.

State policies were inadequate to secure economic growth to support the implementation of the RDP and therefore failed to mobilise sufficient tax revenue and other funding to meet the RDP objectives. Table 8.3 below illustrates the contracting number of taxpayers in South Africa between 1911 and 2011. (Also see endnote 1). The funding problem was exacerbated by a lack of administrative infrastructure and management oversight.[49] The economic reality that redistribution cannot occur without economic development, forced the ANC government to reconsider the RDP. In 1996, a new policy framework, GEAR (Growth Employment and Redistribution), was announced. This new policy returned to more familiar global economic orthodoxy of financial discipline, strategies to stimulate private and public investment, price stability and policies to pursue a stable exchange rate, such as a reduction of tariffs and export-led growth.[50]

Table 8.3 Taxpayers, 1911–2011

	Number taxpayers Individual	*Number of taxpayers companies*	*Indiv as % of total population*
1914	5542	615	0.09
1951	443 086	3 533	3.49
1960	n/a	n/a	n/a
1970	n/a	n/a	n/a
1980	n/a	n/a	n/a
1996	n/a	n/a	n/a
2001	n/a	n/a	n/a
2011	5 600 000	n/a	10.81
2015	6 500 000		11.8

Source: South African Statistics for Fifty Years, 1960; www.sars.gov.za.

The master plan to address social welfare was based on the 1995 World Summit of the United Nations on Social development in Copenhagen. The important policy shift the United Nations attempted to drive home was to replace the International Monetary Fund and World Bank liberal market policies on economic growth by a style of development embedded in social development.[51] The populist election programme of the ANC mandated swift movement on social welfare. In 1997, the White Paper for Social Welfare[52] priority was given to the policy of social development. This development approach targeted poverty alleviation and inequality by suggesting a social development approach integrating social interventions with economic development. The former approach to social welfare was considered to be 'curative' and not 'pro-active and preventative'. The new social development model was 'based on the strength of individuals, groups or communities and promotes their capacity for growth and development'.[53] The concept of social development vests in the development of individuals and communities that would move them out from social marginalisation and integrate them in broad social development initiatives. Midgley (2001a) states:

> [T]he White Paper seeks to promote the active engagement of people in their own welfare through the creation of community-based and participatory programmes through increased self-reliance and through greater social investment that enhance people's capacities to participate in the productive economy.[54]

There is a resemblance to the National Party idealism of the 1950s, that sought to involve the traditional African communities in the social welfare of their own people. This initiative failed, because of a lack of capacity in the traditional areas, a lack of commitment by traditional leaders and growing urbanisation, which left Africans increasingly distant from their traditional origin. Now, in the 1990s, community involvement as part of a comprehensive social welfare programme resurfaced.[55] suggested that social development meant linking 'social interventions to a dynamic process of economic development. . . (and) integrating economic and social policies'. As Gray observed, the intention was not to transfer productive economic resources to finance welfare services, but to ensure that social policies contribute to development.[56]

The South African society has made gradual progress in transcending social and racial fragmentation since the 1980s as differentiation in social security spending disappeared. Since then, the state still faces the task of promoting economic growth and development to secure sustainable social welfare policies. The capacity of the state to deliver in this respect, depends on two key policy variables. These are non-racialism and governance.

Social welfare provision after 1994 became the sole responsibility of a single non-racial national Department of Social Welfare. Social welfare emerged as a human right and served as a mechanism for the redistribution of wealth.[57] Whereas social welfare was not based on a rights-based approach under the previous governments, social welfare after 1994 was seen as a basic human right.[58] The Constitution of the Republic of South Africa (Section 27[1]c and Section 27[2]) reads:

> *Everyone has the right to have access to . . . social security, including, if they are unable to support themselves and their dependents, appropriate social assistance.*
>
> *The state must take reasonable legislative and other measures, within its available resources, to achieve the progressive realisation of each of these rights.*

These clauses clearly present a potential dilemma – citizens have these rights, but if the state lacks the resources or capacity, it cannot deliver. A state unable to deliver on election promises and expectations created during political electioneering is sowing the seeds of social disillusionment and potential new forms of social fragmentation. This amounts to the state being a 'precarious state' – a state unable to provide in the perpetual demand for social security.[59] Well-intended policies unable to deliver present a serious threat to overcoming social fragmentation.

The implementation of the ideal was hampered by a lack of capacity on central level, as well as uncertainty about detailed aspects of the constituent elements of the social security system. The government appointed a committee to conduct a comprehensive study of poverty and social security. This committee (the Taylor Committee) reported in 2002 and provided the base for all subsequent statutory and policy changes. The Taylor Committee proposed the introduction of a basic income grant (BIG) as social security to the unemployed who did not qualify for unemployment insurance (UIF). By 2002, unemployment was unofficially at 25.2%, and the Gini coefficient had risen from 0.64 to 0.67.[60] The state refrained from introducing the BIG, despite claims that it could 'have the potential to fortify the ability of the poor to manage risk while directly improving livelihoods'.[61] This decision not to pursue the BIG was the exact same phenomenon as experienced by the state with respect to the Social Security Committee report of 1943. This proposal was rejected by the government for the same reason as the United Party under Smuts and the National Party did not implement universal unemployment benefits. To silence its critics, the ANC agreed to more comprehensive child support.[62] Ferguson also describes the proposal as 'one of the radical proposals' of the South African state, which is 'socially demeaning to adult men [African] to become dependent on anyone but themselves'.[63]

The Taylor Committee outlined the entire scope of social security transfers to be administered by the state. This included six social grants, three statutory funds and collaboration with voluntary organisations (non-governmental organisations, NGOs). The Social Assistance Act of 2004 replaced the Social Assistance Act of 1992 by codifying all grants payable in terms of former statutes. Serious delivery constraints placed the successful execution of this grand social security system in jeopardy. The Taylor Committee therefore proposed the centralisation of the administration of all these grants and funds. This resulted in the establishment of the South African Social Security Agency (SASSA) to coordinate social welfare delivery and integrate NGOs working in social services into the comprehensive delivery plan.[64] Since 2005 the social security system consisted of the following:

- **SOCIAL GRANTS:**

  Child Support Grant
  Old Age Disability
  Foster care

Grant-in-aid
War veterans grant
Care dependency

- **STATUTORY FUNDS:**

  Unemployment Insurance Fund [UIF]
  Compensation Funds
  Road Accident Fund [RAF]

- **VOLUNTARY FUNDS:**

  Medical schemes
  Retirement funds

Social grants are funded by the Government from taxes, the statutory funds are funded by road users, workers and employees and taxpayers, and the voluntary funds by workers and employees. It shows the comprehensive social welfare net to which taxpayers contribute and from which the poor benefits.[65] During the crucial period of transition to a unitary democratic society, the South African state extended the former redistributive social security programme to benefit a much larger proportion of the total population than ever before in its history. In this manner, the new state addressed the populist call of its constituency during the so-called liberation struggle, for a redistribution of wealth. Poverty and inequality were put forward as the outcome of conquest and policies of racial segregation, especially the National Party policy of separate development since the early 1950s.[66] In fact, crucial demographic trends complicated delivery.

The South Africa population reached 55 million in 2015, and only about 6.5 million pay taxes (i.e. 11% of the population).[67] In June 2017, the number of people qualifying for social grants outnumbered those in employment.[68] The exceptionalism of the social security provision in a country where population growth exceeds economic growth, and where the tax base remains 'extremely small' was placed under tremendous strain since 1994 in the name of 'alleviating poverty'. As is illustrated in Table 8.4, expenditures on social services and welfare (this are transfer payments as social grants within the six categories of social grants outlined earlier) increased from R16.7 billion in 1995 to R188.1 billion in 2015 – this is an annual compound growth of 113.58% (or simply 1026%

Table 8.4 Expenditure on social services and welfare, 1995–2015

	R'bn	*% Total G expenditure*	*% of GDP*
1995	16.7	11.1	1.1
2000	20.9	15.8	2.4
2005	72.2	16.7	4.8
2010	130.7	15.6	4.8
2015	188.1	15.1	5.0

Source: National Treasury, Budget, 1995–2016.

overall growth in the 20 years between 1995 and 2015). Economic growth is insufficient to sustain such transfers – GDP growth rates slumped from 5.2 % in 2005 to 1.3% in 2015 (See Table 8.5).[69] Despite claims to a reduction in poverty, the Gini coefficient rose since 2002 to between 0.66 and 0.68.[70]

The precarious nature of the state seeking to develop this comprehensive social security framework in South Africa manifests in the threatening fiscal cliff, illustrated by the negative growth of the economy (Table 8.5). Real growth rates have dropped significantly from 5% in 2005 to 1.3% in 2015. Per capita growth has slumped even further to less than 1% in 2015. At the same time, the government deficit has returned to about 4%, which is almost at the level of 1995. Public debt has risen to 47.3%. The population grows at a rate of about 1.68%, which exceeds economic growth. The escalation in social welfare expenditure at a rate of 17% on average since 2005, indicates a high potential for catapulting off the fiscal cliff.[71] The state failed to adhere to economic growth strategies, neither GEAR nor Accelerated and Shared Growth Initiative for South Africa, or ASGISA. With social welfare expenditure at

Table 8.5 Gross domestic product (GDP) and government expenditure, debt, 1995–2015*

	GDP Real R'bn	*% Growth*	*Real GDP per capita*	*% Change*	*G deficit/ surplus as % GDP*	*Public debt % GDP*
1995	1 704	3.1	43 267	1.09	-5.0	49.5
1996	1 777	4.3	44 193	2.1	−4.8	47.3
1997	1 824	2.6	44 420	0.5	−3.6	46.8
1998	1 834	0.5	43 720	−1.6	−2.7	46.8
1999	1 877	2.4	43 826	0.2	−2.1	44.4
2000	1 955	4.2	45 735	2.1	−1.9	40.9
2001	2 008	2.7	45 075	0.8	−1.4	40.1
2002	2 082	3.7	45 798	1.6	−1.0	34.1
2003	2 143	2.9	46 287	1.1	−2.2	33.5
2004	2 241	4.6	47 605	2.8	−1.4	33.2
2005	2 359.0	5.3	49 335	3.6	−0.3	31.4
2006	2 491	5.6	51 331	4.0	0.7	29.0
2007	2 625	5.4	53 334	3.9	0.9	26.6
2008	2 709	3.2	54 322	1.9	−9.7	26.0
2009	2 667	−1.5	52 838	-2.7	−5.1	31.5
2010	2 748.0	3.1	53 823	1.9	−4.0	35.1
2011	2 836	3.2	54 930	2.1	−4.8	38.6
2012	2 899	2.2	55 508	1.1	−5.3	41.0
2013	2 963	2.2	56 047	1.0	−4.6	43.9
2014	3 009	1.5	56 185	0.2	−4.6	46.2
2015	3 055.1	1.3	56 304		−3.8	47.3

Source: South African Reserve Bank time series data, www.resbank.co.za accessed 10/10/2016.

* 2010 Prices.

15% of government expenditure and population growth exceeding economic growth, the domestic economy will fail to uphold the expectations created by the system. The persistent growth in total social welfare spending issues a warning that social dependency is not reduced but rather enhanced and embedded.

Reintroduction of race

A serious threat to bridging social fragmentation is delivered by the reintroduction of racial discrimination in South Africa. In the name of RDP 'redistribution', statutory racially entrenched discrimination was enacted. This included the immediate assumption of corporate power and assets by black people. As part of the developmental welfare approach the state after 1994 introduced policies of statutory enforced transfer of ownership and control of corporate entities in South Africa to blacks. This was motivated as 'dealing with the legacy of Apartheid'.[72] The policies to transfer ownership of the South African economy to black people[73] passed through different stages of ideological intensity. Prior to the political change in government in 1994, private business had taken the initiative in facilitating transactions whereby blacks acquired stakes in big business. Sidiropolous (1993) wrote:

> Black economic empowerment [BEE] encompasses, among other things, black entry into business as owners and as managers, advancement in the workplace through the erosion of the industrial colour bar, unionization, acquisition of equity, redistribution of existing wealth, and the rise of the black consumer.[74]

Cyril Ramaphosa defined Black economic empowerment as 'economic empowerment for all South Africans – (it) is a very deliberate programme to achieve meaningful participation of disadvantaged South Africans in the mainstream South African economy'.[75] The first BEE transaction was performed by SANLAM, the Afrikaner-owned life assurance company, in 1993.[76] By the middle of 1998, the market capitalisation of BEE companies listed on the Johannesburg Stock Exchange (JSE) comprised 6% of the JSE, adjusting to R58.7bn/US$9.8bn, or 5.5% of the JSE market capitalisation in January 1999. The decline was the result of the 1998 emerging market crisis. Many of the BEE companies had financed their deals through debt instruments. Most of the BEE financial engineering was conducted to encourage a high degree of deal flow that caused those companies to build a debt base rather than an asset base. The 1998 market crisis thus left them with unsustainable gearing ratios. Furthermore, the special purpose vehicles (SPVs) established to facilitate the empowerment transactions were premised on a bull market. These assumptions failed during the emerging market crisis of 1998. Cargill argued that the SPVs protected the empowerment companies from capital risk and thereby contributed to the distortion of normal business practice. These funding weaknesses compromised their direct hold over operations.[77]

Concern over the actual empowerment effects of the ownership acquisition deals of corporate entities in South Africa[78] led to the report by the Department of Trade and Industry (DTI) in 2003 outlining proposals for the effective empowerment of black people. The underlying principle was that ownership should be distributed more widely to benefit a broad base of the black population and that skills must be transferred in order to facilitate black participation in the management of business. The report *South Africa's Economic Transformation: A Strategy for Broad-based Black Economic Empowerment*[79] introduced the principle of economic sector–based charters to manage the transfer of ownership, managerial control and skills to the broad black community in South Africa. These transfers occurred in accordance with a DTI Code of Good Conduct, assessing the degree of compliance with prescribed targets. These targets included black ownership of enterprises, the number of black directors, black management, skills transfer to enable black managers to take control and the number of black employees, as well as the effective empowerment of the broad black community through compulsory procurement of goods and services from exclusively black enterprises. The incentive to comply with the Code of Good Conduct (scorecards) is to achieve a B-BBBEE score between 1 and 4 (4 was fully compliant). Such a score secured enterprises public contracts, preferential procurement by government, and a general positive image as a business concern contributing to the economic transformation of the country.[80] The impact of the B-BBEE Code of Good Conduct institutionalised market distortion. The adverse effect on free-market conditions in the South African economy institutionalised corruption.

As a strategy to facilitate black participation in the economy, statutory enforcement effectively reinstated racism in South Africa. The B-BBEE strategy in principle intended to facilitate ownership and control of the formal economy by black people. In practice, the first BEE transactions benefitted only the black elite in power or those linked to the ANC seat of power. The elite, those close to the leadership in exile, were institutionally advantaged in two ways. The first mechanism was the absorption of skilled community leaders from the NGO sector into the public sector (as directors, managers and executives in state departments, state-owned enterprises and political positions).[81] The second mechanism was empowerment business transaction whereby black people were assisted in acquiring stakes and managerial positions in big business to secure goodwill between the incoming ANC government, which had threatened the nationalisation of big business after ascending to power and corporate South Africa. The initial populist political ambition of alleviating the plight of the poor, in fact, turned out to ensure the income of the poorest 80% of black people, deteriorating substantially, while the top 20% of the black population secured themselves substantially increased wealth and power.[82]

Atkinson et al. (2017) established that the earnings of the top decile of the South African population as a percentage median rose by 320% in 2000 to 500% in 2015. The Gini coefficient rose to 0.71 in 2015. The percentage of the top 1% in gross income (of individuals post-1990 and tax units before excluding capital gains), rose from 10% in 1990 to 20% in 2015.[83] These findings point to growing income inequality in South Africa since the implementation of economic redistribution policies, especially B-BBEE policies. As empowerment strategies were important, the intention was not to create another super-rich elite, but to eradicate poverty (as explained in the RDP), but in practice the most affluent 10% of black households took home more than 50% of the total income accruing to blacks, while the poorest 10% earned less than 1%.[84] The anomaly of the empowerment strategies was that unemployment increased while the beneficiaries of the empowerment deals (upwardly mobile professionals, skilled workers, entrepreneurs) contributed to growing inequality in black household income.[85] In a statutory manipulated business context, the B-BBEE Act of 2008 was used to enforce transactions whereby black people were appointed in oversight positions as company directors, as business executives, acquired substantial stakes in big companies and, through that avenue, secured preferential access to state tenders, procurement transactions and service contract. Of course, a great deal of fronting occurred, but the system of statutory enforced empowerment enabled the rise of super-rich black businessmen, such as Patrice Motsepe, Tokyo Sexwale and Cyril Ramaphosa. Table 8.6 lists the empowerment transactions between 1994 and 2009. These transactions have contributed to entrenching a powerful position to an elite group of black persons who subsequently emerged as the new black businesspeople, often supported on the lower executive or management level by competent, experienced white entrepreneurs. As shown in Figure 8.1, BEE penetration in

Table 8.6 BEE transactions, values, 1995–2009

	No BEE Transactions	*Value R'bn*	*Total value of transactions*	*BEE deals % Total deals*
1994	0	0	30	0
1995	23	12.4	31	38.7
1996	45	7.0	45	15.6
1997	52	8.3	158	5.1
1998	111	21.2	293	7.2
1999	132	23.1	213	10.8
2000	126	28.0	343	8.2
2001	101	25.1	477	5.2
2002	104	12.4	230	5.2
2003	189	42.2	108	38.9
2004	243	49.9	116	42.2
2005	238	56.2	213	26.3
2006	221	56.0	228	24.6
2007	125	96.0	418	23.0
2008	83	60.7	251	24.3
2009	58	36.5	145	25.5

Source: Ernst & Young Mergers and Acquisitions, A review of activity for the year 2008/2009; 2009/2010.

Information Classification: General

Sector	SD 2007	SD 2008	SD 2009	SO 2010	SO 2011	ED 2007	ED 2008	ED 2009	ED 2010	ED 2011	SED 2007	SED 2008	SED 2009	SED 2010	SED 2011
Resources	7.98	6.27	3.51	7.95	8.55	8.71	4.24	2.61	7.26	10.86	4.46	2.41	3.01	4.83	5.21
Financials	6.9	7.1	6.66	7.2	9.12	11.4	11.23	9.56	14.1	14.91	4.46	3.68	3.43	4.25	4.51
ICT	5.42	8.01	5.57	6.24	6.95	10.19	12.62	9.83	12.05	13.63	3.52	3.57	3.77	4.25	4.96
Retail	5.42	8.38	7.27	7.79	8.03	8.43	9.87	10.22	12.93	13.61	4.5	4.57	4.9	5	4.15
Health & Pharm	4.98	8.16	7.49	10.22	10.53	12.93	12.12	8.06	9.19	9.9	3.36	2.94	3.92	4.43	4.63
Travel & leisure	4.56	4.02	6.01	7.6	8.18	9.72	3.82	3.76	13.59	11.25	4.29	3.5	2.86	5	5
Services	3.03	4.16	4.69	7.61	10.08	5.34	7.17	7.53	11.9	15	2.48	2.79	3.78	3.71	5
Food & beverages	2.79	3.34	4.03	5.24	8.82	4.69	6.76	10.59	13.47	13.58	3.96	2.99	3.68	3.69	4.49
Basic Industrials	2.36	4.92	5.02	7.2	9.2	5.24	7.01	10.91	10.67	14.04	3.17	2.86	2.08	3.72	4.91
General Industrials	2.24	2.26	2.48	7.36	7.82	4.74	3.19	8.02	13.41	13.89	2.82	2.84	2.47	4.33	4.62
Media	1.25	1.28	4.79	6.11	5.53	5	4.86	9.82	12.15	10.03	2.56	2.08	3.25	5	4.32
Transport	1.14	6.45	2.69	7.63	9.26	4.29	10.5	9	15	15	1.71	3.13	2.13	4.49	5

Figure 8.1 Broad-based Black Economic Empowerment (BBBEE) sectoral penetration, 2007–2011

the economy had reached almost 5% in each of the sectors. This is primarily ascribed to the statutory enforcement of B-BBEE scorecards as prerequisites for doing any business with the state. The value of BEE transactions by 2009 rose significantly (see Table 8.6) to more than one quarter of all transactions on the Johannesburg Securities Exchange. This policy constraint has a similar impact on business as exchange controls since the 1960s and 1970s.

Comparing key variables of social transformation and social, and income equality across similar countries such as Brazil, India, Indonesia and Malaysia, it reflects negatively on the social transformation policies of South Africa. The South African Gini coefficient in 2015 is 0.71%, compared to 0.5% in Brazil in 2015, 0.41% in Indonesia in 2015, 0.47% in India in 2015 and 0.4% in Malaysia in 2015. Furthermore, the percentage of the population below the absolute poverty line in South Africa in 2015 is more than 40%, but in Brazil in 2015, it is just over 20%; in India, just below 30%; in Indonesia, 12%; and in Malaysia, about 3%.[86] In each of the comparable nations significant progress with transcending social fragmentation was made between 1990 and 2015, except for South Africa. The only area where South Africa sets the trend, was in the growing wealth of the top 1% of gross income earners. The number of persons dependent on social grants of some kind in South Africa has risen to 16 991 634 in 2016.[87] State resources were allocated to secure positions of power, ownership and control to a clique of black persons, emerging as the super-rich. These persons are very silent on matters of state corruption.

The adverse effect of the magnitude of BEE entrenched business was that less attention was afforded to employment-creation strategies and growth-enhancing policies than to changing the face of business. The imperative to comply with DTI B-BBEE scorecards, resulted in the misallocation of resources to ensure such transactions, rather than investing in productive opportunities. These specific empowerment strategies failed to extend true economic empowerment to the mass of ordinary black persons but enriched a few. On the other hand, these empowerment policies resulted in white entrepreneurs, executives and professionals emigrating. The new statutory entrenched racial discrimination discouraged aspiration of some and created a sense of entitlement with others, also disincentivising individual achievement and excellence.[88] A double-adverse effect on labour supply and employment is delivered by the consistently escalating social security dependency. The escalating cash transfers of the social security system in South Africa has impacted negatively on labour supply and labour force participation rates.[89] In Africa the experience under growing social security transfer payments is that people developed a dependency resulting in disincentives to productive farming and wage employment.[90]

Transcending out of fragmentation and eradicating poverty?

Transitioning from social fragmentation to social inclusion, increased equality and social cohesion depends on policies to address division. If the source of social fragmentation is economic, or culturally or racial, specific dedicated policies to address the source of fragmentation are called for. The welfare state model and the developmental state model are two strategies towards bridging social fragmentation. Both are premised on enabling recipients or empowering people out of dependency. In South African history, forces of racial division contributed only partially to social fragmentation. Diverse cultural constitutions resulted in different degrees of social want as a result of political conflict, natural calamities, wars or own economic inclination. State policies to address these were therefore also differentiated, because of the cultural diversity of the people. Politically the democratic ambitions of the African population were frustrated while the strongest and most advanced economy on the African continent developed under white rule. This political context perpetuated social and economic division and levels of development. Social fragmentation characterised the South African society, where ethnic, cultural and language differences were entrenched in the socio-political landscape. Social marginalisation of the poor was addressed differently by the different cultural entities. After the formation of the Union in 1910, the direction of policy decision-making and implementation was from the centre – from the state to the rest of the population. Non-state agents addressed social fragmentation, manifesting in poverty and unemployment, before 1920, with the Afrikaner DRC and cultural organisations organising strategies to empower Afrikaners. At the same time, the state labour policies assisted in alleviating white poverty.

The simultaneous manifestation of a growing African urban population resulted in the rise of the urban African poor and destitute, while in rural areas faltering productivity and high population growth exacerbated living standards and the ability to sustain the growing population.[91] The process of transition out of social fragmentation in South Africa was delayed by the stark differences in culture, ethnicity, socio-economic development and race. On one hand, ethno-cultural self-determination of an indigenous white community in Africa led to policies of political segregation based on race. Mobilising state resources to address social fragmentation and development was determined by the minority state. This in itself constituted a seed for future confrontation. South Africa did not embark on the development of a unitary democracy before 1990. Therefore, the process of democratisation did not inform social welfare strategies between 1910 and 1990. The advances in the provision of social security since the 1920s nevertheless placed the country well ahead of any other country in Africa.[92] Despite the calls for social security in Africa since the beginning of the century, the rest of the continent lags South Africa substantially.[93]

South Africa made considerable advances in developing a modern economy in Africa during the twentieth century. Political marginalisation did nevertheless not withhold the state from introducing Commonwealth-leading universal social security provision since the 1920s. The self-determination aspirations of the Afrikaner people in South Africa contributed to policies of racial segregation. Afrikaner economic empowerment was unique and successful, but the sense of responsibility towards people of colour within the borders of South Africa, precipitated the introduction of national social security programmes. Two conditions determine the successful implementation of social security programmes to bridge social fragmentation – economic performance enabling growth and wealth creation and an able state.

The National Party state implemented and expanded universal social welfare provision, until the gap in allocation was closed by the early 1980s. Constraints of affordability prevented the introduction of comprehensive social and health security by the Smuts government in 1944, the successive National Party governments and finally also the ANC government in 2004. A persistent threat to the full eradication of social fragmentation in South Africa is economic capacity. Population growth, especially amongst the non-contributory portion of society and the most dependent segment of society, undermines consistently the bridging of fragmentation. The capabilities of the state to deliver on policy is the second condition. The state delivered consistently, and increasingly, up to the end of the twentieth century. The social differentiation on racial and ethnic grounds was only temporarily overturned by the political changes of the 1990s. The incumbent leaders of the new South Africa promised the eradication of poverty and unemployment through 'meeting the basic needs, developing . . . human resources, building the economy, democratising the state and society and implementing the RDP'.[94] The disjuncture between political ideology and economic development under ANC Government led to successive economic policies (the RDP, GEAR in 1996 and much later ASGISA in 2006) but failed to secure growth to facilitate extensive social security provision. In fact, as Seekings (2005) noted, the state failed in its own development agenda, because of self-enrichment BEE empowerment policies that scooped empowerment benefits off benefitting a new elite. State capacity to deliver on its own extended social security policies was undermined not only by a failing precarious state mechanism, incapacity and corruption but also by the demographic explosion of dependent people. The relatively unconditional access to transfer payments nurtured dependency,[95] while the failing economy undermined capacity and human capital development. The state development goals were forfeited for BEE targets. An enabling state, growing non-racial human capital, stimulating economic activity and skills accumulation within the development state model, hold the key to successful transcending remaining social fragmentation. Instead, the state simply threw cash at the problem of poverty. Social security transfers rose by 328% in 15 years to 17 094 331 recipients, while the number of people in jobs increased only by 24%.[96]

Despite the comprehensive social security programmes introduced after 2003, claiming to be social developmental, dependency increased. Limited social development occurred. The state eventually undermined its ability to deliver on its social developmental welfare programmes through institutionalised market distortion. State intervention increased proportionally to the size of the private sector. The B-BBEE strategy entrenched state intervention in all aspects of employment, labour organisation, enterprise development, funding for enterprise development and education and training. The legacy of social fragmentation based on race was re-introduced and entrenched by statute. A mismatch between the forces of democratisation, socio-political modernisation and liberalisation resulted in economic underperformance and failure to address social fragmentation. Fedderke (2009) argues:

> The development of the social security system has been possible only because fiscal and monetary policy created the space to raise welfare payments; and it has been the rising fiscal burden of the welfare payments that has squeezed the ability of the state to address the delivery of vital services in education, health, policing and housing.[97]

South Africa is therefore faced with an interventionist state, but a failed developmental state (Seekings, 2015) or as Leveson (2017) calls it, 'precarious state', because of state capture by the new political elite. This elite was created through public offices, a massively increased civil service, inflated remuneration packages and statutory enforced employment quotas based on race rather than capacity. In the name of 'transformation', persons with skills, capacity and experience were retrenched *en masse*. This left civil service across all three levels of government (central, provincial, municipal) incapable of delivering on promises, resulting in managerial and service delivery collapse. The lack of capacity in the wake of massive financial flows made fertile ground for irregularities, malpractice and ineffective expenditure.[98] State capacity after 1994 was therefore used to 'discipline' business through B-BBEE, and its fiscal capacity to extract taxes, but failed to apply those to ensure economic growth to bridge social fragmentation. With economic policies focused on wealth extraction and not growth and empowerment, or social development, the fragmentation in society deepens.

The growing interventionist state in South Africa has gained legitimacy as a democratically elected government but failed to re-engineer the transition across social fragmentation by creating a new power elite able to use its fiscal capacity to extract resources, which are only partially distributed to address social fragmentation. The substantial growth in the number of recipients of the various social transfer payments institutes an insurmountable burden on the economy and perpetuates dependency on the state. Re-instituted statutory racism after 1994 undermines the ability of the state to perform its developmental function.

Notes

1 Gosden (1973); Hopkins (1996).
2 Leveson (2017).
3 Bottomley (1990).
4 Raper (1978), 235.
5 Vosloo (2012).
6 Hellmann (1948), 233–239.

7 Hellman (1948).
8 Verhoef (2001, 2002).
9 Verhoef (2006).
10 Cape of Good Hope Parliamentary Debates: Hansard (1895): Col 345–346.
11 Houghton (1976); Nattrass (1982); Beinart (2001).
12 Seekings (2005).
13 Vosloo (2012), 5.
14 Duncan (1995).
15 Sagner (2000); Seekings (2005), 44; Verhoef (2006), 615.
16 UG 21–1927.
17 Von Wielligh (2014), 53; Rheinallt-Jones (1949), 413–415; Duncan (1995), 109.
18 Seekings (2005).
19 Duncan (1995), 106.
20 Burrows et al. (1942), 193.
21 UG 9–1943.
22 Rheinallt-Jones (1949), 423.
23 Rheinallt-Jones (1949), 423.
24 NASA: NTS 24/349A.
25 Rheinallt-Jones (1949), 425.
26 Batson (1943).
27 Seekings (2005), 4.
28 Rheinallt-Jones (1949), 423–424; Duncan (1995), 114; Seekings (2002), 11–12.
29 UG 14–1944.
30 Hansard (1945): Col 2160; Marks and Anderson (1992).
31 Verhoef (2016a, 2016b).
32 Fage (2002), 465–490; Cooper (2002), 24–26.
33 Freedom Charter (1955).
34 Sadie (1971), 206.
35 Maasdorp (2002), 9; Jones and Müller (1992), 233.
36 Nattrass (1982), 239.
37 Jones and Müller (1992), 233, 296–299; Feinstein (2005), 145–146.
38 Mthetwa (1993), 30–33.
39 SAIRR Survey (1954/55), 221; SAIRR Survey (1956/57), 217.
40 SAIRR Survey (1961/62), 268; SAIRR Survey (1965/66), 295–296.
41 Brown and Neku (2008), 303; Haarman and Haarman (1998); Haarmann (1999); Haarmann (2000), 13.
42 Abedian and Standish (1984), 256–258; Seeber and Dockel (1978), 227–228; Mthetwa (1993), 31.
43 Nattrass (1982), 233; Jones and Müller (1992), 227, 298; Seeber and Dockel (1978), 228.
44 Lindert (1996), 3–5; Lindert (2004).
45 Davenport and Saunders (2000), 666.
46 Van der Berg (1997), 487; Brockerhoff (2013), 21.
47 ANC (1994).
48 Gray (2006), 14–15; Midgley (2001a), 270.
49 Lombard (2007), 295–296; Potts (2012), 75; Lombard (2008), 156–157; Midgley (2001a), 270.
50 Parsons (2013), 51; Brockerhoff (2013), 23.
51 Midgley (1996, 1998); McKendrik (1998); Haarmann (2000); Gray and Lombard (2001); Bak (2008), 85.
52 GG386, No 18166; Lombard (2007), 295; Gray (2006), 4–6.
53 Lombard (2007), 300.
54 Midgley (2001a), 272.

55 Midgley (1996), 2.
56 Gray (2006), 9–10.
57 Gray (2006), 13.
58 Patel (2005); Lombard (2008), 160–162; Bak (2008), 86.
59 Leveson (2017), 475.
60 Taylor Report (2002).
61 Samson (2002), 92.
62 Schmid (2012); Brockerhoff (2013).
63 Ferguson (2003), vii, ix.
64 Lombard (2008), 162–163.
65 Brockerhoff (2013), 16–22; Haarmann (2000), 10–28; Van der Berg and Bredenkamp (2002), 39–60; Seekings (2002), 6–12.
66 Wilson and Ramphele (1989), 5, 190–195.
67 The number of registered individual taxpayers rose from fewer than 2 million in 1993 to 16.3 million in 2015, and the number of companies registered as taxpayers rose from 1.8 million in 1993 to 10.2 million in 2015. See Hattingh et al. (2016), 450–451. A substantial portion of registered taxpayers do not actually pay tax, as is reflected in the small number of only 6.5 million taxpayers in South Africa in 2015.
68 www.businesslive.co.za.
69 Ferguson (2003), 78–79.
70 Bhorat (2015); Statssa (2015); World Bank (2015); Noyoo (2016), 6; Atkinson et al. (2017).
71 Roussouw et al. (2014); Fedderke (2009).
72 www.anc.org.za/ancdocs/history/charter.html.
73 'Black' here refers to all 'previously disadvantaged persons', which are Africans, Coloured persons and Indians.
74 Sidiripoulos (1993), 1.
75 Ramaphosa (1997), 12.
76 Verhoef (2003), 36–44; Verhoef (2004), 97–98; Kruger (1998), 7–8.
77 Cargill (1999), 3; Kruger (1998), 11–16.
78 Jack (2003); Verhoef (2020).
79 DTI (2003).
80 DTI (2003), 11–14; Jack (2007), 108–109; Verhoef (2020).
81 Lodge (2002), 68.
82 Terreblanche (2002), 414; Empowerdex (2012).
83 Atkinson et al. (2017), 47.
84 Emerick (2004).
85 McGrath and Whiteford (1994), 18.
86 Atkinson et al. (2017), 13, 25, 27, 33.
87 Dawood (2016).
88 Potts (2012); Gray (2006); Seekings (2015).
89 Leibbrandt et al. (2012); Ardington et al. (2009); Fedderke (2009); Surender et al. (2010).
90 Ferguson (2003), 105–107.
91 Hellman (1950).
92 Monyai (2011).
93 Fedderke (2009); World Bank (2009); Weigand and Grosh (2008).
94 ANC (1994), 7.
95 Ferguson (2003), 79.
96 www.businesslive.co.za/bd/national/2017-06-210.
97 Fedderke (2009), 21.
98 Atkinson (2007), 63.

References

Abedian, I., & Standish, B. (1984). An Analysis of the Sources of Growth in State Expenditure in South Africa, 1920–1982. *The South African Journal of Economics, 52*(4), 256–267.

African Nationalist Congress (ANC) (1994). *The Reconstrudtion and Developemnt Programme.* Johannesurg: Umanyano Publications.

Ardington, C., Case, A., & Hosegood, V. (2009). Labor Supply Responses to Large Social Transfers: Longtitudial Evidence from South Africa. *American Economic Journals: Applied Economics, 1*(10), 22–48.

Atkinson, A. B., Hasell, J., Morelli, S., & Roser, M. (2017). *The Chartbook f Economic Inequality.* Institute for New Economic Thinking. Oxford: Oxford Martin School.

Atkinson, D. (2007). Taking to the Streets: Has Developmental Local Government Failed in South Africa? In S. Buhlungu, J. Daniel, R. Southall, & J. Lutchman (eds.), *The State of the Nation 2007* (pp. 53–77). Pretoria: Humans Sciences Research Council Press.

Bak, M. (2008). Can Development Social Welfare Change an Unfair World? The South African Experience. *International Social Work, 47*(1), 81–94.

Batson, E. (1943). Some Points of Comparison between the Social Security Proposals for the Union and for Southern Rhodesia. *South African Journal of Economics, 13*(1), 43–51.

Beinart, W. (2001). *Twentieth Century South Africa.* Oxford: Oxford University Press.

Bhorat, H. (2015). *Is South Africa the Most Unequal Society in the world?* http://mg.co.za/article/2015–9–30-si-south-africa-the-most-unequal-society-in-the-world.

Brockerhoff, S. (2013). *A Review of the Development of Social Security Policy in South Africa.* Studies in Poverty and Inequality Institute. Working Paper 6.

Brown, M., & Neku, R. J. (2008). A Historical Review of the South African Social Welfare System and Social Work Practitioners' Views on its Current State. *International Social Work, 48*(3), 301–312.

Bottomley, J. (1990). *Public Policy and White rural poverty in South Africa, 1881–1924.* Unpublished PhD thesis at Queens University, Kingston, Ontario.

Burrows, H. R., Halliday, I. G., De Vos, P. J., & Smith, R. H. (1942). Social Security. *South African Journal of Economics, 10*(3), 193–247.

Cape of Good Hope Parliamentary Debates: *Hansard* 1895, Col 345–346.

Cargill, J. (1999). Empowerment 1999. A Moving Experience. *Business Map*, Johannesburg.

Cooper, F. (2002). *Africa since 1940.* Cambridge: Cambridge University Press.

Davenport, T. R. H., & Saunders, C. (2000). *South Africa: A Modern History.* 5th edition. Basingstoke: Macmillan.

Dawood, Z. (2016). *Eating from the Poor- SA's Social Security Agency*, www.biznews.com/throught-leaders/2016/12/01/social-secirity-agency-poor/ (accessed 2 December 2016).

Department of Trade and Industry (DTI) (2003). *South Africa's Economic Transformation: A Strategy for Broad-based Black Economic Empowerment.* Pretoria: DTI.

Duncan, D. (1995). *The Mills of Gold: The State and African Labour in South Africa, 1918–1948.* Johannesburg: Witwatersrand University Press.

Emerick, N. (2004). Entitlement Bubble about to Burst. *Business Day*, 15 November 2004.

Empowerdex (2012). *Cannot be the Only Aspect of Transformation.* Johannesburg: Empowerdex.

Fage, J. D. (2002). *A History of Africa.* London: Routledge and Kegan Paul.

Fedderke, J. (2009). Social Welfare: Social Stasis. *Focus, 55*, 15–25.

Feinstein, C. H. (2005). *An Economic History of South Africa: Conquest, Discrimination and Development.* Cambridge: Cambridge University Press.

Ferguson, J. (2003). *Give a Man a Fish: Reflections on the New Politics of Distribution.* Durham: Duke University Press.

Freedom Charter (1955). www.sahistory.org.za/sites/default/files/Freedom%20Charter-reduced.pdf.

Gray, M. (2006). The Progress of Social Development in South Africa. *International Journal of Social Welfare, 15*(Supplement 1), S53–S64.

Gray, M., & Lombard, A. (2001). The Post-1994 Transformation of Social Work in South Africa. *International Journal of Social Welfare, 17*(1), 132–145.

Gosden, P. H. J. H. (1973). *Self-Help: Voluntary Associations in Nineteenth-century Britain.* London: B.T. Batsford.

Haarmann, C., & Haarmann, D. (1998). *Towards a Comprehensive Social Security System in South Africa.* Working Paper for the Congress of South African Trade Unions (COSATU). Cape Town.

Haarmann, C. (1999). *South Africa's New Child Support Grant: A Developmental Perspective.* Cape Town: Applied Fiscal Research Centre, University of Cape Town.

Haarmann, C. (2000). *Social Assistance in South Africa: Its Potential Impact on Society.* Unpublished D.Phil. thesis, University of the Western Cape.

Hattingh, J., Roeleveld, J., & West, C. (eds.) (2016). *Income Tax in South Africa: The First 100 Years, 1914–2014.* Cape Town: Juta.

Hellman, E. (1948). *Rooiyard; a Sociological Survey of an Urban Native Slumyard.* Cape Town: Oxford University Press.

Hellman, E. (1950). The Native in the Towns. In I. Schapera (ed.), *The Bantu-speaking Tribes of South Africa: An Ethnological Survey.* Cape Town: Maskew Miller.

Hopkins, E. (1996). *Working Class Self-help in Nineteenth-century England: Responses to Industrialization.* London: UCL Press.

Houghton, D. H. (1976). *The South African Economy.* Cape Town: Oxford University Press, www.anc.org.za/ancdocs/history/charter.html.

Jack, V. (2003). *From the Starting Bloc: A Decade of Black Economic Empowerment.* Johannesburg: Empowerdex.

Jack, V. (2007). Unpacking the Different Waves of Black Economic Empowerment. In X. Mangcu, G. Marcus, K. Shubane, & A. Hadland (eds.), *Visions of Black Empowerment* (pp. 105–117). Johannesburg: Jacana Press.

Kruger, W. G. (1998). *Black Empowerment: An Economic Evaluation of Future Investor Attractiveness.* Unpublished M Com dissertation, University of Cape Town.

Jones, F. S., & Müller, A. L. (1992). *The South African Economy, 1910–1990.* London: Macmillan.

Leibrandt, M., Lilenstein, K., Shenker, C., & Woolard, I. (2012). *The Influence of Social Transfers on Labour Supply: A South African and International Review.* A Southern African Labour and Development Research Unit Working Paper, No 112. Cape Town: SSALDRU, University of Cape Town.

Leveson, Z. (2017). Precarious Welfare States: Urban Struggles over Housing Delivery in Post-apartheid South Africa. *International Sociology, 32*(4), 474–492.

Lindert, P. (1994). The rise of social spending, 1880–1930. *Explorations in Economic History, 31*(1), 1–37.

Lindert, P. H. (2004). *Growing Public: Social Spending and Economic Growth since the Eighteenth century.* Vols 1 and 2. Cambridge: Cambridge University Press.

Lombard, A. (2007). The Impact of Social Welfare Policies on Social Development in South Africa: An NGO Perspective. *Social Work/Maatskaplike Werk, 43*(4), 295–316.

Lombard, A. (2008). The Implementation of the White Paper for Social Welfare: A Ten-year Review. *The Social Work Practitioner-Research, 20*(2), 154–173.

Lodge, T. (2002). *Politics in South Africa: From Mandela to Mbeki.* Cape Town: David Philip.

Maasdorp. G. (2002). Economic survey, 1970–2000. In F. S. Jones (ed.), *The Decline of the South African Economy* (pp. 7–30). Cheltenham: Edward Elgar.

Marks, S., & Anderson, N. (1992). Industrialization and health and the 1944 national health services commission in South Africa. In S. Feierman, & J. M. Janzen (eds.), *The social basis of health and healing in Africa* (pp. 132–161). Collection No 3. Berkeley: University of California Press.

McGrath, M., & Whiteford, A. (1994). *Inequality in the Size Distribution of Income in South Africa*. Stellenbosch: University of Stellenbosch Economic Project.

McKendrik, B. W. (1998). Social Work Education and Training: From Preparing for Apartheid to Training for a Democracy. *Social Work/Maatskaplike Werk, 34*(1), 99–111.

Midgley, J. (1996). Promoting a Developmental Perspective in Social Welfare: The Contribution of South African Schools of Social Work. *Social Work/Maatskaplike Werk, 32*(1), 1–7.

Midgley, J. (1998). Social Development and Social Welfare: South Africa in An International Context. *Social Work/Maatskaplike Werk, 34*(1), 90–98.

Midgley, J. (2001a). South Africa: The Change of Social Development. *International Journal of Social Welfare, 10*, 267–275.

Midgley, J. (2001b). The Critical Perspective in Social Development. *Social Development Issues, 23*(1), 42–50.

Monyai, P. (2011). *Social Policy and the State in South Africa: Pathways for Human Capability Development*. Unpublished D.Phil. thesis, University of Fort Hare.

Mthetwa, N. R. (1993). *Government Expenditure Growth in South Africa, 1960–1993*. Unpublished M.Sc. dissertation, University of Natal.

National Archive of South Africa (NASA): Native Affairs Department (NTS): 24/349A: *Memorandum on Social Benefits for Natives*, 1947.

Nattrass, J. (1982). *The South African Economy: Its Growth and Change*. Cape Town: Oxford University Press.

Noyoo, N. (2016). *Social Policy after Two Decades of Democracy in South Africa: A Call for Social Re-engineering?* Unpublished paper: Wednesday Seminar, UJ Sociology, Anthropology and Development Studies, 13 April 2016.

Parsons, R. (2013). *Zumanomics Revisted. The Road from Mangaung to 2030*. Johannesburg: Jacana.

Patel, L. (2005). *Social Welfare and Social Development*. Cape Town: Oxford University Press.

Potts, R. (2012). Social Welfare in South Africa: Curing or Causing Poverty? *Penn State Journal of International Affairs*, 74–92, https://psujia.files.wordpress.com/2012/04/social_welfare_final.pdf (accessed 14 October 2016).

Ramaphosa, C. (1997). Empowerment: The Future of Black Business. *Boardroom*, 2.

Raper, R. E. (1978). Dictionary of Southern African Place Names. *Human Science Research Council*, 235.

Roussouw, J., Joubert, F., & Breytenbach, A. (2014). Suid-Afrika se fiskale afgrond: 'n Blik op die aanwending van owerheidshulpbronne. *Tydskrif vir Geesteswetenskappe, 54*(1), 144–162.

Sadie, J. L. (1971). Population and Economic Development in South Africa. *South African Journal of Economics, 39*(3).

Sagner, A. (2000). Ageing and Social Policy in South Africa: Historical Perspectives with Particular Reference to the Eastern Cape. *Journal of Southern African Studies, 26*, 523–553.

Samson, M. J. (2002). The Social, Economic and Fiscal Impact of Comprehensive Social Security Reform for South Africa. *Social Dynamics, 28*(2), 69–97.

Schmid, J. (2012). *Trends in South African Child Welfare Reform*. Centre for Social Development in Africa. Johannesburg: University of Johannesburg.

Seeber, A. V., & Dockel, J. U. A. (1978). The Behaviour of Government Expenditure in South Africa. *The South African Journal of Economics*, *46*(4), 227–236.

Seekings, J. (2002). The Broad Importance of Welfare Reform in South Africa. *Social Dynamics*, *28*(2), 1–38.

Seekings, J. (2005). Visions, Hopes and Views about the Future: The Radical Moment of South African Welfare Reform. In S. Dubow, & A. Jeeves (eds.), *South Africa's 1940s: Worlds of Possibilities* (pp. 44–63). Cape Town: Double Storey.

Seekings, J. (2015). *The "Developmental" and "Welfare" State in South Africa: Lessons for the Southern African Region*. CSSR Working Paper No 358. University of Cape Town.

Sidiripoulos, E. (1993). Black Economic Empowerment. *South African Institute of Race Relations. Spotlight* (2), September.

South Africa (1997). Government Gazette, 386, No 18166. *White paper for Social Welfare*. Pretoria: Government Printer.

South African Institute of Race Relations (SAIRR) Survey: 1951/52. Johannesburg: SAIRR.

South African Institute of Race Relations (SAIRR) Survey, 1954/55. Johannesburg: SAIRR.

South African Institute of Race Relations (SAIRR) Survey, 1956/57. Johannesburg: SAIRR.

South African Institute of Race Relations (SAIRR) Survey, 1961/61. Johannesburg: SAIRR.

South African Institute of Race Relations (SAIRR) Survey, 1965/66. Johannesburg: SAIRR.

Statistics South Africa: Mid-2015 Term Population Estimates, www.statssa.gov.za/publications/P0302/P03022015.pdf.

Statistics South Africa (Statssa): Poverty Trends in South Africa, www.statssa.gov.za/?p=2591.

Surender, R., Noble, W., Wright, G. N., & Ntshongwana, P. (2010). Social assistance and dependence in South Africa: An analysis of attitudes to paid work and social grants. *Journal of Social Policy*, *39*(2), 203–221.

Taylor Report (2002). *Report of the Committee if Inquiry into a Comprehensive System of Social Security for South Africa*. Pretoria: Department of Social Development.

Terreblanche, S. (2002). *A History of Inequality in South Africa 1652–2002*. Pietermaritzburg: University of Natal Press.

UG 9–1943. *Social and Economic Planning Council. Report No 1. Re-employment, Reconstruction and the Council's Status*. Cape Town: Government Printer.

UG 14–1944. *Report of the Social Security Committee and Report No 2 of the Social and Economic Planning Council Report*. Social Services and the National Income. Cape Town: Government Printer.

UG 21–1927. *Report of the Commission of Inquiry on Old Age Pensions and National Insurance*. Cape Town: Government Printer.

Union of South Africa (1942). *Debates of the South African Parliament* (Hansard). Cape Town: Government Printer: 12/1/1942: Column 5–6; 6/3/1942; Column 3316–3321.

Union of South Africa (1945). *Debates of the South African Parliament* (Hansard). Cape Town: Government Printer: 14/2/1945; Column 2160.

Van der Berg, S. (1997). South African social security under apartheid and beyond. *Development Southern Africa*, *14*(4), 481–505.

Van der Berg, S., & Bredenkamp, C. (2002). Devising Social Security Interventions for Maximum Poverty Impact. *Social Dynamics*, *28*(2), 39–68.

Verhoef, G. (2001). Informal Financial Service Organisations for Survival: The Case of African Women and Stokvels in Urban South Africa, ca. 1930–1998: *Enterprise and Society: The International Journal of Business History*, *2*(2), 259–296.

Verhoef, G. (2002). Stokvels and Economic Empowerment: The Case of African Women in South Africa, 1930–1998. In B. Lemire, R. Pearson, & G. Campbell (eds.), *Women and Credit: Researching the Past, Redefining the Future* (pp. 91–114). Oxford: Berg Publishers.

Verhoef, G. (2003). "The Invisible Hand": The Roots of Black Economic Empowerment, Sankorp and Societal Change in South Africa, 1985–2000. *Joernaal vir Eietydse Geskiedenis, 28*(1), 28–47.

Verhoef, G. (2004). Economic Empowerment and Performance: Strategies towards Indigenisation/Black Economic Empowerment and the Performance of Such Enterprises in Nigeria and South Africa, since the early 1970's to 2002. *Joernaal vir Eietydse Geskiedenis, 29*(2), 92–118.

Verhoef, G. (2006). From Friendly Societies to Compulsory Medical Aid Association: The History of Medical Aid Provision in South Africa's Public Sector. *Social Science History, Special Issue: The persistence of the Health Insurance Dilemma, 30*(4), 601–627.

Verhoef, G. (2016a). 'Sonder onderwys, geen bevryding': Die vestiging van 'n grondslag vir swart onderwys in Suid-Afrika, 1952–1968. *Tydskrif vir Geesteswetenskappe, 56*(2–2), 627–640.

Verhoef, G. (2016b). 'Sonder onderwys, geen bevryding': Moedertaalonderrig en gemeenskap in die ggrondslag vir swart onderwys in Suid-Afrika, 1952–1990. *Tydskrif vir Geesteswetenskappe, 56*(3), 746–762.

Verhoef, G. (2020). "Settlers and comrades". The Variety of capitalism in South Africa, 1910-2016. *Business History, Special Issue: Varieties of Capitalism, 63*(8), 1413–1446. https://doi.org/10.1080/00076791.2020.1796972.

Von Wielligh, N. (2014). *'n Vergelykend studie van maatskaplikewerk-praktykopleiding vanuit die perspektief van praktykopleiers.* Unpublished MA dissertation, University of the North West.

Weigand, C., & Grosh, M. (2008). Levels and Patterns of Safety Spending in Developing and Transition Countries. *World Bank*, SP Discussion Paper No 0817.

Wilson, F., & Ramphele, M. (1989). *Uprooting Poverty: The South African Challenge.* Cape Town: David Philip.

Vosloo, R. (2012). The Dutch Reformed Church and the poor white problem in the wake of the first Carnegie Report (1932). *Studia Historiae Ecclesiastica, 37*(2).

World Bank (2009). *World Development Report.* Washington, DC: World Bank.

World Bank (2015). *Global monitoring report 2014/2015: ending poverty and sharing prosperity.* Washington: World Bank.

www.businesslive.co.za/bd/national/2017-06-21-recipe-for-chaos- . . . 2-17/06/21.

Index

Note: Page numbers in *italic* indicate a figure and page numbers in **bold** indicate a table on the corresponding page.

Printed in the United States
by Baker & Taylor Publisher Services